RELIGION
IN CHINA

China Today series

RELIGION IN CHINA

Ties That Bind

Adam Yuet Chau

polity

First published in 2019 by Polity Press

Polity Press
65 Bridge Street
Cambridge CB2 1UR, UK

Polity Press
101 Station Landing
Suite 300
Medford, MA 02155, USA

ISBN-13: 978-0-7456-7915-0
ISBN-13: 978-0-7456-7916-7(pb)

A catalogue record for this book is available from the British Library.

Library of Congress Cataloging-in-Publication Data

Names: Chau, Adam Yuet., author.
Title: Religion in China : ties that bind / Adam Yuet Chau.
Description: Medford, MA : Polity, 2019. | Series: China today | Includes bibliographical references and index.
Identifiers: LCCN 2018045222 (print) | LCCN 2018051512 (ebook) | ISBN 9781509535682 (Epub) | ISBN 9780745679150 (hardback) | ISBN 9780745679167 (pbk.)
Subjects: LCSH: China–Religion.
Classification: LCC BL1803 (ebook) | LCC BL1803 .C43 2019 (print) | DDC 200.951–dc23
LC record available at https://lccn.loc.gov/2018045222

Typeset in 11.5 on 15 pt Adobe Jenson Pro
by Toppan Best-set Premedia Limited
Printed and bound in Great Britain by CPI Group (UK) Ltd, Croydon

For further information on Polity, visit our website: politybooks.com

To my grandparents

Contents

Figures

Map

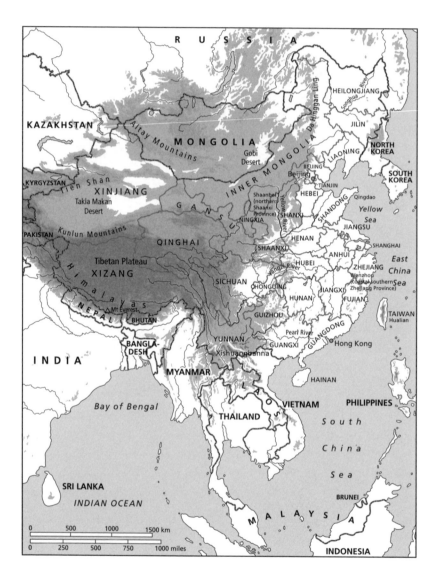

Chronology

1911	Fall of the Qing dynasty
1912	Republic of China established under Sun Yat-sen
1927	Split between Nationalists (KMT) and Communists (CCP); civil war begins
1934–5	CCP under Mao Zedong evades KMT in Long March
1937–45	Invasion of China by Japan
1945–9	Civil war between KMT and CCP resumes
October 1949	KMT retreats to Taiwan; Mao founds People's Republic of China (PRC)
1950–3	Korean War
1953–7	First Five-Year Plan; PRC adopts Soviet-style economic planning
1954	First constitution of the PRC and first meeting of the National People's Congress
1956–7	Hundred Flowers Movement, a brief period of open political debate
1957	Anti-Rightist Movement
1958–60	Great Leap Forward, an effort to transform China through rapid industrialization and collectivization
March 1959	Tibetan Rebellion in Lhasa; Dalai Lama flees to India

1959–61	Three Hard Years, widespread famine with tens of millions of deaths
1960	Sino–Soviet split
1962	Sino–Indian border conflict
October 1964	First PRC atomic bomb detonation
1966–76	Great Proletarian Cultural Revolution; severe suppression of religion and destruction of religious buildings and artifacts
February 1972	President Richard Nixon visits China; "Shanghai Communiqué" pledges to normalize US–China relations
September 1976	Death of Mao Zedong
October 1976	Ultra-Leftist Gang of Four arrested and sentenced
December 1978	Deng Xiaoping assumes power; launches Four Modernizations and economic reforms
Late 1970s	The beginning of the revival of religious life, especially in the countryside
1978	One-child family planning policy introduced
1979	US and China establish formal diplomatic ties; Deng Xiaoping visits Washington
1979	Sino–Vietnam border conflict
1980s–98	The blossoming of *qigong* (vitality-enhancing exercise) in the PRC
1982	Census reports PRC population at more than one billion
December 1984	Margaret Thatcher co-signs Sino–British Joint Declaration agreeing to return Hong Kong to China in 1997
Late 1980s	The end of Martial Law and the liberalization of religious life in Taiwan

1989	Tiananmen Square protests culminate in June 4 military crackdown
1992	Deng Xiaoping's Southern Inspection Tour re-energizes economic reforms
1993–2002	Jiang Zemin is president of PRC, continues economic growth agenda
1998	The suppression of *qigong* practices, including the Falungong
2000s onwards	The rise of the Confucian Classics movement
November 2001	WTO accepts China as member
2002–12	Hu Jintao, General-Secretary CCP (and President of PRC from 2003 to 2013)
2002–3	SARS outbreak concentrated in PRC and Hong Kong
August 2008	Summer Olympic Games in Beijing
2010	Shanghai hosts the World Exposition
2010s	The demolition of a number of churches and the removal of exterior crosses from many church buildings, especially in Wenzhou (southeastern coastal China)
2012	Xi Jinping appointed General-Secretary of the CCP (and President of PRC from 2013)
2015	China abolishes one-child policy
2017	Xi Jinping reappointed General-Secretary of the CCP's Central Committee (and President of PRC from 2018)
2018	National People's Congress removes two-term limit on China's Presidency

Acknowledgments

I thank the University of Cambridge and St. John's College for providing a supportive and intellectually stimulating environment in which to think, conduct research, teach, share and experiment with ideas, and write. A sabbatical year (2017–18) allowed me to complete this book that had been many years in the making. Among the many wonderful colleagues in Chinese Studies at Cambridge I would like to thank in particular the following for their constant support and many inspirations: Joe McDermott, Hans van de Ven, David McMullen, Roel Sterckx, and Michael Loewe.

I am also grateful to all my colleagues, friends, and students (some within Cambridge and the United Kingdom but many far beyond) who have taught me things. The precious opportunities to share various strands of my work in lectures, seminars, workshops, symposia, and conferences in many parts of the world have contributed to the formulation of, and connections among, many of the ideas contained in this book. I thank all those colleagues who have invited and hosted me. I feel incredibly fortunate to belong to a vibrant, worldwide community of scholars working on religion in China.

I would also like to thank Jonathan Skerrett, Karina Jákupsdóttir, Emma Longstaff, Neil de Cort and others at Polity for having shepherded the book from inception to finish with professional skill and grace, and Ian Tuttle for his expert copyediting. Three anonymous reviewers of the book manuscript made numerous suggestions for improvement, for which I am thankful.

Last but not least, I thank Hideko for her always wise counsel.

Notes on Orthography and Pronunciation _____

In this book I have adopted the *pinyin* (literally "spelling sounds") system of romanizing Chinese words without the tone marks, which has become standard practice in Western (especially Anglophone) Chinese Studies scholarship in the past two or three decades (replacing the Wade–Giles romanization system). For words with their conventional romanization in non-*pinyin* forms (e.g. place names and persons' names in Taiwan and Hong Kong), I will either use these conventional forms (e.g. place names in Hong Kong) or provide these conventional forms in parentheses following the *pinyin* form (e.g. Ciji (Tzu Chi)). The following short guide on pronouncing a few of the many Chinese words that will appear in the text is for readers who are unfamiliar with how to pronounce words in Mandarin Chinese using *pinyin*. The approximation in sound is derived from English. *Pinyin* has a few "tricky" consonants and vowels; most other letters and letter combinations are with pronunciations similar to those in English.

Ciji: tsu jee ("jee" as in "jeep") (not "chee jee")
fengshui: fong shuey (not "fan shueei")
jiachi: jia chr (as if you are saying "church" but stopping right before "ur")
qigong: chee gung (not "key gone")
re'nao: You can produce the "e" sound by saying the English word "nerd" but without the "n" and "rd." Unfortunately the "r" in Mandarin has no close equivalent in English so please ask a Mandarin speaker to say this word for you! (But it is definitely not like the English "r"; therefore not "ray nao")
xiu: sheew [close to "show"]

Introduction: Relationality at the Heart of Religion in China

This book is about religious lives in Chinese societies (primarily mainland China but also Taiwan and Hong Kong). Its potential readership can be very diverse, and each kind of reader will bring something different to the reading and get something different from the book. Are you a university student taking a course on Chinese or East Asian religions to fulfill a general education requirement? Are you a Religious Studies major who has taken courses on monotheisms (Judaism, Christianity, Islam) but is now ready to discover religious traditions that are radically different? Are you a seeker of spiritual wisdom who has read *Zhuangzi* and *Daodejing* (*Tao Te Ching*) and wants to know more about the strange worlds of *qi, fengshui, yinyang*, and "the *Dao*"? Or are you a New Age guru who wants to incorporate insights from Chinese religions to enrich your repertoire? Have you fallen in love with Chinese art but feel you cannot really appreciate it unless you become familiar with the deeper religious symbolisms hidden behind the brushwork? Have you visited China or will visit China as a tourist and feel an urge to understand more about the religious traditions that sustain the vibrant religious lives you have seen in some documentary or feature films? Are you a Christian missionary who wants to understand the Chinese people's own religious traditions (i.e. "check out the competition") before heading out to convert them to Christianity? Are you a Protestant pastor or Catholic priest who has been engaging in inter-faith dialogues? Are you a human rights activist who is concerned about the supposed lack of religious freedom in China? Are you a China watcher who is worried that with the rise of China's political and economic power in recent decades, the Chinese Communist Party's particular brand of Confucianism is going to take over the world? Are you a specialist on religion looking for a new way of understanding religious life, not just in China but in other cultural contexts as well? Or are you simply curious about how one fifth of humanity might be practicing religion differently from yourself and those around you? Whatever your motivation in picking up this book, I hope that reading it will be a rewarding experience for you.

But this book is not a run-of-the-mill introductory survey text on Chinese religion (with one chapter on Buddhism, another on Daoism, etc.). It has a particular approach and a particular intellectual agenda. I hope that reading this book will not only enrich your knowledge about religious life in China but change the way you understand religion and the world more generally. Before proceeding to the substantive chapters, I would like to explain my approach – what I have called the "relational approach" – as well as set out the parameters of the study. Here I will introduce a range of essential concepts and analytical frameworks that can serve as a mental "toolkit" at the ready for tackling (i.e. understanding) any potentially baffling religious phenomena. Along the way I hope to dispel a number of commonly held misconceptions about religion in China. I will also tell the reader a little about myself and the sources I have used.

A RELATIONAL APPROACH TO UNDERSTANDING CHINESE RELIGIOUS LIFE

"So, tell me, how many religions are there in China?" "What is the biggest religion in China?" People tend to press me with these kinds of questions when I tell them I am a specialist on Chinese religion. These are legitimate questions, but they are not the best or the most interesting questions because they anticipate easy answers (i.e. people seemed to be satisfied if I answered them with "Five," "Buddhism"), and easy answers are never the best or the most informative answers. Indeed, one of the most important goals for this book is to show why these are not the best questions. Why not ask instead "How do the Chinese practice religion?," "On what occasions do the Chinese engage in rituals?," "What culturally specific desires and concerns inform the religious world of the Chinese?," "How is religious life embedded in Chinese society?," etc. Good questions lead to further explorations and new discoveries rather than confirm one's received wisdoms and pre-existing categories.

Most people in the West (and in fact most educated Chinese in China as well) have been influenced by the confessional approach to understanding religious life and have thus looked at religion in China as consisting of discrete religions such as Buddhism and Daoism, each as a coherent system of beliefs and practices, as if they are the equivalents of Christianity and Islam (though I would argue that even the coherence of Christianity and Islam is more in the heads of theologians than in the practices of Christians and Muslims). Another equally prevalent approach is to view religion in China primarily in terms of philosophical and religious ideas, as sources of "Oriental spiritual wisdom," useful antidotes to an allegedly overly materialist and rationalist West. These approaches in fact tell us more about ourselves and our own religious sensibilities, spiritual anxieties, and epistemological biases than about how the Chinese really engage in religious activities and what *they* are concerned about when they pray to the deities or go on pilgrimage.

This book proposes to look at religion in China from an entirely different perspective, focusing on the socially embedded and culturally specific "forms" that frame Chinese people's religious practices on the ground, i.e. how Chinese people "do" religion. The key analytical and organizing anchor of this new perspective is the notion of "relationality," which helps highlight and foreground the numerous and most important aspects of Chinese ways of doing religion that have previously been hidden from view due to the above-mentioned blinkers and biases. Studies of *guanxi* ("social relationship") in the China anthropology literature in the past two decades or so have allowed us to have an excellent understanding of this crucial aspect of Chinese society (see, in particular, Yang 1994; Yan 1996; Kipnis 1997). This book argues that the religious realm is one of the most crucial arenas where *guanxi* is played out (hence "ties that bind," the subtitle of this book), not just between people in sociopolitical life (e.g. kin, co-villagers, neighbors, colleagues, superior–inferior, patron–client, briber–bribed, party comrades, ex-schoolmates, friends, social media groups) but also between people and spirits, between people and sites of worship and spiritual empowerment, among religious co-practitioners (and co-religionists), between deities, between ritualists and their customers, between masters and disciples, and between the state and religious groups and traditions. These relationships can be long-lasting or transient, local or translocal in scale, collaborative or contestatory, vertical or horizontal, voluntary or compulsory, free or commoditized, convergent or scattered, implicit or explicit, relatively simple or extremely complex, but they are being made and re-made all the time and they constitute the "stuff" of Chinese religious life. In other words, the ultimate aim of this approach is not religion in China *per se* but to show how Chinese people make their lifeworlds through *doing* religion.

WHAT IS RELIGION? DO SPIRITS EXIST?

In this book I deploy a rather broad definition of religion: any form of interaction with spirits, be they God, gods, ancestors, ghosts, or evil spirits. Some scholars and readers will look upon some of the religious practices discussed in this book as "magic," "sorcery," or "superstition," not quite belonging to the category of "religion." However, this kind of distinction between "proper religion" and "primitive magic" is a product of epistemological biases that privilege particular "modalities of doing religion" (more on this in chapter 2) and hinders greatly a broad-based understanding of religious life in any society. Such a bias grants more dignity and legitimacy to religious traditions that are believed to be "higher" on an imagined evolutionary trajectory of religions, denigrating those that are supposedly less institutionalized, less systematic, more "ritualistic," therefore "primitive" and "lower" (if not barbaric and repulsive). This is a well-known Protestant triumphalist prejudice that unfortunately still pervades most understandings of religion. Discarding this prejudice is essential for any sympathetic yet objective understanding of religion.

But do "spirits" exist? What if I am an atheist who does not believe in the existence of God, gods, ancestors, ghosts, or evil spirits? What if I am a Christian who believes in the Christian God but cannot accept the existence of these other kinds of spirits (except as objects of idolatry)? This book is certainly not meant to be an intervention in the "Does God exist?" or "Is religious belief a delusion?" debate. There are no easy empirical tests for the veracity of most religious suppositions and propositions. Since we are interested in understanding Chinese people's religious practices, all we need to do is to treat Chinese people's interactions with spirits as sociocultural practices and phenomena. So if I write later in this book (in chapter 4) that a spirit medium is possessed by the Azure Cloud Immortal (Qingyundaxian), this statement needs to be understood in the sociocultural context of the society in question (somewhere in rural northern Shaanxi Province), where the villagers participating in this séance act as if they believe in the existence of the Azure Cloud Immortal and his ability to possess the spirit medium and speak through the latter. There is no need for us to identify with and share the beliefs informing these religious practices (e.g. beseeching the gods for divine assistance, the exorcism of an evil spirit, making offerings to ancestors). In fact, some of the Chinese people engaging in religious activities premised on such beliefs might themselves hold a "healthy" dose of skepticism or do not make a conscious connection between what they do ritually (e.g. hiring a Buddhist priest for a funeral) and all the theological and symbolic implications evoked in these rituals (e.g. the existence of a Western Realm of Supreme Bliss, the practice of reincarnation).

Having a personal religious or spiritual orientation in whatever form might potentially aid one's understanding of other people's religious practices because one might discover resonances between the two (but hopefully not just the clichés such as "all religions guide people to lead a moral life" or "all religions provide an explanation of the meaning of life"). But it could equally hinder one's understanding because one might too easily identify the familiar and thus overlook the radically different, or one might feel threatened by practices that are so different from one's own, bringing into doubt the validity of one's faith or spiritual pursuit. On the other hand, being a staunch atheist also has its advantages and disadvantages in the cross-cultural study of religion.

SPATIAL EXPANSE AND TIME FRAME

The entity that is popularly known as China or mainland China refers to the People's Republic of China (the PRC), which is the main geographical setting of this study. Though having very different political trajectories in the modern era, culturally speaking Taiwan and Hong Kong are largely Chinese, therefore I will also draw illustrative cases from these two places when appropriate.

China covers a landmass almost ten million square kilometers in size and has a population of around 1.4 billion people. There is an immense diversity of languages and cultures within China, the so-called officially recognized 56 nationalities (*minzu*) being only one way of understanding this diversity. Other differentiating axes include coastal versus inland, urban versus rural, closeness to politically sensitive national borders, priority status in the country's developmental strategies, transnational links, historical legacies (e.g. having been a major treaty port in the past), etc. Religious diversity is not a simple "reflection" or merely an aspect of this immense diversity; it actually contributes to this diversity while constantly absorbing new elements from its varied and ever-changing societal environments (more on religious diversity in chapter 1). The map of China at the beginning of this book shows its provinces and autonomous regions, major topographical features and cities, and its surrounding regions. It also indicates some of the places from which some of the illustrative cases in this book have been drawn (not comprehensive).

The focus of this study is on religious practices in the contemporary period (i.e. the reform era in China, which began in the late 1970s). But there will be occasional mentions of the dynastic period (or the late imperial period, which mainly covers the Ming and Qing dynasties) and the Maoist period (1949–76). Therefore a good sense of the basic chronology of modern Chinese history will be useful. Giving the year of major watershed historical events, the abbreviated chronology at the beginning of this book can serve as a temporal reference.

STATISTICS: THE NUMBERS GAME
[WARNING: USER BEWARE!]

Statistics is not an innocent science (see Liu 2009). Its very name indicates that it was originally conceived as an essential tool of statecraft: In order to better govern a polity, the ruler or its modern equivalent (regimes of various ideological persuasions) needs to acquire, through the census as well as all kinds of quantitative studies, intimate knowledge of the human and non-human resources (e.g. mineral resources) within the territorial boundaries of the nation. The statistics on human resources (often called demography) includes the size of the population as well as its composition: age and sex distribution, geographical concentration, occupational makeup, significant patterns of population movements (e.g. rural–urban migration; in-migration and out-migration), and, relevant for this book, "religious makeup." Some countries do not take census data on religious affiliation (e.g. France, its Republican values being against particularistic affiliations). Many countries are characterized more by non-confessional kinds of religiosity for the majority of their populations (e.g. China, India, Japan, etc.) (see chapter 1). In the PRC there are added challenges of the sensitive nature of religious beliefs (not only due to the political environment), which renders any survey-based quantitative study unreliable. However, these substantial epistemological difficulties have not prevented researchers and policymakers from forcing a confessional-affiliational model onto the statistics and coming up with numbers for each "religion" within each country. Cross-national statistics abhor a vacuum; you cannot have statistics on the religious makeup of one country and not on another, especially if this other country is China. Many foreign observers have an avid appetite for numbers on religion in China, and one of the key points of interest is how fast Christianity is growing in China, which "co-incidentally" is also one of the key points of interest for the Chinese government, but for very different reasons.

In the next chapter (chapter 1) I will explain in more detail why a confessional-affiliational model is not applicable for the vast majority of Chinese people who engage in religious activities. But in order to satisfy those readers who would insist on having "some" (or any!) statistics to hang on to, I will present two sets of statistics on religious affiliations. The first set of numbers are derived from the Pew-Templeton Foundation "Global Religious Futures" project.[1] These Pew-Templeton numbers are from the year 2010: China's total population is 1,341,340,000, among whom 18.2% are Buddhists (i.e. 244.12 million);

5.1% are Christians (i.e. 68.41 million); 21.9% practice folk religions (presumably including Daoism since there is no separate category for Daoism) (i.e. 293.75 million); 1.8% are Muslims (i.e. 24.14 million); 52.2% are unaffiliated (though it is not clear if this means "not religious") (i.e. 700.18 million); and finally, less than 1% are Hindus, Jews, and followers of other religions (fewer than 11 million).

The second set of numbers are from a White Paper entitled "China's Policies and Practices on Protecting Freedom of Religious Belief," released in April 2018 by the Information Office of the State Council.[2] The numbers given by the Chinese government are presumably from more recent studies. Here is an excerpt from the White Paper:

> The major religions practiced in China are Buddhism, Daoism,[3] Islam, Catholicism, and Protestantism; with a total of nearly 200 million believers and more than 380,000 clerical personnel. China has numerous Buddhist and Daoist believers, but it is difficult to accurately estimate their numbers as there are no set registration procedures which ordinary believers must follow as part of their religion. There are around 222,000 Buddhist clerical personnel and over 40,000 Daoist clerical personnel. The 10 minority ethnic groups, the majority of whose population believe in Islam, total more than 20 million, with about 57,000 clerical personnel. Catholicism and Protestantism have 6 million and 38 million followers in China respectively, with 8,000 and 57,000 clerical personnel. China also has many folk beliefs which are closely linked to local cultures, traditions and customs, in which a large number of people participate.

Curiously, while the White Paper gives a number for the total number of Muslims (more than 20 million), it does not give any numbers for Buddhists, Daoists, and those who follow folk beliefs (i.e. popular religion). But if we subtract the numbers of Muslims and Christians from the total number (200 million), we can surmise that the total number of Buddhists, Daoists, and "folk religionists" combined would be around 136 million. If we assume that China's current population is around 1,400,000,000, the White Paper estimates the total number of believers to be at 14.29% of the total population, quite low when compared with the Pew-Templeton figure of 47%. But if the White Paper does not include those who practice folk beliefs as "believers," then the figure 136 million would just include the Buddhists and the Daoists while the "folk religionists" would constitute another, possibly very large number (I would give the number of a few hundred million). The reader needs to keep in mind that the vast majority of these 200 million "believers" have never filled out a form indicating that they are Christians or Buddhists, and the official estimate for the number of Christians will be considered very low by some observers and scholars because it would not include those attending unregistered churches (the so-called "underground churches").

Very usefully, the White Paper also provides some other pertinent statistics:

The State requires the registration of places of worship for group religious activities in accordance with the law, so as to provide legal protection and ensure that all activities are carried out in an orderly manner. At present, there are about 144,000 places of worship registered for religious activities in China, among which are 33,500 Buddhist temples (including 28,000 Han Buddhist temples, 3,800 Tibetan Buddhist lamaseries, and 1,700 Theravada Buddhist temples), 9,000 Daoist temples, 35,000 Islamic mosques, 6,000 Catholic churches and places of assembly spread across 98 dioceses, and 60,000 Protestant churches and places of assembly. ... China has printed over 160 million copies of the Bible in more than 100 different languages for over 100 countries and regions, including 80 million copies printed in the Chinese language, 11 ethnic minority languages and braille for churches in China.

I hope the above figures will satisfy those readers who are statistically inclined. The biggest problem with such attempts at "mapping" religions in China is that it is modeled on a confessional-affiliational understanding of mutually exclusive religious membership. In an important sense the whole point of this present book is to argue against this kind of (mis)understanding.

THE AUTHOR AND THE SOURCES

I think it would be useful for the reader to know a little about where the author of this book is coming from in terms of biographical background, academic training, personal experience with religion, and experience of researching and teaching about religion in China.

I was born in Beijing in 1968, at the height of the Great Proletarian Cultural Revolution (1966–76), and spent my childhood in Beijing during the remaining years of High Maoism (what the West called "Godless China" due to its staunch atheism). It was a China of drab (drab especially to Western observers) blue or green Mao suits for both men and women and a hundred million bicycles. But it was also a China of exuberant political campaigns and socialist festivities. Other than participating in certain socialist rituals (e.g. parades on October First National Day, oath-taking as I was inducted as a Young Pioneer) and some leisure reading and radio-listening (e.g. stories featuring magical battles from classics such as *Journey to the West, Heroes of the Water Margin*), I did not have any exposure to religious life at home or in my surroundings. My early education and socialization were entirely secular (and of course socialist and patriotic). The Chinese state suppressed religious life of all kinds, so whatever religious sentiments and beliefs there were among some people, they had to remain hidden. Because I lived in Beijing, where the presence of the state would be most strongly felt, compliance to the dictates of the state was most likely absolute.

My mother was an Indonesian Chinese. Born in 1937, she grew up in Pekanbaru, Sumatra, when Indonesia was under Japanese occupation, and received Communist-leaning, Chinese-language education after Indonesia became independent in 1945. She went to China in 1952 at the age of 15 to help "build the socialist New China." She married my father, a Shanghainese of Ningbo origin (born in 1936), and had two children, my older sister and myself. Because of my mother's overseas Chinese status, my whole family was able to leave China and move to Hong Kong in 1980, which was then a British Crown colony.

At age 12 I began learning English and Cantonese from scratch. At that time Hong Kong was a bustling capitalist society and a famed center of manufacture of textiles, toys, and electronics for the world market. Things religious finally appeared in my surroundings. Many of my neighbors in the apartment building burnt incense and made offerings daily at the small shrines right next to the metal gates to their apartments. These shrines were most commonly dedicated to the Locality God and the God of Wealth "at the gate" (*menkou tudi caishen*). Sometimes the neighbors burnt paper money in large tin buckets in the stairwell, producing pungent smoke. There were a few small temples and roadside shrines in the neighborhood, but they did not seem to have much going on and I never paid any attention to them. A couple of times a year there would be large festivals celebrating the birthday of deities such as the Empress of Heaven (Tianhou, known as Mazu in Fujian and Taiwan, a most popular goddess along coastal China) at temples not too far from my home (in Shaukeiwan in the northeastern part of Hong Kong island). The streets would be decorated with large colorful flags in red, green, blue, yellow, etc., and a lot of fishing boats in the bay that we could see from our apartment windows would also be decked with flags. We could hear firecrackers and Cantonese opera performances in the distance, but for some reason I never felt the urge to go and take a look. Perhaps it was because we felt unconsciously that these festivals were not for people like us immigrants; they had

a distinctly "indigenous" feel to them. Perhaps we felt a sense of snob-
bish disdain as educated people, and from the capital Beijing no less,
toward these local folks' colorful, exotic, but definitely "low-brow"
cultural expressions. These festivals were simply a world quite alien to
us, but I did not even bother to see with my own eyes just how alien
it might have been. Little did I know that temple festivals just like
these would later become one of my core research interests!

For two years I attended a primary school near my home that was
run by the Church of Christ in China (*Zhonghua Jidu jiaohui*), an
ecumenical Protestant organization active in Hong Kong after having
been forced to leave mainland China following the Communist takeover.
This choice of school was not unusual since a large number of primary
and secondary schools in Hong Kong were run by religious organizations (especially Catholic, Protestant, and Buddhist), as they still are
today, and this particular school had a very good reputation. On numerous occasions each day all the students were required to close their
eyes, hold their hands together, and pray to God. There were also
regular worship assemblies in the school chapel, where we all sang
hymns and listened to sermons. Participation in these religious activities did not turn me into a Christian, and there was no active attempt
on the part of the school or the teachers to proselytize. It was as if we
were assumed to be Christians already. I might not have wholeheart-
edly participated in these Christian rituals, but I do not remember
having ever resisted or rebelled. These activities did not seem to have
made any strong impression on me.

While many of my classmates went on to attend secondary schools
also run by religious organizations (e.g. some having Catholic priests
or sisters as their teachers), I went to a government-run school. There
were no longer any compulsory religious rituals, even though a small
number of my classmates were members of the school Christian fellowship. Five years of busy studying passed, and then one day, during
the summer vacation of 1987, I accepted a Protestant classmate's

invitation to a gospel camp organized by his church (evangelical but non-denominational). At the end of the multiple-day camp (three days or maybe longer) held on the campus of a local university, I became a Christian convert (i.e. "accepted Jesus Christ as my personal savior")!

I quickly turned into a devout Christian, attending church service and youth fellowship every week, avidly reading the Bible and all kinds of Christian devotional literature, and actively trying to spread the gospel to people around me, including my classmates and family members. The church fellowship, small but with many young people, was warm and supportive. There was much socializing beyond things spiritual. I was soon baptized. Hong Kong was at that time undergoing major transformations. China opened up because of the economic reforms, and many factories moved from Hong Kong to the Pearl River Delta region. The Sino-British Joint Declaration in 1984 sealed the fate of the colony, as Hong Kong was to revert its sovereignty to China in 1997.

In 1989 I went to the United States for university education. The changed environment cooled my religious fervor considerably. The Christians in the liberal arts college I was attending (Williams College, in Williamstown, Massachusetts) and in the local church were welcoming, but the overwhelming majority of them were Christians because their family and upbringing were Christian. Very few shared a similar conversion and evangelical experience. I prayed and read the Bible less and less. The courses I was taking in cultural anthropology and comparative religion also led me to wonder why there are so many different religious traditions and kinds of religious practices in the world and how the Christian faith could possibly be the only Truth. My faith gradually faded and one day I told myself I would no longer be a Christian. It is ironic that I would lose my newly acquired faith in one of the most religiously fervent countries in the world, and when so many Chinese students studying in the US would discover and convert to Christianity.

After graduating from university I began doctoral training in socio-cultural anthropology at Stanford University (Palo Alto, California). Through a Chinese visiting professor's introduction, I went to rural Shaanbei (northern Shaanxi Province in northcentral China) for some preliminary fieldwork in the summer of 1995. This was my first encounter with rural China, and I was captivated by the vibrant religious life in Shaanbei, especially its temple festivals. I decided to research on the revival of popular religion in rural China as my doctoral dissertation topic, using one temple in Shaanbei, the Black Dragon King Temple (Heilongdawangmiao), as my primary case study. More systematic and much longer periods of ethnographic fieldwork followed, totaling 18 months. During these months I stayed at temples and inside villagers' homes, attended dozens of temple festivals and numerous funerals and weddings (funerals and weddings always end with elaborate banquets), traveled on the back of trucks with local opera troupes (that were per-forming for one temple festival after another), drank burning liquor accompanied by delicious watermelons, learned how to sing Shaanbei folk songs, helped slaughter sacrificial pigs, observed séances conducted by spirit mediums, listened to folk storytelling, walked or rode on the back of motorcycles along mountain paths, and talked to thousands of locals (peasants, merchants, local officials, opera singers and musi-cians, martial artists, miners, forestry workers, shopkeepers, children and teenagers, students, the elderly, factory workers, contractors, sex workers, restaurant owners, cooks and waiters, truck and bus drivers, stonemasons, construction workers, temple bosses, Daoist priests, spirit mediums, *fengshui* masters, etc.). It was exhilarating. The resulting study became my doctoral dissertation and eventually a monograph (Chau, 2006a).

I subsequently became a professional anthropologist, teaching and researching on religion in China, especially the social aspects of religious life (you will see in the next chapter why I think religious doctrines are not as important for our understanding of how people "do" religion in

China). After the long-term fieldwork in Shaanbei, I have conducted many shorter spells of fieldwork research, over the course of 20 years, in rural and urban China, Taiwan, and among Chinese communities in Southeast Asia (mainly Indonesia, Malaysia, and Singapore) and Europe. These fieldwork trips lasted from a few days to a month. It is this broad range of fieldwork experiences among many kinds of communities that made me appreciate the diversity of Chinese religious practices. This appreciation has been further deepened by my experience as a teacher and a scholar, teaching courses, supervising and examining dissertations and theses, reviewing article and book manuscripts, giving public lectures, interacting with colleagues at academic conferences, and constantly reading and writing. The arguments and insights presented in this book are intellectual products distilled from these experiences. As the many illustrative cases cited in this book will show, I have also drawn heavily upon the works of my scholarly colleagues, who are based in China, Taiwan, Hong Kong, Europe, and North America (the reader can consult the further reading and reference sections for additional explorations). Fortunately, there has been an explosive growth in studies on contemporary religious life in Chinese societies based on fieldwork (published primarily in Chinese, English, and French).

DIVERSE APPROACHES TO STUDYING RELIGION IN CHINA

What distinguishes anthropological approaches to studying Chinese religion from other approaches? What are their advantages and disadvantages when compared to those in other disciplines? Five main academic disciplines have contributed to the study of religion in China: Religious Studies, History, Sociology, Political Science, and of course Anthropology. The boundaries between these different disciplines are sometimes porous, but each has developed its distinct topical foci, methodologies, and analytical frameworks.

The sociology of religion primarily examines how the particular characteristics of a society shape religious life. It is especially interested in broad trends in religious growth and decline. One of the most prominent debates in the sociology of religion has been around the secularization thesis (from Max Weber onward), which predicted that the spread of scientific rationalism would lead to the increasing secularization of society globally. But it turned out religious life has been a lively force in both local and global affairs. More recently, some sociologists of religion have tried to explain the differences in the degree of religious participation in different societies using a religious market model (e.g. Stark and Finke 2000; Yang 2012). Given their research interest in broad societal trends, sociologists of religion tend to work with quantitative data resulting from large-scale surveys (the bigger the better). For theories to have explanatory power, they have to "predict the outcome" accurately given certain conditions (e.g. a more open religious market tends to produce, or at least correlate with, more lively religious life). If sociologists of religion are interested in studying religions themselves, what interests them most are the institutional aspects rather than religious practices *per se*. The sociology of religion has traditionally been developed in studying Christianity in Euro-American contexts (with church membership serving as one of the most prominent "variables"); its adaptation to studying religion in China is an ongoing one. The difficulty of generating reliable survey data on religion is a major stumbling block in the advancement of the sociology of religion in China (not to mention the possibility that many aspects of religious life in China are not quite amenable to being surveyed).

Some political scientists are interested in the study of religion because of the intimate connections between political views and religious affiliations in many contexts. However, the political science study of religion has not been well developed because of the secularist ideologies in Western liberal states that mostly exclude religion from formal politics, while most political scientists focus on politics with a capital "P" (e.g. political parties, the presidency, policymaking, democratic and authoritarian regimes, political movements, etc.). But, just as in sociology, the increasing prominence of religion in contemporary life has forced more political scientists to pay attention to religion. Questions in this field include: Do members of particular religious groups vote in certain predictable ways? How do different countries handle the thorny issues of the separation of church and state? How to identify forces of religious radicalization? How does religion contribute to sociopolitical stability or instability (e.g. violence between different religious groups, religiously inspired protests and resistance)? In the context of China, some political scientists have examined how the state manages the challenge of the rapid growth of Christianity and the extremely active faith-based charities. Just like many sociologists, those political scientists who are used to quantitative analyses are often frustrated by the lack of reliable survey data on religious affiliations in China (partly due to the political sensitivity of such enquiries and partly due to the lack of formal religious affiliations of most Chinese). Similar to the sociologists, political scientists tend to take people's religious identification as a given and are not concerned with the nature and contents of their religious practices.

Religious Studies (also called Comparative Religion) is concerned with the study of the internal contents of different religions. The primary medium of study for Religious Studies scholars is religious texts, especially those that have become "canonical" (thus constructed by the elites of the religious traditions themselves or by their "curators" in the West). The focus is more on doctrines, concepts, religious thinkers, schools of thought than the social and institutional aspects of religion. A legacy of the Western theological and hermeneutics tradition, this approach has partly intentionally and partly inadvertently constructed non-Western religious traditions into coherent systems of religious ideas. This has resulted in our current popular understandings of Buddhism, Daoism, Hinduism, etc. as analogous to Christianity, each with a core of theological propositions and concepts and each with some key texts. Such a "systematic" approach to non-Western religions is reflected in most related university courses and introductory texts. In recent years some scholars in Religious Studies are advocating studying "lived religions," i.e. examining people's actual *experience* with religion (Orsi 2010 [1985]), which brings anthropological approaches to bear upon Religious Studies.

While Religious Studies scholars tend to focus on explaining what a particular religion "is all about" without paying too much attention to changes over time, historians of religion on the other hand make it their duty to trace and account for precisely these changes. Historians of Chinese religions (some of whom are art historians) have tackled questions that include: How did the Chinese indigenize Buddhism, and how did Buddhism impact Chinese society (including other religious traditions)? How did different deity cults evolve over time (some deities changed their identities, iconographies, even sex, over the course of their development)? How did elite and popular forms of Buddhism differ in the Ming dynasty? Was Confucianism invented by European missionaries in the sixteenth and seventeenth centuries? How did reformist Buddhism and modern Daoism emerge in the early twentieth century? In what form did religious persecution and anti-clericalism take in Chinese history? How did the word "religion" (*zongjiao*) in its modern sense come to China via Meiji Japan? What was it like to be a monk or priest in a particular historical period? As social and cultural historians, these scholars make use of a wide range of sources such as dynastic histories and edicts, county and temple gazetteers, diaries and correspondence, institutional charters and minutes, temple inscriptions, mural paintings, ritual manuals, poetry and fictional works, excavated artifacts (e.g. burial inscriptions, tomb offerings), etc.

As an academic discipline, sociocultural anthropology grew out of the Euro-American colonial encounters with peoples in the Americas, Africa, Oceania, and Asia. The earliest professional anthropologists in Europe and the United States (in the late nineteenth and early twentieth centuries) were often advisors to colonial governments in matters relating to ways of life of the natives with a view to better governing the latter. Most of these native peoples were non-literate (not 'illiterate' since they did not have writing), and anthropologists had to live among them over a long period (often many years) to learn their languages, observe and inquire about their customs, and to make sense of their "bizarre" and "primitive" cultural practices relating to material culture, foodways, kinship, rituals, conflict resolution, etc. Long-term "participant observation" became anthropology's hallmark methodology, even as theoretical approaches evolved over time.

In the mid-twentieth century the study of agrarian societies (labeled as "complex societies") came to occupy a prominent place in mainstream anthropology (following wartime studies on the so-called "national characters" as part of the war effort), challenging the previous generations' structural-functionalist treatment of indigenous communities as isolated and bounded wholes. Most significantly, Robert Redfield proposed concepts such as "Great Traditions" and "Little Traditions" (as well as the "rural–urban continuum") to characterize the differences and interactions between literate elite cultural traditions and peasant cultural traditions. During this time, the idea of "folk religion" was born, referring to the religious practices of the common people, as contrasted with the theologically elaborate and textually rich elite religious traditions within the same society, even though it was posited that there had always been interactions between folk and elite religious traditions.

The first generation of anthropological fieldworkers conducting field research in Taiwan and Hong Kong in the 1950s and 1960s (primarily because mainland China was closed to Western researchers until the 1980s) carried with them the training they received during this transition period from British structural-functionalism and the American "culture and personality" approach to a Redfieldian-view on complex societies, further nourished by other theoretical trends such as modernization theories, Marxist theories, symbolic and interpretive anthropology, etc. From that period onward, especially after mainland China was open to foreign researchers again and also because of the vibrant religious life in the different Chinese societies, there have been dozens of fieldwork-based studies on Chinese religious life (many of which have been written by researchers based in mainland China, Taiwan, Hong Kong, and Singapore). Some of the issues investigated include: How have various religious communities revived after the Maoist period? What impact are changing policies towards religion and broader sociocultural transformations such as urbanization and transnationalism having on the ways in which people practice religion? What are the major elements of continuity and change in Chinese religious life and how can we explain them? Why does Chinese ritual life take the forms that it does? What are the attractions of Christianity for the Chinese in rural and urban areas? How do we explain the explosive growth of lay Buddhism in both mainland China and Taiwan? How do Chinese religious forms get globalized? Many of these studies will be featured in the various substantive chapters of this book, so I will not go into details here about the multitude of fascinating topics anthropologists of Chinese religion have investigated.

Even though most of the case studies presented in this book come from anthropology, I have freely drawn upon insights from works in other relevant disciplines. Indeed, anthropology has always been in conversation (i.e. having meaningful relationships) with other disciplines because social and cultural phenomena are complex and ever changing and require a good mixture of methodologies and theoretical frameworks.

The knowledge the reader will gain from this book would be a fortuitous congruence of a number of factors: the objective realities of religious practices on the ground in contemporary China; the disciplinary and Chinese Studies expertise that have been mobilized to describe and interpret the gathered data from the field (hopefully without too much personal and ideological bias); and the particular lens and background the reader has brought into the reading and understanding of the presented materials. There is plenty of room for misunderstanding, but sometimes a little misunderstanding can pave the way for much greater understanding later on. I hope that this book will pique the readers' interest enough for them to wish to explore further the fascinating and rewarding world of Chinese religious life whether through books or "participant observation."

1 Understanding Religious Diversity: Five Modalities of Doing Religion

In the introductory chapter I briefly invoked the notion of religious diversity in China. But in order to understand religious diversity, one has to first decide on the criteria with which one is "measuring" diversity. Many scholars of Christianity are now speaking of the existence of a wide variety of *Christianities* in the world (not only measured by the astonishingly numerous Protestant denominations or the equally numerous Catholic saint cults) (see Cannell 2006; Robbins and Haynes 2014). As Christianity has spread around the globe in the past two millennia, it has taken on all kinds of local cultural flavors and mixed with all kinds of indigenous religions. All other major religious traditions with a global reach have a similar "internal" diversity (e.g. Islam, Judaism, Buddhism).

When we speak of religious diversity in China, are we speaking of the diversity of "religions" (e.g. Buddhism, Daoism, Christianity, etc.)? Or the number of deities worshiped? Or the variety of religious practices? Or the range of different kinds of religious communities? Or the number of lines of transmission of ritual techniques?

A further question that is worth bearing in mind is whether or not you believe that religious diversity is intrinsically a good thing. The answer to this question would in some way betray our ideological orientations. A firm believer in political and economic liberalism would say "Let a hundred religions bloom!" because religions are like commercial products that should be allowed to compete with one another in a religious marketplace. An advocate of cultural diversity or multiculturalism would view religious diversity as having intrinsic value and thus call for the encouragement and protection of religious diversity for its own sake (in fact taking care to not let cruel market principles wipe out "weaker" religions and produce the religious equivalents of global franchises). This is a religious-pluralist position that treats religious diversity not just as an empirical fact but as a policy goal. But Christian missionaries and other kinds of believers of any ultimate religious Truth would prefer to see their own religion triumph over all the others. And staunch atheists would want to see a completely secularized world with no religions at all. Political leaders of authoritarian regimes would grudgingly tolerate a certain degree of religious diversity, if only for maintaining checks and balances, and for as long as religious groups constitute an easily manageable minority of the population and do not cause any trouble (for the regime or for one another). Borrowing a term from economics, the sociologist of religion Fenggang Yang has characterized this last scenario as a religious "oligopoly" (Yang 2012: chapter 7).

China has always been a religiously diverse country, but this diversity is more evident as different "modalities of doing religion" (explained below) rather than as discrete confessional religions. For the vast majority of Chinese people historically and today, the presence of a wide variety of modalities of doing religion is simply a fact of their daily lives. However, "religious diversity" as a concept is alien to most Chinese people because their approach to religion is primarily instrumental and occasion-based (what can be called an *efficacy-based religiosity*) rather than confessionally-based, and their experience of religious diversity is embodied in the employment of different religious service providers on various occasions rather than abstract systems of religious doctrines and teachings. Being an anthropologist rather than an intellectual historian, I will look at the issue of religious diversity in China from the perspective of ordinary people engaging in religious activities on the ground rather than religious elites engaging in high-power theological debates. Next, I will explicate what I have called "five modalities of doing religion" in China.

MODALITIES OF DOING RELIGION

In the long history of religious development in China, different ways of "doing religion" evolved and cohered into relatively easy-to-identify styles or "modalities."[1] These are relatively well-defined forms that different people can adopt and combine to deal with different concerns in life. However, the specific contents within these forms can vary widely. These modalities of "doing religion" are:

1. *Discursive/scriptural*, involving mostly the composition and use of texts.
2. *Personal-cultivational*, involving a long-term interest in cultivating and transforming oneself.
3. *Liturgical*, involving elaborate ritual procedures conducted by ritual specialists.
4. *Immediate-practical*, aiming at quick results using simple ritual or magical techniques.
5. *Relational*, emphasizing the relationship between humans and deities (or ancestors) as well as among humans in religious practices.

Even though these modalities of doing religion are also products of conceptualization and schematization, I would like to argue that they are far more "real" than conceptual fetishes such as "Buddhism," "Daoism," and "Confucianism." The Chinese people have engaged with these modalities of doing religion in real practices, whereas no one ever engages with "Buddhism" or "Daoism" because these exist more as conceptual aggregates with only imputed concreteness and cohesiveness. Religious thinkers and scholars of religion have of course attempted to make various religious practices into coherent wholes (including by giving them names such as "Buddhism" and "Daoism"), but such attempts at arriving at cognitive, conceptual, and sometimes institutional coherence have not had much impact on how most people "do religion" on the ground, where they don't care which deity belongs to which religion or which religious tradition inspired which morality book. What happens on the ground "religiously" is very much a congruence of local customs, historical accidents, social environment, personal temperaments, configurations of modalities of doing religion, and the makeup of the local ritual market (e.g. the availability of which kinds of ritual specialists to cater for the need as well as to stimulate the need of which kinds of clients). Below I shall explicate in a little more detail each modality of doing religion found in Chinese religious culture. One thing I need to emphasize, however, is that these modalities are more or less ideal types, and that they sometimes overlap (e.g. with some actual religious practices manifesting multiple modalities).

The discursive/scriptural modality of doing religion

People are attracted to this modality because of the allure of Confucian, Buddhist, Daoist, and other "great texts" (classics, sutras, scriptures, etc.). This modality often requires a high level of literacy and a penchant for philosophical and "theological" thinking. Key practices within this modality include compiling and editing scriptures or discoursing about "the Way" (*dao*), or preaching, and its paradigmatic forms include reading, thinking about, discussing, debating, composing, translating, and commenting on religious texts. Also included in this modality is the composing of morality books using spirit writing and Chan/Zen masters' exegesis on *gong'an* (*dharma* riddles; *koan* in Japanese). The products of this modality are usually textual (or at least eventually appearing in textual forms) that range from a single religious tract to a whole set of scriptures and liturgical texts (*keyi*) (e.g. the so-called Buddhist Canon or Daoist Canon compiled under imperial patronage). These texts form the basis of the classical "Religious Studies" approach to studying Chinese religions, which was derived from Western religious/theological exegetical traditions. Because of this textual bias, for a long time Chinese religious practices were understood in the West as exclusively this textually transmitted esoteric knowledge or, in the context of New Age or Orientalist consumption of exotic texts, "Oriental wisdoms."

The personal-cultivational modality of doing religion

Practices such as meditation, *qigong*, internal or outer alchemy, the cultivation of the "Daoist body," personal or group sutra chanting, the morning and evening recitation sessions in a Buddhist monastery, merit-conscious charitable acts (e.g. volunteering to accumulate karmic merit), and keeping a merit/demerit ledger belong to this modality. This modality presupposes a long-term interest in cultivating and transforming oneself (whether Buddhist, Daoist, Confucian, or sectarian). The goals of this transformation and cultivation are different in each religious tradition: to become a so-called "immortal" (*xian*) in Daoism,[2] to be reincarnated into a better life or to achieve *nirvana* in Buddhism, and to become a man of virtue or to be closer to sagehood (*sheng*) in Confucianism. But the shared element is the concern with one's own ontological status and destiny, something akin to a Foucauldian "care of the self." In other words, the practices in this modality provide "technologies of the self." Within this modality of doing religion there are both elite and popular forms. For many, working on scriptures itself constitutes a form of self-cultivation. However, ordinary and even illiterate people can pursue personal-cultivational goals without esoteric knowledge or high literacy or much religious training. For example, illiterate peasants can practice self-cultivation by chanting "precious scrolls" (*baojuan*) which are in metered rhymes and often memorized. The simplest self-cultivation technique is the repeated utterance of the mantra *namo amituofo* (*namo amitabha*) thousands of times a day. Though aiming at securing a better reincarnation for the next life or simply to exit the cycles of reincarnation altogether, such chanting practices help cultivate a particular kind of individual-oriented religious subjectivity. Charismatic movements sometimes precipitate out of these personal-cultivational pursuits. The modern *qigong* movement also exemplifies the personal-cultivational modality of doing religion. When Falungong practitioners let the "*dharma* wheel" (*falun*) rotate in their lower abdomen day in and day out as instructed by their master Li Hongzhi, they are engaged in the personal-cultivational modality of doing religion. The key words in this modality are "to cultivate" and "to craft" (oneself).

The liturgical modality of doing religion

This modality includes practices such as imperial state rituals (e.g. the Grand Sacrifice), the Confucian rites, the Daoist rites of fasting and offering, exorcism (e.g. a Nuo ritual drama), sutra chanting rites, Daoist or Buddhist rituals for the universal salvation of souls, the Buddhist grand water and land *dharma* assemblies (*shuilu fahui*), and funeral rituals. Compared to the personal-cultivational modality, practices in this modality aim at more immediate ritual intervention conducted in complex and highly symbolic forms, and are commissioned by and conducted for collective groups – be they families, clans, villages or neighborhoods, temple communities, or the state. This is the modality that features religious specialists (monks, Daoist priests, *fengshui* masters, Confucian ritual masters, spirit mediums, exorcist-dancers, etc.) and often involves esoteric knowledge and elaborate ritual procedures.

Figure 1: Buddhist monks conducting a Water and Land Dharma Assembly at a temple in Shanghai. Photo: Adam Yuet Chau

The immediate-practical modality of doing religion

Practices in this modality also aim at more immediate results, but compared to those in the liturgical modality they are more direct and involve shorter and simpler procedures. There is minimal ritual elaboration. Examples include divination (oracle rod, moon-shaped divination blocks, divination sticks, coins, etc.), getting divine medicine from a deity, using talismans (*fu*) (e.g. ingestion of talismanic water), consulting a spirit medium, calling back a stray soul, begging for rain, ritual cursing, or simply offering incense, etc. Because of its simplicity and low cost, this modality is the most frequently used by the common people (peasants, petty urbanites). The key concepts in this modality are "efficacy" (*ling*) (or miraculous power) and "to beseech for help" (*qiu*). The practices included in this modality are usually called "magic" in the writings of those scholars who would not want to give them the dignity of the label "religion." Many of these simpler religious services are also provided by specialists for a fee, and they are much cheaper than the more elaborate rituals in the liturgical modality. I will be discussing this modality and the liturgical modality in more detail below as I would argue that developments within these two modalities can best illustrate how Chinese religious culture is so prominently characterized by the provision and consumption of ritual services through the payment of fees.

The relational modality of doing religion

This modality emphasizes the relationship between humans and deities (or ancestors) as well as relationships among worshipers. Examples are building temples, making offerings (i.e. feeding ancestors, deities, and ghosts), taking vows, spreading miracle stories (i.e. testifying to the deities' efficacy), celebrating deities' birthdays at temple festivals, going on pilgrimage, imperial mountain journeys, establishing religious communities, and forming affiliations between temples and cult communities. This modality also emphasizes sociality, the bringing together of people through ritual events and festivals. Obviously, the other modalities all exhibit some relational and sociality aspects, but the making and maintaining of relations and the production and consumption of sociality seem to be at the foundation of those practices that I have grouped under this modality. The key concepts in this modality are "social comings and goings" (*laiwang*) and social relations (*guanxi*), or connectedness.

These five modalities of doing religion are frameworks for religious practice and action. They both restrain and enable people to express their religious imagination in words, images, sculptural and architectural forms, and actions. More importantly, these modalities lend people readily recognizable forms to adopt and practice, not unlike the ways in which the differentiation and consolidation of various literary genres such as the novel, the essay, and poetry have facilitated their production and consumption as literary forms. At any one time in any locale of the vast late imperial Chinese empire – and to some extent today as well in the larger Chinese world – all of these modalities of doing religion were in most probability available to be adopted by individuals or social groups, though factors such as class, gender, literacy level, accidents of birth and residence, position within different social networks, temperament, local convention, and the configuration of various modalities might channel some people toward certain modalities and not others. Most peasants in China have traditionally adopted a combination of the relational and the immediate-practical modalities into their religiosity; sometimes they adopt the liturgical modality and hire religious specialists when the occasion requires them, such as funerals and communal exorcisms. Illiteracy and lack of leisure would preclude them from most of the discursive and personal-cultivational modalities. The traditional educated elite tended to adopt a combination of the discursive and the personal-cultivational modalities, but they, too, often needed the service of the liturgical specialists.

IMPLICATIONS FOR OUR UNDERSTANDING OF RELIGIOUS DIVERSITY

This modalities framework focuses our attention on the ways in which people "do religion" rather than their religious conceptions. Studying people's religious conceptions is important, but it yields a bewildering diversity, whose explanation often lies more in human imagination than social processes; on the other hand, there are only a limited number of forms (modalities) that permeate the Chinese religious landscape. The varieties of Chinese religious life – i.e. the reality of religious diversity – have resulted from the elaboration of differences *within* these modalities as well as the different configurations of various modalities. The limited number of modalities and their lasting stability and versatility, no less than the great variety in the symbolic contents of the Chinese religious world, have been a great achievement in the history of world religious cultures.

Religious rivalry in Chinese history has not taken the form of competition between membership-based churches as is common in societies with confessionally-based religiosity; rather, there has been more typically competition *between* the different modalities of doing religion and especially *within* each modality of doing religion, in particular the liturgical and immediate-practical modalities. Religious diversity in China is not manifested as the coexistence of, and competition between, confession- and membership-based denominations and churches but rather primarily as the coexistence of, and competition between, various ritual service providers with different (though sometimes convergent) liturgical programs. From the religious consumers' perspective, more differentiation in religious service provision (in terms of types of services and pricing) would mean a wider choice, which might be seen as a good thing compared to religious monopoly.

The Chinese case of religious diversity does present a challenge to our conception of religious diversity. It is a somewhat messier kind of religious diversity, with no readily identifiable religious leaders, religious organizations, or systems of religious thought. But should we sacrifice true understanding for apparent clarity? The religious elite and modern state regulatory apparatus in China have a vested interest in constructing certain Chinese religious traditions in the image of monotheistic religions; however, such a construction is carried out at the expense of the vast majority of the providers and consumers of religious services in China, as it favors the discursive modality of doing religion and suppresses most of the practices encompassed by the other four modalities (especially those in the liturgical and immediate-practical modalities), many of which are labeled as superstition or counter-revolutionary sectarianism. The modern Chinese state in mainland China recognizes and approves five major religions: Buddhism, Daoism, Protestantism, Catholicism, and Islam. However, it is primarily the discursive modality within these religious traditions that is granted legitimacy. As a result, for example, the Daoist Association is completely dominated by the Quanzhen monastic Daoists since they can "discourse" much better than the Zhengyi ritualists (and they appear more "properly religious" because of their monasticism), and on the national stage the Buddhists prevail over the Daoists thanks to, among other reasons, the superior Buddhist discursive apparatus (not to mention organizational prowess and transnational links; see Ashiwa and Wank 2002). Not so incidentally, the religious pluralism and inter-faith dialogue paradigms in the liberal West also favor the discursive modality of doing religion, as all religious traditions have to meet the demand of coming up with reasoned and communicable discourse in order to even enter the dialogue with the much more theologically and discursively sophisticated Abrahamic traditions. The vast majority of the world's population who "do religion" in other ways are thus silenced (or whose efficacy-oriented religiosity was forcefully twisted to conform to a confession-oriented understanding of religion). A true religious pluralism will have to acknowledge the full range of modalities of doing religion in all societies, even though this will be an immensely challenging task since our world has been so entrenched cognitively and institutionally in the prevailing paradigms.

Interacting with Gods, Ghosts, and Ancestors

EFFICACY AND DEITY-WORSHIPER RELATIONSHIPS

The ways in which Chinese people conceive deities are very different from those in the Christian tradition. In the Christian tradition, the church authorities and theologians, over the course of more than 2,000 years, have maintained the semblance of a monotheistic religious tradition. In this tradition there is only one supreme, transcendental God; the worship of any other deity is idolatry and condemned. This is largely the case for all three so-called Abrahamic faiths (Judaism, Christianity, and Islam). Of course, we have to ignore the saint cults in Catholicism, the Sufi saint cults in Islam, the belief in angels and holy persons, etc., in order to uphold the monotheism illusion. In Catholicism, for example, theologically speaking the saints only intercede on behalf of the worshipers rather than perform miracles themselves, but in popular practice worshipers believe that the saints themselves are the miracle-performing agents. Therefore the cult of venerating the saints is quite similar to the way Chinese people worship their deities. On the other hand, it is true that in some religious traditions there are literally tens of thousands, if not millions, of gods and goddesses (the myriad divine manifestations in Hinduism, the *kami* in Shinto, gods and goddesses in China, etc.). As we will see in the course of this book, for most Chinese only a small number of deities are truly relevant.

New deities are being produced all the time in China (for example, Mao Zedong has been deified in some rural areas in mainland China in recent years). Traditionally, ordinary humans could cultivate themselves both during their lifetime and after they died, and eventually became gods. The imperial court had an official registry of spirits to make offerings to (including Heaven [*tian*], imperial ancestors, etc.), and canonized many local worthies (e.g. a particularly virtuous magistrate) and other locally produced deities. Some of these deities with humble human origins could even become extremely popular deities, e.g. Mazu (with the title Empress of Heaven), the most widely worshiped goddess in southeastern coastal China. Daoist priests and literati Daoist aficionados had a range of mechanisms for creating new deities and immortals (e.g. through self-divination; see Goossaert 2017). The introduction of Buddhism into China brought with it a wide variety of Buddhas and bodhisattvas (some of which had been created indigenously or transformed in China, e.g. the change of Guanyin from male to female). Both Daoism and Buddhism, through their more translocal vision and more elaborate liturgical frameworks, attempted to incorporate more local and minor cults (e.g. by absorbing local deities into the Buddhist or Daoist pantheons) while the latter developed ways to resist or subsist. Because the majority of Chinese people engage in what scholars have characterized as popular religion, for the rest of this chapter I will be primarily speaking about popular religious practices that do not make a sharp distinction between Buddhism and Daoism.

The single most important concept in understanding the Chinese deity–worshiper relationship, especially at the grassroots level, is *ling* (magical efficacy) (see Feuchtwang 2001: 84–9). It refers to the ability of the deity to respond (*ying*) to the worshipers' problems, for example curing an ill family member, pointing to the right course of action for conducting business, enlightening one on a knotty personal dilemma, bringing down ample rain after a bad drought, awarding exam success, granting a good spouse, and so forth. Therefore, we can characterize

Chinese popular religion as essentially a religion of efficacious response (*lingying*, i.e. miraculous response). Most thanksgiving plaques or banners hung at popular religious temples have the following stock expressions: *youqiu biying* (whatever you beg for, there will be a response), *shenling xianying* (the divine efficacy has manifested), and *baoda shen'en* or *dabao shen'en* (in gratitude for divine benevolence).

Whether or not we accept the possibility of real divine power, we need to understand *ling* as a sociocultural construct (i.e. it is through sociocultural processes that *ling* is endowed with its attributes). Even though *ling* is constructed by human actions, people's experience of *ling* is real and is an empirical fact accessible by observers (the same as Christians' experience with God).[1] A deity is *ling* because people experience his power and therefore say that he is *ling*. One deity is more popular and "powerful" than another because more people say the first one is more *ling*. A perceptive Taiwanese informant told the anthropologist Emily Ahern:

When we say a god is *lieng* [*ling*] we mean the god really does help us. Word is then spread from person to person, each telling the other that the god helped. So it is really a matter of relations among men. ... A change in the popularity of temples is not a result of change in gods' abilities. The abilities of gods don't change. People's attitudes toward them do, however. (Ahern 1981, quoted in Sangren 1987: 202)

This understanding of deities' power would apply in other parts of China as well. In other words, the more people experience a deity's *ling*, the more *ling* is attributed to the deity, which in turn contributes to the intensity of people's experience of the deity's *ling*, and so on in a mutually re-enforcing spiral. One deity's decline in popularity is usually caused by the rise in people's *ling* claims for another deity and the subsequent defection of incense money to the other deity. On the one hand, *ling* is a deity's power in the abstract. On the other hand, *ling* inheres in concrete relationships, between the deity and an individual worshiper or household, or between the deity and a community. It is meaningful to worshipers mostly in the second sense because *ling* in the abstract is only latent power, not manifest power, and the only meaningful way a deity manifests his or her power is through aiding a worshiper who is in trouble or who needs the blessing to weather life's many trials and tribulations. An allegedly powerful deity whom a person has nonetheless never consulted (e.g. because of geographical distance) is without significance to this particular person. Like social relationships, the relationships people have with deities also need maintenance and frequent renewal, hence the visits to the temple in the first lunar month and participating in the festival that celebrates the deity's "birthday."

Despite the great variety of deities worshiped in China, there seem to be some very basic principles or postulates that inform Chinese people's religious beliefs and practices and form the core of their religiosity. These basic postulates are:

1. That there are gods (or that it does not hurt to assume that there are gods);
2. That people should respect the gods and do whatever pleases the gods (e.g. building them beautiful temples, celebrating their birthdays) and should not do anything that displeases the gods (e.g. belittling them);
3. That the gods can bless people and help them solve their problems;
4. That people should show their gratitude for the gods' blessing and divine assistance by donating incense money, burning spirit paper, participating in temple festivals, presenting laudatory thanksgiving plaques or flags, spreading the gods' names, and so forth;
5. That some gods possess more efficacy than others (or have specialized areas of efficacious expertise); and
6. That one is allowed or even encouraged to seek help from a number of different gods provided that one does not forget to give thanks to all of them once the problem is solved.

These six basic postulates underlie most of Chinese people's religious beliefs and practices, even though they are not systematically thought about or articulated as I have done here. Scholars of Chinese popular religion have attempted to categorize temples and their cults using criteria such as the deities' functional specialties or the temple cult's membership spread, i.e. local or translocal. Yet, despite these differences, most Chinese people seem to practice popular religion with the above-mentioned general postulates or principles.

Different people must have different degrees of faith in the power of different deities depending on their personalities and personal experience with these deities. In their comparative study of a Chinese person's and a Hindu Indian person's religiosity, Roberts, Chiao, and Pandey (1975) put forward the concepts of "personal pantheon" and "meaningful god set." According to them, a personal pantheon is "the aggregate of gods known to a single believer" (1975: 122), whereas this same person's meaningful god set refers to the most important subset and core of his personal pantheon, which comprises "gods who are particularly meaningful for the believer in the sense that they have personal significance and salience for him, but not necessarily in the sense that he loves or treasures them" (1975: 123). This perspectival approach is immensely useful to the proper understanding of Chinese people's religiosity. Even though the popular religious landscape in China consists of a large number of deities, sacred sites, and religious specialists, each Chinese person's set of meaningful deities, sacred sites, and religious specialists is a limited one, constrained by his or her personal experience. The makeup of each person's "religious habitus" (a concept inspired by the French sociologist Pierre Bourdieu's notion of "habitus") – that is, his or her attitudes toward, and behavior concerning deities, sacred sites, religious specialists, religious rituals, and supernatural forces in general – is determined by whether or not, in what way, and to what degree the events in his or her personal life have brought him or her, in a meaningful way, to which of the deities, sacred sites, and religious specialists. It also goes without saying that each person's religious habitus changes over time. Children and young people tend to treat deities with less reverence because of their lack of life's many responsibilities and experience with deities' assistance, and they also know much less about different deities' legends and magical exploits.

Many Chinese people have a practical approach to deity belief. In Shaanbei (northern Shaanxi Province), for example, where I conducted extensive fieldwork in the 1990s on popular religious revival, some people told me that insofar as supernatural powers and stories of efficacious responses are concerned, "one should not *not* believe [what others say about the power of deities and other supernatural occurrences], nor should one believe everything [they say]" (*buke buxin, buke quanxin*). Another saying also testifies to the flexible attitude Shaanbei people hold toward deities and worship: "If you worship (literally "honor" or "respect") him, the deity will be there; if you don't worship him, he won't mind" (*jingshen shenzai, bujing buguai*).

WORSHIPING DEITIES

The first thing that a Chinese person does when approaching a deity or spirit is to burn sticks of incense. Hawkers and shops sell incense and spirit money in front of every temple, and worshipers don't buy incense by the stick but rather by the bundle (though sometimes there are giant, two-meter-tall incense sticks that one can buy by the stick). Normally one needs to put only three sticks of incense in the incense pot in front of a deity (though there are also those who light up the whole bundle at the same time); many worshipers would leave the rest of the incense with the temple keeper so that he can keep the incense burning during times when there are very few worshipers. Other times the worshiper does need so many sticks of incense because there are often many deities being enshrined in each temple and each should be

Figure 2: Worshipers burning incense at a Buddhist temple in Shanghai. Photo: Adam Yuet Chau

offered incense as a matter of respect even if the worshiper has no particular relationship with the majority of these deities (in fact many would not go to the trouble of finding out these deities' names). Most worshipers burn incense the way they do out of custom and without reflection, and they might not be able to tell an outsider what incense-burning means exactly. But from its usage an investigator could venture some interpretations.

Burning incense is a sign of respect for the deity, and the fragrance of the incense is supposed to please the deity (the Chinese word *xiang* means both incense and fragrance). The ethereally rising incense smoke is also thought to communicate the worshiper's thought and prayers to the deities. Typically, the worshiper raises the incense sticks with both hands toward the deity statue in a gesture of respect before planting them into the incense pot; many murmur prayers or words of gratitude while holding the incense. Many worshipers bring offerings of fruit, meat, and other items to lay out on tables, and sometimes burning incense sticks are stuck onto these offerings as if the fragrance of the incense also transports the spiritual essence of the offerings up to the deities. After the deities have taken their share of the food offerings (i.e. their spiritual aspects), the worshipers would bring the food items back home for their family members as these are now considered blessed by the deities and have beneficial properties. Incense is also offered to ancestors and ghosts.

Every year the Chinese burn an enormous amount of incense and paper offerings to the spirits, including tons and tons of spirit money (see Scott 2007; Blake 2011). The mountains of ashes left behind (and particles flying in the air) contribute to environmental pollution. Because of increasing environmental consciousness, more and more temples in Taiwan are fitting smoke-processing vents on top of the paper offering burning furnaces and prohibiting the burning of incense inside the temple halls – a few even go so far as implementing virtual burning of incense and spirit money on the internet! The environmental protection bureau of the local government also sends officers around during religious festivals to persuade people to not burn as many paper offerings. This is a difficult issue. The advocates of environmentally conscious worship say that what matters is "one's sincere heart," not how many offerings one burns or how much money one spends. But Chinese religion would not feel the same without the burning of incense and spirit money. During my visit to the festival of the Black Dragon King Temple (the temple I worked on during my doctoral research in the 1990s) in 2016, I saw that, instead of allowing worshipers to burn incense and spirit money at the temple, they were instructed to throw the bundles of incense sticks and spirit money into a big truck parked next to the steep stone staircase going up to the temple. When full, the truck would bring its contents to an open area outside the Dragon King Valley to be burned summarily. And setting off firecrackers was completely forbidden. I was told by the festival organizers that these measures were put in place to prevent injuries, fire, and pollution. The temple grounds were definitely much cleaner and more orderly, but I did miss the more chaotic, noisier, and smokier festival of the old days.

DIVINATION

Consulting deities for divine advice or prognostication is another important way for the Chinese to interact with deities. The Chinese have

Figure 3: A worshiper (kneeling) consults a deity who responds by commanding the palanquin through possession (held by four persons). The person behind the worshiper is the intermediary who poses questions to the deity on behalf of the worshiper. Photo: Adam Yuet Chau

developed divination techniques since antiquity. The oracle bones from more than 3,000 years ago are the best known. The other well-known divination method is drawing divination lots (*qian*), where a worshiper with a particular problem goes to a temple, burns incense in front of the deity, and then shakes a box of divination sticks until one "jumps" out. He or she then consults the corresponding divination poem or message for the divine message and inspiration. There are also many divination methods that involve specialists such as a spirit medium or Daoist priests. Here I will introduce a divination method which is widespread in North China.

The method involves the use of an oracle roller called the *gua* (with obvious reference to the Daoist octagram *bagua*). And our example comes from the Black Dragon King Temple in Shaanbei (northern Shaanxi Province) where I conducted fieldwork in the 1990s. The *gua* is a short, fat wooden roller (reminiscent of a rolling pin used by bakers) with eight flattened segments along its length (so the two ends, also flattened, are octagon-shaped). It is about 10 inches long, and is a little thicker in the middle section than at the ends. Each segment has a different four-character message inscribed in the wood. The consultee with a particular problem holds this roller in both palms and rolls it horizontally in a wooden tray about 12 inches wide and 22 inches long. This action is called *tanggua* (Shaanbei dialect expression, which literally means "rolling the *gua*"). When the roller stops, the characters on the top segment are the message Black Dragon King wants to communicate to the consultee. The eight four-character messages are respectively:

+ Extremely auspicious (*shangshang daji*);
+ Not so good (*xiaxia zhongping*);
+ Not clear how you would thank me for the help (*kouyuan buming*);
+ Go home soon if traveling (*xingren zaohui*);
+ Not in accordance with god's ways (*buhe shendao*);

+ Pray with a sincere heart (*qianxin qidao*);
+ Bring the medicine with magical water (*quyao daishui*);
+ Will get well after taking the medicine (*fuyao nenghao*)

The simplest application of this oracle is to ask a yes or no question. For example: "My brother and I are planning to take a trip to Wushen Banner [of Inner Mongolia] to sell some clothes. Your Highness the Dragon King, do you think we will make some good money? If yes, give us 'extremely auspicious'; if no, give us 'not so good'." Then the consultee rolls the roller. If Heilongdawang's answer is "not sure how you would thank me for the help," the consultee either puts more money in the donation box or makes a vow, promising that he will bring a certain amount of incense money if he makes money on the trip with Heilongdawang's blessing. Sometimes the consultee promises 10 percent of his profit or even more. It is like entering a partnership with Heilongdawang. If the answer is "not in accordance with god's ways," the consultee needs to reflect on whether his business plan is going to break the law or offend the god. Other yes or no questions can be: "Has my marriage luck come?"; "Will grandma get better?"; "Will I get a promotion?"; and so forth.

The reference to medicine and magical water on the oracle roller indicates that this *gua* is the medicine oracle, most often used when consultees want to request Heilongdawang's divine intervention in treating their own or their family members' illnesses. The "water" on the oracle roller refers to the spring to the side of the temple that is believed to have magical healing powers, and the "medicine" on the roller refers to "divine medicine" collected at the base of sticks of incense, which is to be dissolved in the spring water and taken by the patient. Heilongdawang has another *gua* that is only used when, on increasingly rare occasions, there are requests for rain. It is called the rain oracle. On it, the two medicine-related messages on the medicine *gua* are replaced by two rain-related messages: "will rain today" and "will rain within three days." To my knowledge all dragon kings in Shaanbei have a similar rain *gua*.

APPEASING "HUNGRY GHOSTS"

In the Chinese religious imagination, ghosts (*gui*) are an important category of supernatural beings. Generally speaking, ghosts are spirits of men and women (and sometimes children) who have died but have no one to make offerings to them so they become the so-called "orphaned souls" (*guhun*). Some ghosts are spirits of identifiable persons. For example, a bullied daughter-in-law might kill herself and become a vengeful ghost going after her cruel mother-in-law; a daughter who has died without having been married might come back in her parents' dreams asking for a husband, upon which a young man would be found who would agree to become her "husband" through a "ghost marriage" (*minghun*) in exchange for monetary compensation (this does not prevent the young man from eventually getting a real wife later on, though often he is unwilling to reveal to his fiancée that he has had a ghost bride in the past!); a man who was killed in a traffic accident might linger around (i.e. haunt) the spot where he died until someone takes pity on him and commissions a ritual to appease his soul.

The vast majority of ghosts are anonymous and are most often addressed as a collective group (e.g. during a ritual): orphaned souls and wild ghosts (*guhun yegui*). An important source of these ghosts is wars in the past since so many young men died on the battlefield without proper burial. Another important source is natural disasters that caused mass deaths. These pitiable spirits roam around hell, trying to grab whatever food they can lay their hands on, such as those offerings laid out for other people's ancestors. Because they are so numerous they fight among themselves for these leftovers. Many of them are in a kind of hell that's called "flaming mouth" (*yankou*) which means that whatever they put in their mouths immediately turns into a ball of flame. Even if they can grab onto some scraps of food, they are still always hungry – hence their name. In both Buddhist and Daoist liturgy, a ritual segment is designed to relieve the hungry ghosts from the flaming mouth so that they can actually eat the offerings, but this only provides sporadic and temporary relief.

The hungry ghosts are released from hell for the entire seventh lunar month each year so that they can roam around the human world. This is when many people feed them with all kinds of offerings so that they can feel sated and don't bother the humans and cause them trouble. During this month households and businesses put tables of offerings on the pavements outside the doors for them to feed on (because they are so lowly and dangerous they are never invited into the homes). These offerings include (uncooked) ducks, chicken, slabs of pork, beef jerky, instant noodles, potato chips, candies, biscuits, and cakes. After the hungry ghosts have finished feeding on the "immaterial aspects" of the offerings through the rising incense smoke (lit incense sticks are stuck onto the offerings), people would take the food items back and eat them. In Taiwan, because people buy so many food items during this month, the supermarkets during this time of the year all have "ghost month" sales to compete for customers. Often members of the household or business would choose their favorite food items to use as offerings. Apparently, the hungry ghosts are not that picky about what kinds of food are put out as they are grateful that people put out any offering at all. The Southern Fujianese and Taiwanese call the hungry ghosts "good brothers" (*haoxiongdi*) and treat them with respect to make sure that they do not cause trouble.

But the offering tables households and businesses put out for the hungry ghosts are small meals compared to the massive feasts that communities put out collectively for them. On the fifteenth day of the seventh lunar month, it is the Middle Prime Festival (*zhongyuan*) (or Yulanpen Festival for Buddhism), which is when communities stage collective offerings to the ghosts, with rows and rows of food offerings and dazzling shows such as folk operas and fireworks. Different communities would hire Buddhist monks or Daoist priests to conduct rituals, which last for days, culminating in the final "feeding the hungry ghosts" (or "relieving the flaming mouths") segment on the night of the grand offering. Through the priests' ritual manipulation, the already abundant offerings are further multiplied miraculously a million-fold. It is a veritable feast for the hungry ghosts. But after the banquet the ghosts have to go back to hell. They will suffer from the "flaming mouth" for another year before the next round of feasts.

Sometimes ghosts can be upgraded into minor gods, such as the so-called "righteous martyrs" (*yimin*) among the Hakka (*Kejia*) in Taiwan. These were young men who died defending Hakka communities against other ethnic groups (e.g. the aboriginals and Hokkien settlers during

Figure 4: The annual Righteous Martyrs temple festival in Xinzhu (Hsing-chu) County, northern Taiwan. Photo: Adam Yuet Chau

the settlement of Taiwan by Chinese migrants) or who died fighting alongside Qing government troops against rebels. These battles and fights happened in the eighteenth and nineteenth centuries, and thousands of young Hakka men died without getting married and produced heirs, which means that they had no descendants to burn incense for them or feed and clothe them on a regular basis. So they risked becoming hungry ghosts. But thanks to the initiatives of some Hakka community leaders in the past, their bones were gathered and buried together and temples were built to honor them, thus ensuring that they would receive regular offerings and not go hungry like the hungry ghosts. Every year the communities celebrated the Righteous Martyrs Festival to commemorate their forebear's bravery, sacrifice, and contribution to the Hakka communities and to make offerings to them.

The Xinpu Righteous Martyrs Temple in northern Taiwan (Xinzhu county) has served as the center of the cult of righteous martyrs for the whole island of Taiwan. In the past hundred years or so, the temple has spawned dozens of branch temples through the practice of "incense division," where a new community wishing to establish their own temple would bring the fire and incense ashes from an older temple to their new temple. During the annual festival a lot of branch temples would send representatives to their "ancestral temple" to pay respects. And these branch righteous martyrs temples have their own festivals and rotational hosting communities. Scholars studying the cult of righteous martyrs have mostly treated the righteous martyrs as a sub-genre of ghosts, but in recent years many Hakka community activists are contesting this view, saying that they are more like deities. The grand scale of the festival rivals the festivals of many deity cults, but there are many details in the rituals during the festival that betray the righteous martyrs' proximity to ghosts (e.g. the date of the festival being in the "Ghost Month"). Meanwhile, in order to appeal to younger people, some Hakka cultural workers have been engaging in efforts to "cute-ify" the righteous martyrs, even making smiley righteous martyr dolls.[2]

RELATIONSHIPS WITH ANCESTORS

The traditional Chinese kinship system was what anthropologists call patrilineal, which means that descent was traced through the male line (father to sons). Daughters were married out to other patrilines so they did not retain a place in their natal homes. Daughters-in-law were brought in from other patrilines for the purpose of producing male descendants. Even though mothers were honored and respected, they were only members of the patriline as wives and mothers. The patrilineality was also a political economic arrangement, where property was passed onto sons only (equally divided among the sons). In some regions of China (especially in South China), patrilines were joined together to form lineages, complete with genealogies, lineage regulations, lineage ancestral halls (where ancestral tablets are kept), lineage-run schools, and ancestral estates whose rental income supported the annual communal lineage rituals and other activities (including issuing loans to lineage members). But in most other regions only the elite had lineages, while ordinary people had simple ancestral veneration rites but not lineage halls and accompanying elaborations.

In traditional practice, when a parent died, a funeral would be organized. Members of the immediate family would don mourning attire, and neighbors, relatives, and other close associates would come and pay their respects. A *fengshui* master would be hired to locate the most auspicious spot for the grave (which could be on a hillside or even in the middle of a piece of cultivated field), and a troupe of either Daoist priests or Buddhist priests would be hired to conduct rituals (more on this in chapter 4) in addition to a folk music band. While the body of the deceased would be buried, the soul would be "seated" in an ancestral tablet (*paiwei*; *zhu*) that received daily offerings in the

Figure 5: A public cemetery near Ningbo. It would be crowded with people making offerings to their ancestors on or near the Qingming (literally meaning "clear and bright") Festival. Photo: Adam Yuet Chau

home of the eldest son and later that of the eldest grandson. After that, he would join the collective ancestorhood and receive seasonal rather than daily offerings. If the family was wealthy, the funeral and subsequent commemorative rituals could be very elaborate and expensive. Every year in spring (Qingming, or "tomb-sweeping festival") and autumn (Chongyang) members of the family would visit the ancestors' graves, make offerings, and share a meal together with the ancestors. The Chinese New Year was also an important occasion for all lineage households to gather at the lineage hall for collective rituals, which included taking home sacrificial meat shared with, and blessed by, the ancestors.

The social reform movements of the modern era (from the Republican era onward) as well as broader societal changes (e.g. urbanization, migration, the one-child policy, increasing gender equality) over more than a hundred years have brought about major transformations to the Chinese kinship system and rituals associated with funerals and ancestors. Nuclear families have now become the norm, even in most rural areas. Many lineages have not been revived after decades of assault by modern family ideologies and socialist policies; even when they have been revived, their functions are primarily symbolic (e.g. the compilation of genealogies) without the traditional political economic powers. Many urban families practice a kind of minimalist ancestor veneration, with photographs of deceased parents and grandparents displayed in an altar-like place (e.g. on top of a cabinet) but without any offerings. Tomb-sweeping practices have been revived in recent years, even meeting official approval as it is seen as an expression of traditional Chinese filial virtues. The traffic jams created by cars going to the cemeteries during Qingming times are second only to those created by the massive movement of people across China during the Chinese New Year season.

THE HOUSEHOLD AS BASIC UNIT OF RELIGIOUS ENGAGEMENT

The Chinese engage in religious activities (i.e. interacting with gods, ancestors, and ghosts) at three different levels: the individual, the household, and the community. Traditionally, anthropologists and historians of Chinese religious life have primarily focused on aspects of communal religious life such as collective rituals and temple festivals. On the other hand, the personal aspects of religious life, admittedly much more difficult to access, have been studied primarily through the lens of discursive productions of elite religious practitioners. The household has not been the focus of serious investigation, but it is the *most* fundamental unit of religious engagement in Chinese religious life.

The household as a discrete sociopolitical unit is a product of, and constitutes the most foundational component of, agrarian societies. The traditional agrarian empire in China depended on the patrilineal household and the household patriarch for proper governance, and considered all kinds of social actors outside the household framework suspect (such as celibate monastics, prostitutes, bachelors not belonging to any households, Jesuit missionaries, members of celibate sisterhoods). This pattern of household-centered governance has persisted in important ways until today (despite brief interruptions during the Maoist period).

In addition to facilitating the management of taxation and security, the household also operates as a sovereign political-economic and ritual unit. Budgeting and most production-consumption decisions (including division of labor, assignment of tasks, migration, household division, and marriage) are made at the household level. All members of the household are the responsibility of the head of the household until the sons divide the household and form new households of their own. But the most salient expressions of household sovereignty are the interactions between, on the one hand, the household as a discrete ritual unit and, on the other, all kinds of spiritual forces (gods, ghosts, and ancestors) and ritual specialists.

Because the household is the most basic political economic and moral-religious building block of Chinese society, any individual engaging in religious activities would be doing so as a member of the household, which is an intimate collectivity whose welfare is interdependent (the hermit who is too concerned with his own spiritual pursuits and leaves his family behind will inevitably damage the wellbeing of the household). There has been a long-held misconception about Chinese religious life, that since women seem to participate more in religious activities, they must be more religious (or superstitious, depending on one's attitude toward such activities). But the truth is that most women participate in religious activities on behalf of all members of their households; they are simply representatives of the household as a unit of religious engagement. The same is true when only the names of heads of households are written on the memorials to be sent (through burning) to the celestial court in communal rituals; on these occasions

the heads of households do not act as individuals but rather as representatives of their respective households.

The household is the site of the worship of various deities and spirits
(e.g. ancestral and deity worship at domestic altars, the stove god). On
the more obvious, basic, and prosaic level, the household is host to the
stove god (*zaojun*), Heaven and Earth (*tiandi*), the immediate ancestors,
and perhaps some other common deities found in domestic settings
(e.g. the God of Wealth, Guanyin). Usually represented in the form
of spirit tablets (*shenzhupai*) on domestic altars, these are some kind
of permanent lodgers in the home, to be cared for on a daily basis,
usually in the form of incense (freshly offered in the morning), red
electric lamps in the shape of candles, and offerings that need not be
replaced too frequently (e.g. fruits or even fruits made of wax, biscuits,
and candies in wrappers). Familiarity has made it unnecessary for the
host household members to be too ceremonious in interacting with
these deities and ancestors. Typically, the matron of the household (i.e.
wife of the head of the household) assumes the responsibility of this
kind of "everyday forms of hosting." These minor yet recurrent hosting
occasions mirror those minor social hosting occasions (e.g. friends and
neighbors dropping by for a visit). At certain nodal points during the
lunar calendar year, the family makes more elaborate and special offerings with more ostentatious gestures of being the host to these spirits
and deities, collectively or individually, e.g. on the first day of the lunar
New Year, on the anniversary of the birth and the death of an immediate ancestor, on the "birthday" of one of the deities such as Guanyin
(somehow extremely generalized deities such as Heaven and Earth,
the stove god, and the God of Wealth don't have birthdays), or during
the "ghost month" (for banqueting the "hungry ghosts"). To be sure,
not all of these rituals physically take place within the household – for
example, the lineage ancestral rites take place at the lineage hall – but
there is no mistaking that the household is always the most basic unit
of hosting these various kinds of spirits.

When the village or neighborhood community stages a communal religious festival such as a temple festival or New Year's festival, it is the households that serve as the basic participatory building blocks in the form of contributing funds and/or labor. In fact, in most communal rituals, the households stage their own household-based mini-rituals that are embedded in the larger framework of the communal ritual but are nevertheless expressions of the household idiom of religious engagement. For example, during a large-scale Daoist communal cleansing ritual (*jiao*), there are usually two distinct sites of ritual actions. In the temple the main group of Daoist priests and musicians conduct the long and drawn-out rituals for the community at large – but also, significantly, read aloud the names of the heads of households before submitting the communal requests to heaven (i.e. the Jade Emperor) – while individual or small groups of ritualists (usually lower-ranking) conduct much briefer and simpler small rites from house to house at the invitation of individual households, receiving separate "red packets" with cash in them as payment for their services. The impulse to engage in religious practices at the household level is so strong in many parts of China that there are even "temple festivals" that take place within the houses of the spirit mediums, whose tutelary spirits constitute the divine guests to be hosted on these occasions (see Yue 2010).

Another important aspect of the household makes it the most basic unit of religious engagement. In Chinese religious life, the most common and most important activities are in the form of households hiring ritual specialists to conduct rituals on behalf of the household, especially at funerals. The overwhelming majority of these specialists-for-hire are not regular members of any larger religious institution and do not live in special dwellings separate from the common people; rather, they are mostly householders themselves who live among the people who constitute their clientele base. In contrast with clerics who live collectively in cloisters (e.g. monasteries, nunneries, Daoist belvederes and temples), these religious specialists are atomized, living within the community of their prospective clients but sometimes far removed from other, similar specialists. These specialists include *yinyang* master, the *huoju* (or *sanju*) Daoist priest, the spirit medium, and other similar types of householder religious specialists (or householder religious service providers). We will look at these specialists in more detail in chapter 4.

The revival of household-based political economy and the cash nexus during the post-Mao reform era has provided the material and socio-structural basis for the revival of Chinese petty capitalism (Gates 1996; also D. Yang 2005) and its concomitant household-based "petty" religiosity. This has provided a fertile ground for the flourishing of householder religious service providers as well as household-based religious engagement. The vitality of the household idiom of religious engagement will probably persist for as long as the household remains the key structural component of the Chinese political economic, social, and moral order.

THE HOSTING IDIOM IN
CHINESE RELIGIOUS PRACTICES

One particular social form characterizes much of how Chinese people interact with various kinds of spirits: hosting. The Chinese host gods, ancestors, and ghosts at specific points in the annual ritual calendar and during periods of special needs (e.g. communal exorcism, temple dedication). It is through highly formalized and structured rituals such as "hosting" – where banquets are laid out for the supernatural visitors – that Chinese households and communities establish and maintain long-term relationships with these different categories of supernatural forces. What is more, and perhaps even more importantly, these occasions are also for hosting human visitors from other households and other communities. Indeed, the cost of hosting these human visitors (with elaborate banquets) often far outweighs that of hosting deities.

In this section I will focus only on the role of the household in hosting funerals since they are the most elaborate and expensive household-level "event productions," with the host household receiving and banqueting hundreds of guests.[3] The idiom of hosting refers to receiving guests (human or spirits) who are known and familiar to the host. It contrasts sharply with the more commonly employed concept of "hospitality," which primarily refers to receiving and being kind to strangers (see Heal 1990; Derrida and Dufourmantelle 2000; Candea and da Col 2012).[4]

Peasant household event productions such as funerals are essentially "host/guest rituals" that fashion the host household (*zhujia*) as a sovereign social unit and the head of the household as the sovereign or master (*zhu*) of this unit.[5] The host household exudes "pre-eminence" (one of the key meanings of sovereignty) over and above other households. The structural meaning and position of each host household are derived from its being situated within the constellation of households in the community and beyond, each of which is entitled to host at some point in the course of its "lifespan." During these hosting occasions, even though the guests (including both humans and spirits) have to be well treated and respected, it is the *zhujia* that accrues recognition, social prestige, "face," and symbolic capital by being the host. For the brief period of the event production (two or three days), it is as if the whole world revolves around the courtyard of the *zhujia*. The "red-hot sociality" (*honghuo/rènao*) produced by the convergence of so many people, noisy firecrackers and music, steamy dishes, colorful decorations and loud banqueting makes the *zhujia's* house unquestionably pre-eminent (Chau 2006a: chapters 7 and 8).

This kind of important hosting (which a household stages only a few times in its "lifespan") is a moral event production because a recognition and acknowledgment of social worth is communicated between, and co-produced by, host and guest, and the hosting event always entails morally inflected judgments of all the details of the whole event (behavior, utterances, gestures, the level of courtesy, the degree of politeness and generosity, the number of guests, the presence of important guests, the quality of banquet dishes, the elaborateness of rituals, the ability to mobilize helpers, and so on). By being host, a household is putting its status and reputation on the line. A well-hosted event production maintains or augments the host household's status and reputation, while a badly hosted event production can drastically drain its store of social-relational goodwill and affect its standing in the social universe of inter-household relations. Successfully hosting major household event productions most importantly constitutes the personhood and identity of all members of the household and by extension establishes and confirms the standing and "sovereignty" of the household in the community.

A significant amount of the attraction of Chinese religious activities for the Chinese derives from their employing the idiom of hosting in framing ritual actions. The hosting idiom is attractive because it is a common idiom found in many domains of Chinese social life. In other words, the familiar idioms and models prevalent in Chinese social life have informed and enframed Chinese religious life. More than a cognitive resonance between the religious and the social, the actual "doing" of religion employs certain key organizational and conceptual idioms that underlie much of Chinese social life. Hosting is one of these key idioms that have been imported to, or have been captured by, the religious domain. Hosting is a major structuring idiom through which the staging of many ritual actions and event productions in Chinese religious life is made possible. Yet capturing a key social idiom such as hosting has its costs for the development of Chinese religious traditions. In Chinese religious actions, the emphasis is put on being a good host and on orthopraxy rather than being a good theologian and on orthodoxy. Hosting occasions produce "hosts" who would embody gestural and other related protocols of hosting, who need not memorize any catechism or understand any theological arguments. In hosting, practice trumps theory. Through embodying the roles of host and guest in countless social occasions (religious and non-religious), most Chinese act out the hosting idiom without conscious reflection; the idiom becomes part of their "habitus" (social as well as religious, if indeed these two domains can ever be disentangled from each other). As a result of the prominent role hosting plays in Chinese religious culture, Chinese religious practices cultivate a kind of social subjectivity (i.e. hosts and guests) rather than religious subjectivity (i.e. the Judeo-Christian "believer"). Of course, Chinese religious life is far richer and more varied than the hosting model can summarize. In other words, Chinese religious life cannot and should not be reduced to the hosting idiom. Yet one can hardly picture Chinese religious life without the hosting idiom. Take away hosting from Chinese popular religious life and the entire popular religious life at the level of practice will simply collapse or become entirely unrecognizable.

It would be very instructive to contrast the hosting idiom in Chinese religious culture with the hosting idiom in Christianity. In Christian theological formulation, God is the ultimate host in heaven ("the Kingdom"), and this conception is translated into this-worldly practice in the idiom of the church (physically as the church building but also as the collectivity of all believers), which represents the body of Christ. When worshipers go to church for mass or the communion, the Church and church personnel are always the host and the worshipers are always the guests. Instead of "feeding" the deities, as in Chinese popular religion, Christian worshipers are fed the body and blood of Christ at communion in the form of bread and wine.[6] Instead of acting as members of a household engaging in ritual activities as a collective unit, Christians as individuals come together to constitute a congregation, and the believers engage with God, at least in theory, as individuals.[7] Christians stage important life-event productions such as weddings and funerals at the church, again relegating sovereignty to the church. This church-centered event production structure vitiates the importance of the households as loci of hosting. As a result, the household loses its sovereignty.

But because of the centrality of the household as a social-organizational and ritual unit, many Christians in China have not completely relinquished their household sovereignty. There is certain tantalizing evidence suggesting such household-centric Christian practices in China. For example, in some places worshipers belonging to officially sanctioned churches who attend the Sunday services at church would gather even more frequently in small groups in one another's homes for small-scale worship and fellowship. And some elderly converts are still in the habit of inviting "the Lord" to come and consume offerings in their homes (i.e. hosting God) (see Wang 2011). In many ways the so-called "house churches" in China have resulted not simply from the state's unwillingness to let the worshipers build proper churches but rather the worshipers' desire to keep worshiping in their own homes, to "host God" (at least in form if not in theology), and to express and assert their household sovereignty.

3 | Festivals and Pilgrimages

Temple festivals and pilgrimages are the most spectacular and concentrated expressions of religiosity. They are also where we can find the most varied forms of relationships and sociality. This chapter is divided into two parts. The first part is on temple festivals. Through case studies from both northern and southern China I hope to show not only how relationships are built and maintained (between humans and deities as well as between deities) but how worshipers construct and consume collectively a particular kind of sociality ("red-hot sociality"). The second part is on pilgrimages. The case studies for this part include: (1) the famous Mazu (a sea goddess) pilgrimage network in Taiwan; (2) the pilgrimage of lay Buddhists in the Ciji Merit Society who are followers of the charismatic nun Master Zhengyan; (3) a new form of pilgrimage in Taiwan for people who seek to cultivate their "original spirit" by visiting a series of temples; (4) Chinese Muslims' hajj pilgrimage to Mecca; and (5) the hosting of a tree-planting event by the Black Dragon King Temple.

I will conclude with a discussion on the concept of "capture" that can be best used to understand how worshipers are bound by their temples and how sometimes seemingly incongruent social elements can be brought together by religious sites through temple festivals and pilgrimages.

TEMPLE ASSOCIATIONS AND
TEMPLE FESTIVALS

In addition to building a beautiful temple, the other most important thing worshipers do for their deity is to organize temple festivals. All temple festivals are expressly to celebrate the gods' birthdays, to show gratitude for a year's peace and prosperity or a good harvest, or simply to make the gods happy. A "red and fiery" (re'nao, honghuo) temple festival is the most visible manifestation of the sense of being blessed felt by the sponsoring ritual community. It is also the best form of public relations the community has with other communities because temple festivals are occasions for extensive hosting of visitors (including visiting deities from neighboring communities). Below I will use my Shaanbei case study to illustrate the amount of work that goes into the organization of temple festivals and the cultural logics behind the form it takes. There are practices that are unique to Shaanbei, but a similar range of practices is found in most places in China.[1]

As tradition dictates, Shaanbei people stage temple festivals at least twice a year, one during the Lunar New Year and the other for the deity's birthday. These temple festivals are organized by temple associations (hui), which comprise a small group of responsible and generally respectable adult men who are approved by the deity through divination. If the deity has a medium, he will usually become a core member of the temple association. The members of the association are called "association heads" (huizhang), and the head of the association is called the "big association head" (dahuizhang). In the past these associations were ad hoc groups, formed for the specific purpose of organizing the festival and dissolved when all the work was done. In recent years, most of these associations (especially those of bigger temples) became permanent organizations because the local state requires them to register and have a formal organizational structure. This statist requirement has ironically led to the increasing professionalization of temple associations.

Traditionally, every year, in the first half of the first lunar month, the temple association organizes a temple *yangge* troupe (traditional folk dance troupe with musical accompaniment of drums, cymbals, trumpets, etc.) to "visit door by door" (*yanmenzi*) around the villages in the vicinity of the temple to greet the villagers and to collect donations for the temple. On the fifteenth day of the first lunar month, the association oversees the communal festival at the temple. The temple festival on the deity's birthday is a much larger event, lasting typically for three days, and thus requiring much more organizational effort. Depending on the degree of wealth of the temple community, different folk performing arts are staged for the deity as well as for the community. The goal of every temple festival, like that of other festive occasions, such as weddings and funerals, is to produce "excitement and fun" (*honghuo*). If the temple commands a large sum of donations, the temple association will invite an opera troupe to perform folk opera, the culturally ideal choice for temple festivals in honor of deities' birthdays. But if the temple endowment is modest, the temple association will then only invite a folk music band or a storyteller to enliven the atmosphere. Lots of firecrackers are also a must. As in other parts of China, traditional dynastic and mythical stories are the most prevalent in folk opera repertoires. Traditional stories also provide the most common themes in Shaanbei storytelling at temple festivals (e.g. the martial exploits of military heroes derived from famous vernacular novels). Folk music bands play a variety of festive music, with many tunes common to those they play at weddings and funerals.[2]

Many temple festivals in Shaanbei also serve as occasions for commerce, following a long tradition typical of such festivals in north China. Itinerant traders would bring their commodities to sell to temple festivalgoers (everything ranging from pots and pans to clothing and toys), and villagers from communities running the temple would normally have priority in occupying the best spots around the temple to sell incense, spirit money, firecrackers, and food. Itinerant entertainment troupes of all kinds (e.g. circuses, song-and-dance shows, freak shows, etc.) also come from far and wide. With much improved transportation, even the most modest temple festivals in today's Shaanbei would attract a few thousand festivalgoers.

TEMPLE FESTIVALS AND SOCIAL RELATIONSHIPS

All temple festivals entail some kind of pilgrimage, when people from outside of the regular temple community come to pay homage to the deity, meet old friends and relatives, and enjoy the excitement and fun. Daughters who have left through marriage come back to their natal villages, and parents visit their daughters when their in-laws' villages are having temple festivals. When long-distance pilgrimage is involved and the number of outside visitors is high, the temple associations have to arrange accommodation for them. Large temples often have dormitories or build temporary structures for pilgrims. Sometimes, when a large number of pilgrims come from one particular locale, they will organize into groups to take care of themselves. A famous example of a locale-based pilgrimage organization in Shaanbei is the "eight big congregations" (*badahui*) for going to the biggest and most famous temple festival in Shaanbei, Baiyunshan (the White Cloud Mountain) in Jia County. Because the Baiyunshan festival is so crowded, different congregations in different areas have to arrive on different days over the one-week festival period to be accommodated, fed, and received properly (but of course there are plenty of individual festivalgoers who would go without joining one of these congregations). The Miaofengshan temple festival in the "Western Hills" of Beijing is famous for its many "festival associations" that come from a wide geographical area.[3] In a section below on pilgrimages, I will present the Mazu pilgrimage network in Taiwan, which best exemplifies the vitality and complexity of temple networks.

TEMPLE FESTIVALS AND SOCIAL HEAT

When worshipers converge at a particular temple festival, they will find themselves bombarded by an overwhelming amount and variety of sensory stimulation. Below I will try to evoke the sensory ambience of the temple festival at the Black Dragon King Temple, also known by its location, the Dragon King Valley (Longwanggou) (the "ethnographic present" is the summer of 1998). Admittedly the Longwanggou temple festival is a lot grander in scale and richer in sensory stimulation than most other Shaanbei temple festivals, but the difference is only in degree, not in kind. All temple festivals are *honghuo* events, replete with noises, sights, smells, tastes, and ambient sensations.

Figure 6: Worshipers converging onto the Black Dragon King Temple in Shaanbei during the annual temple festival. Photo: Adam Yuet Chau

Noises. Tractors, motorcycles, minivans, and buses are constantly bringing people into and out of the festival site; on the roads leading to Longwanggou the bus operators are shouting: "Longwanggou! Longwanggou!"; at the mouth of the valley the bus operators heading out shout out the destinations or directions: "Mizhi! Mizhi!" "Yulin! Yulin!" "Zhenchuan! Zhenchuan!"; the diesel motors are relentless with their staccato "tok tok tok tok tok tok tok," rhyming with the different pitches of honking; loudspeakers tout people into freak show or song-and-dance tents; people are shouting, laughing, chatting, playing games, gambling; firecrackers explode; drums, gongs, trumpets of the *yangge* troupes are playing; the sacrificial pigs and goats squeal; the sounds of opera singing and music pierce the air. ...

Sights. People are everywhere, people in festive, colorful clothes; an ocean of people, some one knows but most one doesn't; game stands, trinket sellers, incense and firecracker sellers, watermelon stands, noodle tents, freak show tent, song-and-dance tent, fortune-tellers, folk music bands; men, women, children, old people; people climbing up the steps to the main temple hall; people kneeling down in front of the deity, burning incense and spirit money, praying and offering thanks, and putting money into the donation box or bowl; the pile of bright yellow spirit money burning like a bonfire; the brightly lit opera stage and the opera singers in colorful costumes; the *yangge* performances; the fireworks at night; the dazzling chaos. ...

Smells and tastes. The smells and tastes of all kinds of food: noodles made of wheat and potato flour, griddle cakes, goat intestine soup, stir-fried dishes, garlic and scallion, vinegar and red pepper, watermelons, small yellow melons, icicles, soft drinks, burning liquor, beer; the pungency of diesel exhaust, exploding firecrackers, the warm raw blood of freshly slaughtered pigs and goats; the mixed fragrance and pungency of incense and burning spirit money; the faint smell of sweat from so many people squeezing through the main temple hall. ...

Figure 7: Festival-goers at the annual temple festival of the Black Dragon King Temple in Shaanbei. Photo: Adam Yuet Chau

Ambient sensations (heat, proprioception, kinesthetics, etc.). The worshiper gets off the bus or tractor-truck, whichever is his means of transportation to get to the temple festival, follows the swarms of other worshipers up and along the valley, passing through noodle stands, watermelon stands, gambling circles, song-and-dance tents, buys a few bundles of incense and spirit money from the incense hawkers, climbs up the steps to the main temple hall, throws the spirit money into the bonfire, lights a string of firecrackers, kneels and prays, burns incense, puts some money in the donation bowl, shakes the divination cylinder and gets his divination slip number, gets immediately pushed aside by worshipers coming up from behind, goes to the divination slips room and has the divination poem interpreted, then squeezes his way through the crowd to catch a glimpse of the opera performance, and wanders through different parts of the festival ground, snacks or eats a bowl of noodles, chats with acquaintances and co-villagers or complete strangers, plays a few rounds of games, watches the fireworks at night, and always finds himself in the company of tens of thousands of other worshipers. ...

Describing the high-spirited, chaotic scenes typically found at local temples in Taiwan and invoking the southern Hokkien term *laujiat* ("noisy and hot," i.e. *re'nao, honghuo*), the anthropologist Robert Weller aptly calls Chinese popular religion "hot and noisy" (1994: 113–28). As Weller observes, "[a]ny successful large event in Taiwan, from a market to a ritual, provides plenty of heat and noise – it *should be* packed with people, chaotically boisterous, loud with different voices, and clashingly colorful" (emphasis added). This "should-beness" captures the often tyrannical force of such a cultural imperative. We might call this cultural imperative of *honghuo*-making the "festive regime." A large event that is not hot and noisy is a failed event; people have to produce heat and noise on a festive occasion. Similarly, a market is a successful market when it is hot and noisy. Temple festivals epitomize such an aesthetics of "heat and noise" (Weller 1994: 118). But what take place at a temple festival that makes it *honghuo*?

The key component of *honghuo* is people; the more people the more *honghuo*. Embedded in this belief is a premium put on the warmth or heat (not necessarily a physical sensation) generated from human sociality. Shaanbei people make a sharp contrast between the dull and bland drudgery of everyday life and the lively and exciting social events such as funeral and wedding banquets or temple festivals. These social events are *honghuo* because there are always large gatherings of people, people doing any number of things: milling around, talking and shouting, eating and drinking, smoking, playing, singing, dancing, drumming, setting off firecrackers and fireworks, burning incense, gambling, or simply watching and being part of the scene. Crowdedness is the necessary condition for *honghuo*-making. It is as if the simple convergence of many people will generate *honghuo*, which is why I choose to translate *honghuo* (or *re'nao*) not simply as "exciting," but also as "social heat" or "red-hot sociality." The convergence of people generates *honghuo*, and *honghuo* generates a greater convergence of people because people are predisposed to be attracted to the noise and colors of *honghuo*. A small crowd is sure to generate a bigger crowd. The Daoism scholar John Lagerwey once remarked: "For religion is people coming together, assembling: we might say, the Chinese love to form a crowd, therefore they are religious" (Lagerwey 1987: 4).

Each temple festival is an elaborate event production rather than a ritual. At a temple festival there might be a pre-arranged program for the opera performance or a set sequence for some organized groups to pay homage to the deity, but there is no strict plan for individual worshipers to experience certain things in a certain manner, as is the case for most ritual participants (e.g. at a mass or a procession). There are no prescribed "ritual actions" other than the minimal sequence of paying respect to the deity, which is a small, albeit important, part of the entire temple festival experience for any worshiper. It is utterly impossible to control or predict the many different encounters, experiences, sensations, pleasures, or frustrations of different worshipers. This *absence* of structure (as opposed to Victor Turner's famed "anti-structure") allows one person's trajectory through the time-space of the temple festival to be quite different from that of another; as a result, no one's experience at the temple festival is ever the same as that of another. Also, unlike a ritual, an event production such as a temple festival does not have a clear beginning or a clear ending: the momentum builds up to a crescendo, and then it tapers off and dies out completely. People come and leave as they wish. Each person can have his or her idiosyncratic moments and loci of excitement. But just like rituals, these event productions are also judged as successful or unsuccessful, though not in terms of effectiveness in delivering the desired result as in rituals (e.g. healing, adulthood, exorcized state) but in terms of felt satisfaction: a sense of having been part of intense red-hot sociality.

Many Shaanbei peasants related to me the most *honghuo* funerals, weddings, or temple festivals they had been to, their eyes glowing in excitement as if they were reliving the *honghuo* atmosphere in their minds. It was not uncommon for some members of the audience to recount their experience of *honghuo* events as if in competition to see who had the good fortune of having seen or participated in the most *honghuo* events. *Honghuo* events become memorable events to be savored, and it is almost as if participants or witnesses become imbued with *honghuo* as an intangible quality the way a person is endowed with mana (life force, vitality, spiritual power) in Melanesian societies. Taiwanese pilgrims who go on long and often arduous pilgrimages to centers of divine power to attend temple festivals (e.g. the Mazu temple at Beigang) experience similar feelings of the endowment of renewed energy and personal vitality. They even liken the experience to dead batteries' getting recharged. Even though they believe the power comes from Mazu, it is equally plausible that they derive renewed vitality from the extreme social heat (i.e. *honghuo*, or the Minnan expression *laujiat*) generated at the crowded and exciting temple festival scene. Sangren (2000) has convincingly argued that the masses of worshipers at Mazu festivals constitute a kind of collective testimonialism that confirms and authenticates an individual worshiper's faith in the magical efficacy of the deity. The same can be said about Shaanbei deities, temple festivals, worshipers, and magical efficacy. Temple festivals are not simply expressions of people's relationships with the deities; they at the same time construct and affirm such relationships. The forms and contents of temple festivals in China can be quite varied. Some temple festivals have elaborate formal ritual events while others are minimalist in formal ritual matters. The common denominator of all temple festivals, however, is the attempt of all participants (organizers as well as visitors) to make the atmosphere

Figure 8: A Mazu palanquin passing over prostrating worshipers to bless them with divine power during a Mazu pilgrimage in western Taiwan. Photo: Adam Yuet Chau

as *honghuo* as possible. And ultimately this festive regime is the best expression and carrier of their religiosity and their conceptions of the magical efficacy (*ling*) of their deities.

TEMPLE FESTIVALS AND INTER-COMMUNAL RIVALRY

Many amicable interpersonal, inter-household, and inter-communal relationships are renewed at festivals. But temple festivals are also occasions for inter-communal rivalry. This is most pronounced in southeastern coastal China (including Fujian, Guangdong, Taiwan, Hong Kong) where deity cults take on the most "territorial" characteristics due to a long history of inter-ethnic and inter-lineage competition over land and other resources. In the past there were frequent armed conflicts between many of these communities, and their respective deities became important symbols of their communal identities as well as divine protectors. Nowadays such armed conflicts have long subsided, but the spirit of competition has remained.

The most important activity of a territorial cult is the annual "tour of inspection" of the deity around the communities (framed very much as a festival), especially along the borders of the deity's "ritual territory." Because these borders are necessarily also borders of rival neighboring cult communities, these tours of the deity in a palanquin with a massive human entourage (featuring especially a large number of martial-spirited young men) parading ritual paraphernalia, beating on drums and cymbals, and firing off firecrackers are ostentatious displays of the community's strength. Below is a summary description of one of these recently revived processions (i.e. inspection tours) found in a rural area in Chaozhou (eastern Guangdong Province bordering Fujian Province) in the late 1990s:

The fifth day of the Lunar New Year marks the beginning of six weeks of festivities in the rural area of Chaozhou, a distinct dialect region in Southeast China. Scheduled on separate dates, processions of local deities are staged by different villages. On the morning of the chosen day, villagers flock to the main village temple, where wooden statues of the divine occupants are congregated with those from other local temples. Each family sets up a table in the courtyard, lights incense and candles, and presents its offerings (of chicken, duck, goose, fish, rice, wine, fruits, cakes, and candies) to the statues. With spirit money set on fire, worship and prayers begin.

A few hours later, a thundering blast of firecrackers starts the main event of the day – procession of the deities (*youshen*). Wooden statues of the deities are placed in separate sedan chairs. Each sedan chair is carried by four to eight young male villagers, mostly those who married or had a male child during the preceding year. Firecracker gunners and a gong team lead the way, followed by carriers of lanterns and banners bearing wishful words for good fortune and warnings against evil spirits. The sedan chairs are preceded by children carrying flower baskets and a drum-and-bell ensemble and followed by an assembly of senior villagers representing different families. The slow-moving procession marches through the main roads of the village and encircles its boundaries. A few stops are made at ancestral halls of the village's different clans to receive greetings and offerings. Villagers and spectators from far and near line up along the designated route, where firecrackers are set off from adjacent houses and buildings as the procession passes by or pauses for worship and presentation of offerings. People seeking to have their wishes granted take turns swapping the burning incense sticks held in their hands for those planted in a large incense burner in a separate sedan chair. The procession lasts for several hours before the deity statues are carried back to their temples. On the days before and after the procession, the villagers perform certain rites of initiation and completion and arrange various entertainment activities, such as opera, dragon or lion dance, puppet shows, fireworks, lantern displays, riddle games, and movies. (Eng and Lin 2002: 1259–60)

On this occasion there were no violent clashes with neighboring villagers, which might have happened in the past. James Watson has observed on the modern ritual rivalry between same-surname communities in the New Territories of Hong Kong that they now "fight with operas" (i.e. the elaborateness of the festivals) instead of fists (Watson 1996). In fact, ritual competition and rivalry, which often result in seemingly excessive expenditure of monetary and other resources (see e.g. Yang 2000), are important mechanisms for generating excitement and "red-hot sociality," as are threats of ritual violence (see e.g. Sutton 2003).

GODS VISITING GODS:
MAZU PILGRIMAGES IN TAIWAN

Mazu is one of the most widely-worshiped deities in coastal China, especially in the coastal regions of Fujian and Guangdong provinces (see Chang 2008). The name Mazu literally means "mother ancestor," which is a familiar term of address by her worshipers. Even though she started out as a protection deity for fishermen and seafarers, a role that is still important today, Mazu eventually became a goddess that granted miraculous response to all kinds of requests. Mazu is also known as Empress of Heaven (Tianhou), a title granted by the imperial state. The anthropologist James Watson has studied the history

Figure 9: Devotees welcoming the Mazu deity palanquin passing through their town in western Taiwan. Photo: Adam Yuet Chau

of this goddess's "canonization" by the imperial state over the course of several centuries, calling this process "standardizing the gods" (Watson 1985), with a particular emphasis on how the imperial state tried to impose a certain standardized version of her hagiography. But this kind of standardizing effort never succeeded because in local cult communities all kinds of locale-specific legends and miracle stories were constantly being produced.

The southern Fujianese migrants brought Mazu to Taiwan over the course of their settlement of the island in the Ming and Qing dynasties, and it subsequently became the most popular deity in Taiwan. The various settler groups each had their own patron deities brought from their places of origin, but Mazu as a deity was worshiped by all of these groups, which was the main cause of her popularity. When the Nationalist exile government ruled over Taiwan (1949 until the introduction of presidential elections in the 1990s and the coming to power of the Democratic Progressive Party first through the election of Chen Shui-bien and later Tsai Ing-wen), Mazu became a *de facto* symbol of Taiwanese identity because very few "mainlander Taiwanese" (*waishengren*, literally "those from provinces other than Taiwan") worshiped Mazu. This association between Mazu worship and non-mainlander Taiwan identity, and for some even pro-Taiwan independence identity, has remained strong until the present day. However, in the past two decades or so, the PRC government has mobilized Mazu in its efforts to link Taiwan culturally to the mainland in order to facilitate amity between peoples of the two shores of the Taiwan Strait. This is part of the United Front strategy to soften the hostility felt by pro-independence Taiwanese towards mainland China.

The Mazu cult in Taiwan best exemplifies the vitality and complexity of temple networks and what we might call pilgrimage networks. In southeastern coastal China and Taiwan, one of the most common ways of establishing a new temple is to go to an already established temple and to "divide" the incense and efficacy of the enshrined deity (see Sangren 1987, 2000). This involves making a new statue of the deity, infusing this new statue with the incense fragrance of the older one, scooping up some incense ashes from the older temple's incense burner, lighting a lamp using the older temple's oil lamp fire, and bringing all these back to the new temple building to enshrine the new statue. From this moment on, the new temple and its enshrined statue will have an affiliation with the older temple that puts the new temple in a subordinate position. Even though the deity enshrined in the two temples is the same deity, each has its own power supported by a body of miracle lore testifying to its efficacy. And each statue is named after the place in which the temple is situated, e.g. Mazu of Dajia, Mazu of Lugang, etc. In fact, a deity usually has a large, main statue carved from wood or sculpted from clay and then painted and elaborately clothed that is enshrined in the temple and multiple smaller statues about half a meter in height that can be carried in a deity palanquin or brought home by individual worshipers for in-home consultation (especially when involving a spirit medium) (see Lin 2015). All of these different smaller statues then develop their own special powers and bodies of divine lore resulting in all being treated by worshipers as different deities.

In order to sustain and renew the power of the new statue, it has to visit the "parent" temple periodically to recharge its power, thus necessitating periodic pilgrimage of members of the newer temple community to the older temple. These pilgrimages are called incense-presenting (*jinxiang*) trips. Similarly, members of the older temple community organize periodic pilgrimages to *their* "parent" temple to recharge the power of *their* deity statue. Over time, such relations of affiliation extended both vertically and horizontally (in a fashion resembling a pyramid) and can form an intricate and dense network of dozens if not hundreds of "higher" and "lower" temples and "brotherly" (or "mother-daughter") temples. Important temples with high claims of efficacy and a large number of affiliate temples would assert regional supremacy and become regional centers of pilgrimage, but the most important pilgrimage is always the one that centers on the so-called "ancestral temple," from where all the other temples and their statues have been derived through varying degrees of direct connection.

The Mazu temple pilgrimage network in Taiwan is the most famous and best studied among the incense-division temple networks. The ancestral temple for the Mazu cult is on Meizhou Island in Fujian because that was where the apotheosized girl Lin Moniang first manifested her power and was worshiped. But because of Taiwan's geographical status as an island far from the Fujian coast, Taiwan's cultural and political separation from the mainland during the Japanese colonial period (1895–1945) and the post-colonial period from the mid-1940s until now, among many other factors, the first Mazu temple in Taiwan assumed a quasi-ancestral temple status over the years. Even though there have been disputes between different temples over which is the first Mazu temple in Taiwan, for a long time it was the Chaotiangong in Beigang to which Mazu worshipers from all over the island converged annually to pay respect and to recharge their own Mazu statues' power. After travel between Taiwan and the mainland became possible, rivalry among the main Mazu temples in Taiwan intensified, each trying to reconnect to the original ancestral temple in Meizhou though never actually conceding primacy to the mainland.

Pilgrimage studies (since the anthropologist pioneer Victor Turner) has highlighted the structural and experiential aspects of the so-called liminal state (being suspended in a social limbo) of the pilgrim. But this image of the pilgrim is based on the archetypal case of the long-distance, often once-in-a-lifetime, pilgrimage (e.g. a Catholics' pilgrimage to Rome, Lourdes, Santiago de Compostela, Fatima, etc., or a Muslim's pilgrimage to Mecca). A far more common form of pilgrimage in many religious cultures (including Christianity and Islam) involves excursions to religious sites that are not too far from the pilgrim's own turf and these are likely to be repeated many times during the course of the pilgrim's lifetime. The Mazu pilgrimage culture in Taiwan exemplifies the form of pilgrimage that is done repeatedly and traverses a relatively short distance. However, as it turns out, Mazu pilgrimage is often not about getting to the destination following the shortest route and employing the fastest method. In recent decades two Mazu temples on the west coast of Taiwan (Dajia and Baishatun) have insisted on visiting their "ancestral temple" on foot, deliberately foregoing the convenience of modern transportation. Such pilgrimages would therefore take a few days of grueling brisk walking instead of a quick, leisurely day trip by car or chartered bus. In addition, their pilgrimage trajectories have become increasingly more circuitous, incorporating many more towns and villages, and, as a result, extra days have to be added to accommodate the deliberately stretched itinerary.

The key reason for such spatially and temporally extended pilgrimages is the desire to establish ever wider networks of temples and temple communities through the acts of paying respect and hosting. Like most pilgrimages in Chinese popular religious traditions, these Mazu pilgrimages are not just about people visiting deities; crucially, they are more about *deities visiting deities*, with humans serving as members of the entourage. As deities travel through other deities' territories, the former need to pay respect to the latter and the latter would host the former. The longer the journey the more such respect-paying and hosting occur, thus establishing and consolidating relationships among deities, between deities and humans, and between communities of worshipers. Some of the temples *en route* also serve as rest stops or places for the visiting deity and entourage to spend the night. Some temples would jostle for the honor of hosting the visiting deity, and the visiting temple community would resort to divination to decide on the pilgrimage route and which temples to visit or stop at, etc. Strings of temples and temple communities are thus linked together spatio-temporally by these pilgrimages, forming a complex, ever shifting network of deities, temples, territories, and communities. Indeed, in Chinese religious culture "gods visiting other gods" is one of the most prevalent idioms through which different, sometimes far-flung, communities establish long-lasting relationships with one another.[4] Herein lies the ingenuity of Chinese popular religion.

CIJI PILGRIMAGES: RE-TERRITORIALIZING UNIVERSALISM

We now live in an age of large-scale religious globalization, with a number of so-called world religions as well as a myriad of new religions spreading to all corners of the globe. The majority of these globalized religions are premised on sets of beliefs and practices that are readily de-territorialized (i.e. transferrable to any location of the world) even if they originated in particular historical and geographical settings. Often these major religions get re-worked significantly locally or spur unexpected innovations, but the imprint of a pre-packaged religious tradition getting transplanted onto new soil is very clear (e.g. Tibetan Buddhism, Zen Buddhism, Pentecostalism, etc.). On the other hand, the multiple features of particular locales sometimes exert themselves and yield a multitude of "ritual *terroirs*" (sites empowered by rituals which in turn empower religious practitioners; see Chau under review) despite the universalizing tendencies of organized religions. For example, the Taiwanese lay Buddhist organization Ciji (Tzu Chi) has become a hugely successful transnational religious movement in the past few decades, with branches and aid-relief activities in dozens of countries (even including mainland China despite the very different environment for religious life). Ciji's founder, the soft-spoken yet charismatic nun Master Zhengyan (Cheng Yen), encourages her followers to practice the great love of bodhisattva compassion and to help the needy (e.g. disaster victims, the poor, the sick) via monetary donation and volunteering through many of the organization's volunteering groups (meticulously organized according to gender, age, rank seniority, mission institutions, functional departments and locale/congregation, differentiated by corresponding uniforms).

Ciji's mission is largely independent of geographical constraints, but just as it has grown into a significant global organization, its headquarters in Hualian (Hualien) in eastern Taiwan quickly became a place of pilgrimage for all Ciji followers (see Huang 2009: chapter 3). Ciji followers within Taiwan and overseas Ciji followers all try to go on "homecoming" visits to the Ciji headquarters for spiritual retreat and, most importantly, to see the founder Master Zhengyan. Special chartered trains and buses bring Ciji members from all over the world to the Ciji headquarters, and they engage in all kinds of ritual activities along the way and when they are in Hualian. The center of the pilgrimage is the modest Still Thought Abode (*jingsi jingshe*) where Master Zhengyan and her monastic disciples reside and practice. Sobbing uncontrollably when seeing Master Zhengyan is one of the most memorable experiences for many Ciji members. All of these centripetal movements of people and activities constitute what I have called "rites of convergence" (Chau 2006a; 2012a; 2012b), crucially constructing the Ciji headquarters in Hualian as a ritual *terroir*.

DRAWING POWER FROM MULTIPLE SITES: NEW AGE SPIRIT CULTIVATION IN CONTEMPORARY TAIWAN[5]

In the past three decades or so (since the 1980s) a new ritual practice emerged in Taiwan: groups of seekers converge upon particularly spiritually hospitable temples or other religious sites for collective sessions of spirit possession (the practice is called *huilingshan* or "converging upon spirit mountain"). These spiritual practices take advantage of the existing elements of the religious site (e.g. the power of its enshrined deities, its *qi* field, its reputation in the overall landscape of religious sites, its particular spatial configuration, the deities enshrined and their relationship to the practitioners, etc.) but significantly add an entirely new genre of ritual practice, thus enriching these sites as power-laden places (i.e. ritual *terroirs*).

Spirit mediumism has been a prominent aspect of Chinese religious life (see chapter 4).[6] Spirit mediums are people who have succumbed to divine calling and agreed to be possessed by various kinds of deities in order to serve these deities and to help people with their problems. Their mode of operation typically belongs to the immediate-practical modality of doing religion, where clients consult the mediums for a relatively cheap and quick solution. But in the past few decades a new form of spirit mediumism emerged in Taiwan that has gained popularity. Ordinary people ranging from teenagers to the elderly, many more women than men, would gather in temples (and occasionally other social or private spaces) to get possessed by deities and to cultivate their own spirits. These people call themselves *lingji* (spirit mediums), though it is more appropriate to call them spirit cultivators to differentiate them from the better-known traditional spirit mediums, because the goal of their practice is to get in touch with one's "original spirit" (*yuanling*) and to cultivate this spirit to reach higher and higher forms of spiritual accomplishment. Not belonging to any formal religious organization (e.g. temple cult or sectarian group), these spirit cultivators gather in fluid, informal groups to meditate, seek to be possessed by deities such as the Taiwanese goddess Mazu, the Bodhisattva Guanyin, the Living Buddha Jigong, or even the Christian God, Virgin Mary, and Mao Zedong.

Upon being possessed, the spirit cultivators will start burping (apparently sometimes even farting!), singing, chanting (speaking in stylized "heavenly language"), gesturing (e.g. with Buddhist mudras), dancing, pairing up with each other or staging formations in groups, with various styles depending on the possessing deity and individual practitioner. The higher the level one is at, the wider the range of possessing deities will be. The ultimate goal of cultivating one's original spirit is to reach personal happiness, to reduce suffering, and to help build a harmonious and peaceful world. Unlike the traditional spirit medium, who typically works for a clientele and charges a fee, these spirit cultivators engage in these spiritual pursuits mostly for their own benefit (even given the professed purpose of benefiting the world at large). Self-consciously syncretic in nature, this innovative spirit-cultivation practice echoes the New Age practice of channeling found in the West (cf. Brown 1999) and the many *qigong* innovations in mainland China.

Below I will quote an ethnographic account on an episode of *hui-lingshan* (Marshall 2003: 87–8):

Befitting the lack of structure and informality of New Age *lingji* practice, many performances take place in a variety of places, ranging from ice cream parlours to large temples like the one in the following account. Here, the temple is an urban Buddhist and Daoist (*fodao*) one in southern Taiwan that offers its space to the public for individual informal practice six nights a week. On one of these evenings, *lingji* begin to arrive around 7:30 p.m. and may schedule a consultation with one of the three temple healers and masters, called *zhencai*, one floor down, before they go to the large hall upstairs and move the spirit. On other days of the week people come to the temple for organized group meditation, lectures on Daoist and Buddhist doctrine, and chanting of Buddhist sūtras. All of these activities are free and open to the public, and are not restricted to *lingji* performers. By 9:30 p.m., the large temple hall is full with twenty or more *lingji*, and by 10:00 p.m. on this particular evening forty *lingji* have arrived. The *lingji* teacher who is explaining the practice to me says that sometimes fifty or more *lingji* will come. Most of the *lingji* who perform are women and they are watched by a predominantly male crowd that consists of the *zhencai* and his attendants, other *lingji*, husbands, and friends, who fill the benches around [the] room.

Initially, the *lingji* will sit on blue exercise mats, meditating in silence before the Buddhist deities. Gradually, many of them will begin to move their heads, arms, bodies – some may begin to burp, slowly and gently at first, then more intensely, and sometimes begin to sing. Other individuals will remain sitting on mats, appearing to be lost in trance. Those who begin burping may then move their arms and rise from their mats, first bending one knee and then gracefully standing. Often, they will then walk to a position in the center of the room and begin to dance. Again, the pattern varies for each individual: some will only dance; while the more experienced of the group will quickly move into the stage of dancing and singing. The singing acts as if it is a magnet attracting those sitting nearby to get up and also dance. Eventually, the room is filled with spontaneous partnered *lingji* dancing, singing and burping in various positions. As the *lingji* becomes more proficient in allowing the spirit to move and cultivate her or him, she or he edges closer toward a new existence in which a spirit of cooperation replaces individual desires and motivations. One *lingji* expressed the goal of *lingji* self-cultivation using the traditional Chinese phrase "human and heaven are one" [*tianren heyi*] that describes the harmonious relationship between heavenly and human realms.

Lingji practices seem to be a sort of "person-cosmos resonance." It is intensely individualistic, yet the practitioners always practice in groups and through their practices connect numerous religious as well as secular sites over a large spatial expanse.

According to studies conducted by Ting Jen-Chieh (2005), some *lingji* practices are more organized and structured. Typically, these take the form of groups of spirit-cultivators organized by private shrines (*siren gongtan*) as they visit different temples that enshrine certain deities. Private shrines have been a common feature of the Taiwan religious landscape for many decades, mostly in urban areas. Unlike community temples that are owned and managed collectively by the communities, these private shrines are owned and run by private individuals (often a spirit medium but not necessarily so) but are open to the public for consultation sessions and worship. Starting in the 1980s many of these private shrines (through the enshrined deities during their consultation) began advising their devotees to visit particular temples on the island so that they could cultivate their "original spirit" (*yuanling* or *benling*). These recommended temples tended to be ones that enshrine powerful "mother" deities associated with what is called "former heaven" (*xiantian*) as, according to *lingji* beliefs, the spirit-cultivators are trying to cultivate their original spirits through replugging into the "spirit veins" (*lingmai*; "vein" in Chinese suggesting lines of genealogical and lineage transmission but crucially also used in *fengshui* discourse referring to invisible geo-cosmic lines hidden in the landscape) of these "mother" deities, very much like lost children reconnecting with their mothers. These deities include the Golden Mother (Jinmu), the Queen Mother (Wangmu), the Earth Mother (Dimu), etc. (Ting 2005: 65–7). Often the owner of the private shrine would organize periodic pilgrimage tours of a select number of temples for the followers of his or her shrine. Below is a translated (from Chinese) and redacted summary description of one of these pilgrimage tours that took place in 2004 as recounted by Ting (2005: 106–10).

The private shrine was called Boundless Sacred Treasure Hall (Wujishengbaodian) in the Wanhua district of Taipei City. The main enshrined deity was the Boundless Ancient Mother (Wujilaomu) though there were statues of many other deities as well. The shrine was a two-story house very similar to regular residential houses in the neighborhood. The ground floor housed the deity statues and was used for daily consultation sessions. The first floor upstairs was a hall used for meditation sessions and classes. In the evenings on Tuesdays and Fridays most of the time the spirit medium possessed by the General of the Middle Altar (Zhongtanyuanshuai) (i.e. Nezha) would conduct séances and solve problems brought by visitors. Wednesday evenings were normally devoted to lectures explaining the scriptures revealed through spirit-writing sessions brought in by a "teacher" from an affiliated temple in Danshui (near Taipei). The owner or master of the private shrine (*gongzhu*) was a 55-year-old woman who had been serving the deities for more than 20 years. She founded the shrine about ten years earlier. At first it was modest in scale and it was only recently that she moved to this bigger venue not far from the old site. Most of the devotees were from Taipei City, many attracted to the shrine by word-of-mouth spread of the shrine's reputation (based on the efficacious work by the shrine master and the spirit mediums affiliated with the shrine).

It had been ten years since the shrine master began taking devotees on pilgrimage tours to mother-deity temples. The itineraries were determined by the deities announcing through the spirit mediums. This particular trip was organized for the sixteenth and seventeenth of the second lunar month. The destinations were eight different temples in eastern Taiwan (including Yilan, Hualian, and Taidong counties). The tour was framed as combining both "paying respect to deities with incense" (*jinxiang*) and "converging spirits" (*huiling*). The participants were told that they were to overcome three obstacles (*guo sanguan*) and once they achieved that they would reach yet another level of spiritual cultivation. Altogether 44 people (including the ethnographer) joined the tour (28 female and 16 male). They were aged between 20 and 70, with the middle-aged predominant. Most of them wore white tops and white trousers. All of them had pre-assigned tasks (e.g. holding the incense burner; holding various ritual implements, offerings and deity statues; troupe discipline; managing the trip; etc.). They were also advised to wear a thick yellow fabric band around their waists to protect them against undesirable spirits along the way. The group traveled to each temple on the itinerary by a chartered tour bus.

Upon arriving at each temple, the group would first engage in a "paying respect" ritual routine that is commonly seen in Taiwan when deities visit one another because the deities from the private shrine were traveling with the group and needed to greet and pay respect to the deities they were visiting. This involved setting off firecrackers, passing the shrine deity statues over the smoke and fire of the host temple's main incense burner (thus enhancing the power of the visiting deities), kowtowing to the host deities in the temple hall, etc. Then the individual participants would begin their own worship. They would first burn a confessionary petition (thus sending it to the deity). Then they would one by one enter into a trance state, which would be indicated by making spirit gestures, spirit dancing, and speaking spirit language, etc. The hall would quickly be filled with noises of singing, chanting, and crying. The shrine master and other more experienced spirit-cultivators would be on close watch at their sides, providing guidance when necessary. This kind of guidance was called "receiving the spirit" or "dotting the spirit," which was to help the less-experienced spirit-cultivator get connected to the spirit source (or indeed source spirit). For example, the shrine owner would use her hand to guide the spirit of the host deity toward the top of the spirit-cultivator's head, all the while chanting some formula helping to effect the connection of the spirit-cultivator's "original spirit" and that of the deity's. Each of the spirit-cultivators had his or her own "unfinished business" to take care of. For example, at one of the temples in Hualian that had nearly 200 stone steps leading up to the main hall, three of the spirit-cultivators "climbed" up the steps on their knees, crying the whole way, wishing to deep-cleanse themselves. At the last of the three main temples to visit for "overcoming the obstacle," the spirit-cultivators' spiritual response became even more fervent. Even the ones who hadn't had any spirit responses thus far began to swirl around and speak the spirit language. On the way back on the bus all the participants sang and laughed in high spirits. When the group got back to the home shrine and after the home deities had all resettled onto their altars, one of the spirit mediums became possessed by the General of the Middle

Altar and conducted an assessment of the trip, pointing out some of the shortcomings in ritual etiquette during the trip and urging everyone to do better in the future.

Spirit-cultivation pilgrimages like the one described above are creating new linkages between otherwise unrelated temples and shrines (similar to Mazu pilgrimage networks). Thanks to these organized respect-paying and spirit-cultivation tours, the small private shrines can enhance the power of their own deities, connect with many much bigger and well-established temples, and contribute, with their own human and ritual resources, to the construction of the religious sites in so many different locales all over Taiwan. These bigger temples enshrining different "mother deities" also get strung together by these new ritual networks, reinforcing their renown but also shifting the constituting elements of their overall ritual terroirs.

As these new spirit-cultivators frequent these temples, the temples also need to respond to this new category of visitors. Let us go back to the above case described by Marshall (2003). The temple committee members of this temple in the suburbs of Tainan in southern Taiwan, who were all men (which is typically the case in Taiwan), were very welcoming to the spirit-cultivators, who were mostly women in their forties, fifties, and sixties. The temple had its resident spirit medium who would get possessed by the Bodhisattva Jigong and conduct séances to help people with their problems. The spirit-cultivators who visited the temple brought significant offerings to the spirit medium (i.e. to the deity) and brought their friends and family members as well. The temple not only opened their doors to the spirit-cultivators but even went out of their way to cater to their special needs. The spirit-cultivators constantly suggested new ways to "move the spirit" and the temple staff built outdoor stages, expanded temple space, and made other accommodations to involve the spirit-cultivators in temple activities, create new events (a wild Universal Deliverance ceremony, for instance, dominated by the spirit-cultivators), and enable them to cultivate their spirit in song, dance, mime, or meditation. In fact, the temple made significant structural changes to the temple in order to accommodate the visiting spirit-cultivators.

FROM CHINA TO MECCA: THE HAJJ PILGRIMAGE AND THE CHINESE STATE

Going to Mecca (Maijia) on pilgrimage (called *hajj* in Arabic and *chaojin* in Chinese) is one of the five duties of all Muslims (the other four being recognizing Allah as the only God and Mohamed as his prophet, praying five times each day, engaging in alms-giving, and ritual abstinence), if it is within the means of the individual Muslim and if his or her absence will not cause undue hardship to the family. But over the 14 centuries of its development, Islam has become such a globalized religion that there are now more than 1.8 billion Muslims in the world, most of whom live far from where Islam originated; for example, Indonesia is the country with the largest Muslim population. This means that the vast majority of Muslims of the world, historically as well as today, would never be able to go on the hajj due to the vast distance between their places of residence and Mecca, and the high cost and arduous nature of the trip. In addition, nowadays the Saudi Arabia government has an annual quota for hajj pilgrims by country, calculated by percentage of the overall Muslim population of each country (roughly one out of one thousand). This further limits the number of hajj pilgrims from countries with a large Muslim population and enough Muslims who have the means to finance their trip to Mecca. China has around 21 million Muslims, most of whom are Hui Muslims, widely distributed in China rather than concentrated in a particular region (e.g. the Uyghurs in Xinjiang), though there are a few regions with very large Hui numbers (especially the Ningxia Hui Autonomous Region, Gansu Province, and Yunnan Province).[7] Thanks to the increasing prosperity of China, more and more Muslims in China can afford the high cost of the hajj, so the number of prospective hajj pilgrims is quite high. The annual quota set for Chinese hajj pilgrims is around 20,000 persons, though each year the total number of hajj pilgrims from China is somewhere between 12,000 and 14,000 (12,800 in 2017).

In China, the hajj is organized centrally by the Islamic Association of China (Zhongguo yisilan xiehui or IAC) and is a key manifestation of the involvement of the state in religious affairs (which is why this section could have been presented in the chapter on state–religion relations). According to the number of hajj applications, the IAC apportions the annual hajj quota to different regions of China. A prospective hajj pilgrim has to get certified by the local mosque of his Muslim identity and have his health checked to make sure that he is in good enough health to undertake the hajj before making an application to the local branch of the IAC. The waiting list in some regions can be quite long, and it is not uncommon for a wait of a few years before one's turn is up. The IAC headquarters in Beijing and a few of the main regional branches (Ningxia, Xinjiang, Yunnan, and Gansu) take care of the entire process of the hajj, including coordinating with the Ministry of Hajj of the Saudi Arabia government, sending a preparatory team to Saudi Arabia to get everything set up (e.g. ensuring adequate living quarters, supply of food and water, etc.), working with airlines to arrange special hajj chartered flights from China to Saudi Arabia,[8] running training courses to prepare the hajj pilgrims in religious and safety matters, providing guides, interpreters and medical personnel to accompany the pilgrims, etc. The IAC also publishes a detailed illustrated handbook for all those who wish to know more about the hajj while preparing for it (Islamic Association of China 2005).

In the spirit of financial transparency, the regional Islamic associations are required to post a detailed breakdown of the hajj expenses. For example, the Islamic Association of Ningxia Hui Autonomous Region posted an extremely detailed breakdown of the expenses of the 2016 hajj trip in table form.[9] Here is a summary of some of the major items: flight between China and Saudi Arabia: 18,550 (in renminbi or Chinese *yuan*); supplementary flight expenses (including fuel surcharge and Saudi Arabia airport charge): 1,342; expenses in Saudi Arabia (meals and accommodation, etc.)[10]: 19,298; overall service charge of the Chinese Islamic Association: 192; service charge of the Ningxia Islamic Association: 288; insurance: 120; suitcase: 216; clothing (including hajj robe and head covering): 270 (255 for female pilgrim); *ihram* clothing (ritual robe): 66 (female 0). The total expenses came up to RMB40,342 (female RMB40,261). As each hajj pilgrim initially paid RMB43,000 before the trip, they were each due a refund of RMB2,658 (female RMB2,739).

The "hajj work" (*chaojin gongzuo*) is one of the most important tasks of the IAC each year. Even though the hajj is a religious activity, and the meticulous organization of it seems to be all about attentive service for the hajj pilgrims, for the IAC the whole operation is necessarily a political act as well (as the term "hajj work" suggests, since in Chinese political culture the term "work" carries a heavy connotation of a task assigned by the party-state). Domestically, a successfully organized hajj season would consolidate the reputation and legitimacy of the IAC in the eyes of all Muslims in China as well as among organizations of other religions (which is why the hajj has a high visibility on IAC websites and other media, featuring many news items and pictures). Internationally, an orderly Chinese hajj delegation would strengthen the positive image of China's state-sponsored religious cosmopolitanism and contribute further to Islam-facilitated international relations (e.g. as part of the One Belt One Road initiative) (see Al-Sudairi 2017).

On the morning of August 9, 2017, a group of 385 hajj pilgrims from Inner Mongolia, Henan Province, Hebei Province, and a few other regions would be departing from the Capital International Airport in Beijing.[11] They were the first group of hajj pilgrims of the year flying out from Beijing. A sending-off ceremony was organized by the IAC, where the president of the IAC, the ambassador and visa officer of the Saudi Arabia embassy, the vice-chief of the Islamic Affairs Bureau of the State Administration for Religious Affairs (SARA) gave speeches and expressed their good wishes. Yang Faming, the president of the IAC, impressed upon the hajj delegates that the IAC has always been dedicated to the work involved in organizing the hajj in order to achieve the goal of "safe hajj, orderly hajj and civilized hajj" (ping'an chaojin, youxu chaojin, wenming chaojin). He wished that, while accomplishing their hajj religious duty, the hajj delegates would uphold the wholesome image of their great motherland and Chinese Muslims and come back safely.[12]

While the IAC organizes the hajj pilgrimage each year mostly as a political task, the benefit of such attentive service to the individual hajj pilgrim is also real. The pilgrims are given detailed instructions and guidelines. All their needs during the pilgrimage are taken care of by their guides and interpreters. Because their itineraries are regimented and closely supervised (e.g. where and what to eat, where to rest and sleep, what to do on each day, where to shop, etc.), there are no rude surprises. Even though their contact with non-Chinese pilgrims is limited (these potential encounters would have been difficult anyway due to language barriers), they do have plenty of opportunities to bond with other Chinese pilgrims in their group. Instead of worrying about travel matters, the pilgrims can have the peace of mind to focus on devotional activities. Beside the close involvement of the state, the hajj pilgrimage is not an activity solely concerning the individual pilgrim in another important sense. The families and communities of the hajj pilgrims are all involved. Both before their departure and after they return from the trip, there are elaborate social activities surrounding the pilgrims including sending-off and welcoming-back parties and extensive gift-giving (see Gillette 2003). After returning from the hajj, the pilgrim becomes a respected hajji and is expected to practice Islam in a more devout manner. The hajj pilgrimage is not just a

Figure 10: Chinese Muslims celebrating the Eid at a mosque in Xining, Qinghai Province. Reproduced by the permission of Zhou Yiren

manifestation of each pilgrim's relationship to Allah and the Islamic heartland in the Middle East, it also affirms and transforms the pilgrim's local social relationships.

LONGWANGGOU HOSTS A TREE PLANTING EVENT: THE VISIT OF BEIJING ARBORTOURISTS

In earlier chapters I have already introduced my ethnographic fieldsite Shaanbei (northern Shaanxi Province) and the Black Dragon King Temple. One event related to the Longwanggou civic hilly-land arboretum that I witnessed and participated in during my fieldwork in 1998 is a particularly good example to illustrate how a tree-planting trip is like a pilgrimage, how the temple and temple boss Lao Wang

("Old Wang") tried to capture "the powerful outside" to bolster the temple's legitimacy, how metropolitan and global environmentalism articulated with folk environmentalism, and how a certain kind of tourism (what I call arbortourism) interfaced with a religious site, despite the fact that the site visitors ostensibly ignored the religious attributes of the site all the while with the full corroboration of their local hosts who also elected to only highlight the trees and downplay the temple. As a result of these efforts of mutual dissimulation, a sort of theatre was staged, with a happy outcome for both parties.

The leaders of Friends of Nature (*Ziran zhi you*), a non-governmental environmentalist organization based in Beijing, had heard about the achievements of the Longwanggou arboretum project and decided to bring some of their members as well as some Beijing secondary school students to Longwanggou to plant trees (tree-planting being one of their most important outreach activities). The director of the organization was a certain Dr. Liang Congjie, a university professor and a well-known member of the National Political Consultative Conference (*Zhengxie*). As Lao Wang was elected to be a member of the Yulin County Political Consultative Conference, Dr. Liang and he were also linking up as members of the same nationwide organizational system (*xitong*), though at two very different levels (one national, the other merely local). Lao Wang, the local elite, had control over some local resources (i.e. Longwanggou) to offer the national elite (Dr. Liang and his associates) in exchange for possible favors in the future. It was trees that the Beijingers were coming to Longwanggou to plant, whereas Lao Wang and his associates wished to "plant" crucial *guanxi* (connections) with some potentially useful external forces. The Beijingers were to come in the spring of 1998, during the May Day long vacation (*wuyi laodongjie*).[13]

Lao Wang was very excited about their imminent visit. He made various arrangements to ensure that their visit would be pleasant and successful. Of course, no one can just show up at a place and decide to plant some trees; a lot of preparatory work is needed. At that time, all of the hilly land around the temple had been planted, so Lao Wang ordered the forestry technician and a team of laborers to vacate a couple of patches of the arboretum not too far from the temple to let the Beijingers plant trees. This meant digging up and relocating many healthy trees that had already taken root to some other spots in the arboretum at the risk of killing them. They also needed to purchase tree saplings from some nearby sapling stations and store them at the temple until the day the Beijingers came. Other things they had to purchase were shovels, buckets, hoses, and tags for the Beijingers to mark the trees they would plant as "their trees," so that in the future they could come back and check up on them. The forestry technician warned that it would not be the perfect time to plant those trees (more than a month later than the ideal planting time) and he had serious doubts that they would survive. But the "tree-planting event" as a performance had to succeed, even if the new saplings might not survive and some old trees had to be dug up to make room for some cosmopolitan environmentalist arbortourists.[14]

The members of Friends of Nature and the Beijing students and teachers came in three big rented sleeper buses in the early morning of May 1, after about 18 hours of travel. They even brought a TV crew and a few Chinese and foreign journalists. There were altogether about 120 visitors. They were welcomed warmly by the temple staff and fed a hearty and multi-course Shaanbei breakfast (presented as "revolutionary food" though considerably superior to the real revolutionary diet of the Red Army or that of the high Maoist era). After resting a little while in their dormitory rooms that had been specially readied for them, they climbed up the hill behind the temple with the tools and began planting trees under the supervision and with the help of Longwanggou arboretum and temple staff. It seemed to be a fun activity for the Beijingers, especially the students; they were singing songs, chatting, and laughing. But all worked hard. For them, this was the most suitable activity for a "labor day."

The tree-planting activity occupied the entire first day. On the second day the Beijingers visited the nearby village Batawan on some kind of folk culture tour; the students were assigned to different peasant households to experience Shaanbei life. This kind of rural-life tourism was only beginning to take shape in China in the 1990s. It soon took on the umbrella term "peasant family happiness" (*nongjiale*) (see Park 2008; Chio 2012). Other than some minor incidents, all the activities went smoothly.[15] In the evening a "happy-together" gala (*lianhuan wanhui*) was held on the opera stage where the Beijing visitors and the Longwanggou Primary School students performed songs, dances, *yangge* (a group dance style in local folk tradition), and skits to a large and enthusiastic audience that was composed of villagers from the area.[16] The gala was concluded by a large *yangge* dance in the open area in front of the opera stage in which all the Beijingers participated.

The next morning, before the Beijingers were to depart in their buses, a little solemn ritual was held. A beautiful stone stele was officially "revealed" (*jiebei*) at a prime spot near the temple with inscriptions to commemorate the tree-planting event (the polished black granite stone alone cost the temple 1,000 yuan). The stele was also intended to provide material expression of Longwanggou's far-flung translocal ties and legitimacy. Curiously, the traditional idiom of erecting a stele at a temple ties Longwanggou's arboretum enterprise and the Beijingers' arbortourism back to popular religion (all temples feature steles commemorating the rebuilding or renovation of various temple structures).

The success of this tree-planting event provided Longwanggou yet another organizational idiom or model to interact with outsiders (the other idiom being hosting forestry experts' workshops). In terms of monetary and labor input, the tree-planting event was very taxing for

Longwanggou, but it apparently was deemed worth the effort, at least from Lao Wang's perspective.

What is most interesting about these arbortourists' visits to Longwanggou is how seemingly far tree-planting as an environmentalist-driven activity is from religion. The Beijinger arbortourists seemed to have fastidiously avoided touching anything religious when they were at Longwanggou (most likely because an understanding was reached among the adults, including the teachers, that it would be better to play safe and not to expose the schoolchildren in their charge to "feudal superstition"). It seems that as far as they were concerned, they were visiting the Longwanggou Hilly Land Arboretum and not the Black Dragon King Temple, and the trees they were planting were to benefit the environment conceived broadly rather than the Black Dragon King Temple grounds. This conceptual apartheid between the environment and religion was in fact crucial to the use of the arboretum and the arbortourists in legitimating Longwanggou, which until 1998 was not officially registered as a venue for religious activities, which meant that all the religious activities taking place at the temple (dispensing divine healing water, divination, worshiping and making offerings to the Black Dragon King, providing child-protection rituals, the temple festival, etc.) were illegal "feudal superstition" that should have been suppressed by the Public Security Bureau (i.e. the police). But all the money (lots of money!) that sustained these tree-oriented activities (including the hiring of forestry technicians and laborers; irrigation works; the buying and transportation of saplings and tree-planting equipment; the hosting of arbortourists, forestry experts, journalists, and other site visitors; the rental on the plots; etc.) came from incense donations to the temple, which ultimately were derived from folk religiosity and the belief in the Black Dragon King's magical efficacy, his miraculous response to the prayers of the worshipers. If the Beijingers and other visiting arbortourists were genuinely ignorant of the religious nature of the funding

Figure 11: Small children undergoing divine protection ritual in Shaanbei. Photo: Adam Yuet Chau

that enabled their visits and their tree-planting activities, then they seemed to have come to this encounter with Longwanggou in bad faith (though I am certain some were not so naïve). Lao Wang and the temple, on the other hand, knew perfectly well what they were doing.

Thereafter the Friends of Nature came to Longwanggou for more tree-planting activities. Members of Inter-Asia, the Japanese-funded, pan-Asian, non-governmental organization to which Lao Wang belongs, also came to Longwanggou to plant trees. More commemorative steles were erected. Even though these tree-planting trips to Longwanggou have been framed as environmentalist activities, they are simultaneously pilgrimages made by environmentally-minded cosmopolitans to a far-away, rural place that is special (unlike most tree-planting sites they are accustomed to). Longwanggou's special attributes are in every way connected to the magical efficacy of the Black Dragon King and the broad array of religious activities sustaining this site.

MUTUAL CAPTURING

Temple festivals and pilgrimages foster particular kinds of relationships whose manifestations are spatially heightened. Worshipers are drawn to particular sites, be they temples or historically significant pilgrimage sites (e.g. Mecca). These sites take on and augment their qualities of sacrality over time and continue to draw in worshipers and other kinds of visitors (e.g. tree planters). But why do people converge to these sites? Why do they string together these sites as do the Mazu worshipers and Taiwanese spirit-cultivators? The concept of "mutual capturing" might help us better understand these phenomena.

The French theorists Giles Deleuze and Félix Guattari (1987 [1980]) first introduced the concept of "apparatuses of capture," but the ritual studies scholar Kenneth Dean reworked the concept in the context of analyzing the complex ritual networks and "ritual machines" in southeastern coastal China (Dean 1998: 45; also Dean and Zheng 2010). In explicating the exuberance of ritual performances on the Fujian coast (across the Taiwan Strait from Taiwan), Dean defines "apparatuses of capture" as "the capture and temporary consolidation of social, economic, political, and libidinal forces by cultural forms" (Dean 1998: 45). Temple festivals and pilgrimages are these "cultural forms" that help "capture" diverse forces that include not only human vitality but also physical landscapes, cosmic flows of qi as well as conceptual schemas.

In the event of hosting a tree-planting expedition by the Beijingers presented above, we witness an example of how popular religion and trees "capture" each other: trees are used to protect the temple and in turn the temple's income and religio-physical location (i.e. the temple *as a site*) sustain the trees. We also witness how the folk (i.e. the villagers sponsoring the Black Dragon King Temple) "capture" useful elements of the state (i.e. local state agencies, scientific expertise and endorsement) and transnational environmentalism; and how agents of the state "capture" the folk to further their ends; and how metropolitan and transnational environmentalism "captures" the folk (including the scenic and exotic rural). Had the temple not captured the expanding environmentalist discourse and founded the hilly-land arboretum, it would never have captured the elite visitors such as the Friends of Nature environmentalist-activists and the students and teachers of an elite secondary school in Beijing. Similar processes of mutual capturing are also evident in the cases of Mazu pilgrimage, Taiwanese spirit cultivation, Ciji pilgrimage, and the hajj.

4 Ritual Service Providers and Their Clients

Chinese people "do" religion more through rituals than through interiorized reflections (e.g. a Protestant's reflections on his or her relationship with God). And most of the time these rituals are conducted by ritual specialists who are hired by either a household or a community with a fee for the occasion. I call these ritual service providers, and Chinese people are consumers of such ritual services. These ritual specialists range from *fengshui* masters (geomancers) to Daoist priests, Buddhist monks to sectarian ritualists, fortune-tellers to spirit mediums, and their ritual works deal with funerals, burials, memorial offerings, divination, healing, exorcism, and communal offerings. Some rituals last for days and are conducted by highly trained priests who charge high fees, while there are also "quick-fix" services that cost very little or nothing at all (e.g. dispensing a talisman or consulting the deity through a simple divination session). In this chapter we will meet some of these ritual service providers, have a glimpse into the kinds of ritual service they provide, and attempt an understanding of why such provision and consumption of ritual service are the most prominent form of religious life in China historically as well as in the present day. I have drawn the ethnographic examples from different regions of China as well as Hong Kong and Taiwan even though one might find the entire spectrum of kinds of ritual services in one locale alone. The reader has to be reminded that the rituals presented in this chapter are a tiny sample of Chinese ritual life; the examples could easily be multiplied a hundred-fold even if we only drew from current scholarly literature.

RITUAL SERVICE AND EFFICACY

Most "Han" Chinese throughout China's long history have not had confessional religious identities, with the exception of very small pockets of groups claiming Muslim, Protestant, Catholic, Jewish, and millenarian/sectarian identities.[1] The overwhelming majority of Han Chinese would not call themselves Daoist, Buddhist, or Confucian. They enshrine Daoist, Buddhist, or other kinds of deities on their domestic altars alongside the tablets for their ancestors in a seemingly indiscriminate manner, and they approach in a seemingly opportunistic manner deities or religious specialists of whichever persuasion to exorcize evil spirits, ward off bad fortune, produce a good marriage partner or a long-awaited male descendant, deliver good fortune and blessing for the family or cure for a difficult illness, find lost cattle or motorcycle, or resolve a life dilemma.

A person with a particularly difficult problem might go to a Daoist temple, then a Buddhist temple, then a spirit medium, and then even a Catholic church or a Muslim mosque if the problem is resistant to other interventions. What matters to him or her is not which religious tradition the particular temple or specialist is affiliated with, but how efficacious (*ling, lingying, lingyan*) the deity or specialist is in responding to his or her requests. We have already mentioned some of these in the chapter on gods, ghosts, and ancestors. Typically, a person will make a vow promising that if the problem is solved he or she will bring offerings or money, help with the temple festival by contributing labor or materials, or spread the name of the deity far and wide. For temple festivals that hire opera troupes, a devotee and supplicant can also promise to sponsor a number of opera performances. Depending on the extent of engagement over time one has with these various temples, deities, and specialists, one develops a network of more or less enduring and meaningful relationships with them which might be maintained for a lifetime and even generations. Less efficacious deities and specialists are visited less often and are gradually dropped from the network, while newly discovered, more efficacious ones are added. The temples and specialists might, and do, vie with one another for clientele and donations,[2] but they never take the form of one religious tradition as a whole (e.g. Buddhism) against another religious tradition as a whole (e.g. Daoism), except occasionally at the elite, discursive level and in competition for patronage by the dynastic court (again usually at the elite level) (see Schmidt-Leukel and Gentz 2013).

Below the elite religious practitioners in terms of level of sophistication there are all kinds of religious service providers such as *fengshui* masters, diviners, fortune-tellers, spirit mediums, magical healers, householder Daoist priests, Buddhist ritual masters, and Confucian ritualists who provide their specialist services for a fee or its equivalent. There were also sectarian village-based volunteer ritualists who provide ritual services to fellow sect members and other villagers for free (similar to practices among Catholics and Protestants).

In Chinese religious culture there is usually one kind of specialist for each ritual occasion. For finding the best site for houses and graves one needs a *fengshui* master; for divining one's luck and fortune one consults a fortune-teller; for exorcizing evil spirits one can hire a spirit medium or an exorcist; for a funeral one hires a troupe of Daoist or Buddhist priests. The one ritual occasion that is the most significant in the Chinese world is the funeral, and it is what Chinese do ritually at the funeral that illustrates their strongly efficacy-based religiosity. Unlike standard funerals in most societies, where a specialist belonging to the same religious group as the deceased (or his descendants) presides over the funeral, in China either Daoist priests or Buddhist monks perform the funeral ritual (following different liturgical programs) depending on the availability of ritual specialists locally and locally salient conventional practice.[3] But what is most interesting is that rich people will often hire as many groups of religious specialists as possible to accrue karmic merits and other spiritual benefits for the deceased

Figure 12: A Daoist troupe performing a communal exorcism in eastern Taiwan. Photo: Adam Yuet Chau

(and, by association, his or her kin) as well as to assert the family's social status and prestige. These religious specialists can include groups (always in troupes) of Buddhist monks, Buddhist nuns, Daoist priests, Tibetan Buddhist lamas, and lay sectarian practitioners. In other words, the Chinese funeral exhibits the sharing of the same ritual event by groups of religious specialists belonging to different religious traditions. I have called this condition *ritual polytropy*.[4]

To the majority of the Chinese, it is the efficacy of the rituals (and the ritualists) that matters, not one's religious identity (if that is even discernible). We can call this an *efficacy-based religiosity*, as opposed to the kind of *dharma-based religiosity* that characterizes the way people do religion in the Buddhist countries in Southeast Asia and in monotheistic religions.[5] By hiring ritual specialists from different religious traditions only when one needs them obviates the necessity to adhere to any one of these traditions.

But how did such a ritual polytropy come into being historically? To put it simply, the elite specialists of various religious traditions catered to the needs of a market for rituals by having invented and standardized various liturgical repertoires for various ritual occasions; indeed, one may even say that these ritual occasions (e.g. funerals, exorcisms) were largely constructed by these liturgical inventions. But the liturgical repertoires of one group of specialists as religious products were susceptible to being pilfered or copied by other groups, and that was exactly what happened in China. For example, the Daoist funerary liturgy was in large part inspired and influenced by the Buddhist funerary liturgy, and the Buddhist "water and land dharma assembly" (*shuilu fahui*) liturgy and the Daoist "universal salvation" (*pudu*) liturgy have many elements in common.[6] One consequence of such mutual borrowing of liturgical elements was the increasing convergence of liturgical goals and therefore the apparent mutual substitutability of rituals from different religious traditions. But there were also enough differences between the liturgical programs of various religious traditions so that there was often a division of ritual labor or segmentation of the ritual market, so that everyone could make a living out of providing ritual services and no single ritual tradition could have a monopoly in the entire ritual market (though one ritual tradition might achieve prestige and dominance in a local ritual market). In fact, because most ritual specialists in China worked as householder ritual service providers and could hardly cater for a demand higher than what they could handle as a family troupe, there was little incentive in crowding out other providers (though of course there was plenty of competition for the more lucrative ritual jobs in one's catchment areas).[7] In most cases these various ritual specialists chose a more or less peaceful coexistence. Sometimes arrangements were made so that one family of ritualists would have a monopoly over a certain neighborhood or district, but such arrangements were more common between ritualists of the same tradition providing the same liturgical programs than between ritualists of different traditions, partly because of the division of ritual labor and segmentation of the ritual market mentioned above.

One important thing we have to keep in mind is the wide variation in the configuration of ritual markets in different regions and neighborhoods. In some places, especially rich urban areas, there would be a higher concentration of ritual specialists and therefore more competition for the more lucrative ritual jobs. On the other hand, in some other places, especially poorer rural regions, there is sometimes a dearth of ritual specialists so people had to make do with whomever they could find. In other words, there is a spectrum between, at one end, an extreme efficacy-maximizing ritual polytropy with an abundance of many kinds of ritual specialists in the local ritual market and, at the other end, a sort of involuntary, making-do "monotropy" without the luxury of either choice or "efficacy maximization through ritualist-multiplication." We can speculate that one of the most important reasons behind the popularity of sectarianism in some parts of rural China was the fact that membership in these sectarian groups guaranteed free ritual services, which most of the people would not be able to pay for a professional ritual service provider to do.

But why, one may ask, did Buddhism in China not develop in a way that resembled its trajectories in South Asia, Southeast Asia, and Tibet, where one's religious identity as a Buddhist is much stronger and people's religiosity is more *dharma*-based? In other words, why did Buddhism "behave" differently in China? Two key factors account for Buddhism's different trajectory in China. The first factor is the strong push toward commoditization within the larger religious-cultural tendency toward generating efficacy through rituals. The other key explanatory factor is the attitude of the late imperial state toward religion.

Even though many emperors of various dynasties favored Buddhism during their reign, they stopped short of imposing Buddhism onto the general populace (as opposed to, for example, the case of sovereign-led, population-wide conversion to Christianity in Europe). In fact, many emperors and literati-officials perceived the expansion of Buddhist influence (e.g. in the form of large monasteries with many monks and large tax-exempt monastic estates) as a threat, and launched attacks on the Buddhist establishment. There were waves of decrees confiscating monastic estates and forcefully laicizing monks and nuns. As a result of these persistent attacks, advocates of Buddhism in China never succeeded in converting the Chinese into the kind of *dharma-based religiosity* that more characterized people in Buddhist kingdoms in, for example, Thailand and Sri Lanka. One can say that Buddhism succeeded in penetrating into Chinese society not by making Chinese people into *dharma*-following lay believers but by providing ritual (primarily funerary) services to them, which could be understood as an "amicable" compromise. In fact, such ritual penetration was so thorough that traditionally, for most Chinese, the Buddhist funerary ritual almost became the norm (though the Daoists and the sectarians developed their own funerary rituals and competed for ritual market share).

In the twentieth century as well as today, modernist and purist Buddhist reformers have attacked this legacy of funerary ritual provision and hoped to construct a more *dharma*-based Buddhist religiosity for the masses (i.e. the kind of religiosity fostered in the personal-cultivational modality of doing religion, which will be explored more in the next chapter).

A *YINYANG* MASTER AT A FUNERAL

Here is an ethnographic vignette from my fieldwork in Shaanbei in the 1990s presented in the ethnographic present tense.

The mother of Lu Gang of the village of Huaqu near Zhenchuan has just died. As head of the household, Lu Gang is responsible for staging the most important kind of household event productions in his life: a funeral for a deceased parent. In rural Shaanbei all major household event productions such as weddings and funerals are staged in the homes of the host households (*zhujia*). A funeral in today's Shaanbei typically takes two days and involves mobilizing dozens of helpers, preparing a large amount of banquet food, and hosting more than a hundred mourners (descendants of the deceased and relatives who are not members of the host household) and guests (co-villagers and friends of the deceased and his/her family), not to mention the need to hire a ritual specialist (a *yinyang* master [*yinyang xiansheng*], which is the local term for *fengshui* master) and going through all the intricate rituals demanded upon the mourners. This would be the second such funeral Lu Gang hosts, as he hosted his father's funeral a few years earlier.

The *yinyang* master hired for this occasion, Mr. Zhou, is around 50 years old and lives in a village not far from the bustling town of Zhenchuan in Yulin County, Yulin Prefecture of Shaanbei. He is one of the best known *yinyang* masters in Zhenchuan township and is a top choice ritual specialist when any household in the area plans to build a house, dig a grave (i.e. the *yang* dwelling for the living and *yin* dwelling for the dead), determine marriage compatibility, or set the date and time for key moments such as funeral, burial, wedding, and house construction. Mr. Zhou's ritual tools include a *fengshui* compass (*luopan*) and some handcopied manuals. Unlike a spirit medium (see below), who usually works in his or her own home, Mr. Zhou usually works outside of his own home and mostly outdoors (especially siting graves and homes and supervising funeral and burial rituals). Mr. Zhou's son is in his early twenties and has been groomed to be his father's successor. Little Zhou has been his father's assistant for many years, helping with the preparation of ritual implements. He makes very beautiful "soul-calling canopy" (*yinhunfan*), essential for the funeral and burial.

Mr. Zhou determines that the third day after Lu Gang's mother's death is auspicious for beginning the funeral. During the funeral the dozens of helpers, under the supervision of a director (*zongling*, an experienced older co-villager), make sure everything runs smoothly, including setting up the spirit shed for the deceased, cooking and washing, and catering to the guests. The members of the host household are chief participants of the mourning rituals (including ritually thanking all the guests who have come to pay respect to the deceased), making them too preoccupied to handle any of the practical aspects of the hosting. A band of folk musicians is hired to play during the entire funeral.

The job of one of the helpers is to take care of the *yinyang* master and prepare all the necessary ritual implements (his position is called *kanyinyang*, literally "looking after the *yinyang* master"). Even though the overall procedures of the funeral are under the direction of the *zongling*, the *yinyang* master is present during most of the funeral to provide advice and ritual supervision. His service is needed at the evening procession to feed the soul of the deceased and the hungry ghosts, at the moment of departure of the coffin for the gravesite the next morning, at the gravesite (he aligns the coffin inside the grave "dwelling" according to *fengshui* principles, performs in-grave and graveside rituals, propitiates the disturbed earth god), and after coming back from the burial (he exorcizes harmful influences from the host's and neighbors' homes). After all of these he sits down with the head of the host household and instructs him about the rounds of postburial rituals ("doing the sevenths"). By this time most of the guests have finished banqueting and have left. According to custom the folk musicians and the *yinyang* master are feasted last, and then thanked and seen off with gifts (cartons of cigarettes, bottles of liquor) and the fees.[8]

FUNERAL RITUALS CONDUCTED BY A DAOIST
TROUPE IN SHANXI PROVINCE

The funeral rituals conducted by a *yinyang* master in Shaanbei are much simpler when compared with those done by a whole troupe of Daoist or Buddhist priests. The ethnomusicologist and ethnographer Stephen Jones has given this list of rituals for a traditional-style three-day funeral from his Daoist priest informants in Yanggao County, northern Shanxi Province (Jones 2017: 31):

Day One

am	Opening scriptures
	Delivering the scriptures
	Delivering the scriptures
	Delivering the scriptures
pm	Opening scriptures
	Fetching water
	Opening the quarters
	Delivering the scriptures
	Delivering the scriptures
dusk	Invitation
eve	Escorting the lanterns
	Report to the temple

Day Two

4–7am	Rising at the fifth watch
9am	Hoisting the pennant
	Inviting offerings
	Presenting offerings
	Dispatching the pardon
noon	Noon offerings

pm   Opening scriptures

           Delivering the litanies

           Crossing the bridges

           Judgment and alms

eve   Redeeming the treasuries

           Transfering offerings

Day Three

am   Burial procession: raising the coffin, circling the soul

           Burial

           Exorcizing the house (of inauspiciousness)

Each ritual segment of the above program is at least half an hour long, some lasting well over an hour, involving chanting from ritual texts (mostly memorized) with ritual music accompaniment by *sheng* (a Chinese multitube mouth organ), *guanzi* (an oboe-like wind instrument), *dizi* (Chinese flute), *yunluo* (framed small gong set), gongs, small and large cymbals, and drums. A troupe of six or seven Daoist priests performs each segment either in smaller groups or all together. Most of the liturgy is solemn and awe-inspiring, but there are also fast and lighter segments. One segment requires the Daoist priests leading the mourners on a breakneck chase in some kind of a formation. There are always moments during the ritual program when the Daoist priests introduce a "fooling around" segment when they mess about with their instruments while playing some local opera melodies, making funny faces and comical tunes to entertain the crowd, especially children (which also attracts spur-of-the-moment gratuity money from the host). The ritual program is very tiring work, physically demanding and mentally taxing. Using Western concert performance as an analogy, Jones likens a day of their ritual work to "doing two motets and five cantatas over the course of the day – plus a few oratorios, and (previously, for temple fairs) six long symphonies" (Jones 2017: 312). The troupe typically performs each funeral program with dedication, though the program has been shortened and simplified over the years as fewer households care to pay for the elaborate, fuller version.

The Li family Daoist priests Jones studied, with Li Manshan (born in 1946) as their head, are hereditary householder priests. The skills are transmitted from father to son and are not taught to outsiders except in extraordinary circumstances. Li Manshan was trained by his father Li Qing since he was a boy (interrupted by a few years of schooling and the high Maoist years of suppression of religious life and hardship), and his troupe now consists of his younger brother, his son, and a number of regulars and *ad hoc* members, mostly trained by Li Manshan himself or by his father or uncles. Though Li Qing was labeled as a "rich peasant" despite the poverty of the family, he managed to get a job in a state-run revolutionary music and dance performance troupe in the city of Datong and for a number of years performed as an instrumentalist touring in the countryside. The Li Daoist family troupe performed at temple festivals, funerals, and other occasions before their ritual paraphernalia (ritual texts, musical instruments, etc.) were confiscated. But in the late 1970s ritual life in the countryside revived and the family troupe took up their trade again. It took a long time for Li Qing to copy ritual texts from surviving copies (from an uncle) and for young priests to be trained, but the Li family Daoist troupe soon became the most sought-after troupe in the region, doing rituals almost non-stop. Li Manshan took over the leadership of the troupe from his father when Li Qing had a stroke in 1996 and had to retire. Other than ritual work at funerals, Li Manshan also sites graves, decorates coffins, and determines auspicious dates for important household events (e.g. wedding, burial, building work, opening a business, etc.). The Li family troupe eventually came to be known to Chinese and Western musicologists and the government and has been brought to perform, mostly "concert style" but occasionally outdoors similar to how they would normally stage their performances, not only in Beijing (1990 and 2013) but abroad as well (Amsterdam in 2005; New York City in 2009; Milan, Venice, and Rome in 2012; Hamburg, Geneva, and Leipzig in 2013; Paris and Clermont-Ferrand in 2017). They have also been certified as living embodiments of "intangible cultural heritage" (feiwuzhi wenhua yichan). Despite the fame and glamorous foreign tours, they seem most comfortable performing at funerals back in their home and surrounding villages; so busy are they that they work almost every day of the year.

THE DAOIST RITUAL OF OFFERING OR COSMIC RENEWAL (JIAO)

The ritual of offering or cosmic renewal is an exorcistic liturgical service conducted for the living by Daoist priests. It is commissioned by communities or households on periodic cycles, or at the completion of a building or renovating a temple. Its purpose is to purify and renew the space or the temple of a community by driving away the demons and to ensure prosperity and security against misfortunes. A typical jiao lasts for three days, but it can also be extended to five days or even longer. It is much grander in scale than a funeral.

In a jiao witnessed by the Daoist scholar Kristofer Schipper to consecrate the renovation of the temple of Xuejia town in southern Taiwan,[9] five lay members of the temple board of directors (who were all local notables and businessmen) were selected by throwing divination blocks to represent the community during the ritual service. The five directors were locked inside the temple with the Daoist priests for the entire duration of the liturgical service, which lasted five days and five nights, while, outside the temple, other priests conducted public rites for the masses. The priests and their acolytes conducted most of the ritual procedures inside the temple, while the directors stood quietly, and kneeled when required. At the beginning of the service, the priests and acolytes entered the sacred precincts, conducting sword dances, and sprinkled holy water around in the four cardinal directions. The directors were then instructed to kneel, to inhale vapor from a bowl of vinegar into which a piece of hot iron had been dipped, and then to step over the vinegar and a pot of incense, and to march in procession around the ritual space. Suddenly, firecrackers exploded and filled the temple with smoke, and a masked demon surged into the sacred space, while the horns and percussive instruments produced a deafening noise. The demon jumped around frenetically, peering into all corners of the temple, until he saw the incense pot and grabbed it, and seemed about to flee with it. At this point the head Daoist priest appeared, holding his sword and his bowl of holy water. He gulped some water and spat it onto the demon, jabbed at it with his sword, and the two engaged in mock combat, attacking, pursuing, and dodging and stabbing, until, finally, the exhausted demon dropped the incense pot. At that point the priest blocked his way and "beheaded" the demon by removing its mask. The priest then began a triumphal dance, limping around and symbolically "sealing" the sacred space, and then "buried" the demon (i.e. the mask) in a secret rite in the northeast corner of the temple, called the "demon's gate."[10]

This was only the beginning act of the *jiao*, which lasted several days. Scholar of Daoist ritual John Lagerwey (1987) provides a meticulously timed sequence of ritual actions during the three-day *jiao* he observed in November 1980 in Taidong, Taiwan. Within each named segment there are numerous complex ritual manipulations by different members of the Daoist troupe hired for the occasion. The basic program is as follows:

Preliminary Rituals (the Night before Day One)
  1. Firing the oil to drive away dirt (21:05–21:40; 35 minutes)
  2. Starting up the drum (23:03–23:14; 11 minutes)

Day One

3. Announcement (6:20–7:50; 1 hour and 30 minutes)
4. Invocation (7:52–8:49; 57 minutes)
5. Flag-raising (10:03–10:22; 19 minutes)
6. Noon offering (11:31–12:35; 1 hour and 4 minutes)
7. Division of the lamps (21:27–22:37; 1 hour and 10 minutes)

Day Two

8. Land of the way (6:28–8:18; 1 hour and 50 minutes)
9. Noon offering (11:36–12:53; 1 hour and 17 minutes)
10. Floating the water lamps (16:00–16:30; 30 minutes)
11. Invocation of the masters and saints (16:55–17:40; 45 minutes)
12. Sealing the altar (20:32–21:28; 56 minutes)
13. Nocturnal invocation (22:33–22:52; 19 minutes)

Day Three

14. Renewed invocation (6:43–7:52; 1 hour and 9 minutes)
15. Scripture recitation (8:30–8:50; 20 minutes)
16. Presentation of the memorial (9:30–10:26; 56 minutes)
17. Noon offering (11:00–11:30; 30 minutes)
18. Orthodox offering (16:30–17:44; 1 hour and 14 minutes)
19. Universal salvation (18:50–21:00; 2 hours and 10 minutes)

Each segment of the *jiao* consists of complex liturgical manipulations involving hand gestures, bodily movements (including dances), texts, talismans, swords, seals, scrolls, scriptures, costumes, and even tables and chairs. A large ritual occasion such as a *jiao* often requires more than a dozen ritualists, some in charge of the core liturgical work while others serve as ritual musicians.

There may be some occasions where a very large ritual event production would require the simultaneous service of dozens and sometimes even over one hundred Daoist priests. In Hong Kong, the Daoist community has had a long tradition of conducting large-scale "ritual congregations" or "dharma assemblies" to petition for blessings and to expel evil influences.[11] For example, in 1997 the Hong Kong Daoist Association organized a "Ritual Congregation to Celebrate the Return of Hong Kong's Sovereignty to China and to Petition for Blessings." The service lasted for seven days and seven nights, and the Three Pure rites, the core of the entire service, were simultaneously recited by 250 Daoists, setting a record for the territory in terms of the scale of the event production. In the spring of 2003, during the height of the SARS epidemic in Hong Kong, the Daoist Association combined forces with 16 different Daoist temples and altars to stage a "calamity-dispelling, misfortune-absolving, and blessing-petitioning ritual congregation" (*xiaozai jie'e qifu fahui*) on behalf of the entire Hong Kong population. Again the service lasted seven days and seven nights, and 80,000 talismans to dispel plagues and ensure safety were distributed to people. The venue of this large service was on a soccer field in front of the famous Chegong Temple (Chegongmiao) in Shatin, the New Territories. One prominent Daoist temple was in charge of the main altar on each of the seven days, and an enormous number of scriptures were recited and chanted.

NEGATIVE RELATIONS: DEALING WITH TROUBLESOME SPIRIT TIES

Most of the spirits Chinese people interact with are benevolent and can bring blessings and good fortune (if you treat them properly!). But there are also some occasions where one has the misfortune of being caught in an unwanted relationship with a spirit. This spirit can be a god unhappy with someone who has not fulfilled his or her vow, an ancestor who hasn't received proper offerings or whose grave has been disturbed, or a lonely ghost latching onto someone indiscriminately for offerings or help. Below I will present a case of how Chinese people deal with this kind of troubles by resorting to the help of ritual specialists.

The notion of spirits of dead children (including the stillborn and aborted) has deep roots in East Asian Buddhism, but in recent decades it developed into a serious ritual concern, first in Japan and later in Taiwan, and is well on its way to spread into mainland China and the West. Fetus ghosts (*mizuko*, literally "water babies," in Japanese and *yingling* in Chinese) are those dead children's spirits who feel resentful toward their mothers and sometimes other related people such as family members and boyfriends/husbands. Because they did not live out a full life, and especially because of their status as children, they cannot become ancestors who would receive regular offerings. As a result, they become hungry ghosts suffering in hell or wandering around stealing from other people's offerings and getting bullied by "adult ghosts." Some of them would appear to their "mothers" and demand ritual attention; some others become vengeful and haunt the living; yet some others become so desperate that they would accept offerings from a wicked sorcerer who would train them to commit immoral deeds.

Since its emergence in the 1970s, a wide range of ritual services (with different payment structures) have become available to the Taiwanese who wish to deal with trouble-causing yet pitiable fetus ghosts. Below is a description of some of the ritual solutions provided by anthropologist Marc Moskowitz (2001). Note how the ritual services span the whole range of elaborateness within the liturgical and immediate-practical modalities of doing religion[12]:

I have just outlined the criticism that fetus-ghost appeasement enables greedy religious practitioners to extract large amounts of money from gullible people. The actual picture is more complex. Teacher Lin's temple, for example, charges an annual fee of NT$1,200 (US$35) for three years. A worshiper at Ms. Xu's temple will usually appease a fetus ghost for one or two months, most commonly paying a total of NT$1,480

(US$43). Streetside Daoist temples usually have neither memorial plaques nor statues, often preferring to exorcize the spirit directly and be done with it. Such exorcisms are more individualized and labor-intensive for the Daoist or Buddhist master, and far more expensive for the client. For example, I interviewed one woman who had paid an exorcist NT$20,000 (US$882) for a three-day ceremony to appease a fetus ghost that was repeatedly causing her son to fall ill. Although this is more than the usual fee, no one I spoke with seemed to think that it was an excessive amount to pay for such services. ... To compare the price of fetus-ghost appeasement to other services offered by local temples, I know one woman who paid a Daoist master over NT$10 million (US$293,800) over a period of three years for assistance with a variety of problems ranging from advice on financial investments to her marital difficulties. In the end her investments failed, her husband left her, and the Daoist master, aware of who actually earned the money, sided with her husband. (2001: 56–7)

[The head monk of a large Buddhist temple in central Gaoxiong, the biggest city in southern Taiwan] told me that it was up to his clients to decide how much they wanted to contribute to the temple for this service [note: chanting sutras to appease fetus ghosts that cause trouble]. He declined to estimate an average contribution amount, but the majestic nature of the temple, its obvious wealth, and the fact that a monk would read the scripture for two solid hours, would likely make a worshiper feel embarrassed to contribute too little. (2001: 95–6)

The Noodle Vendor sells noodles and cooked vegetables in a night market in Taibei. ... [He] has started a sideline production, so to speak, working out of his home to appease ghosts, which he claims to be able to see. ... Like many of the religious masters I discuss here, he does not have a set fee but relies on his clients' donations. I suspect the modesty of his station would garner far smaller donations on average than, say, the Gaoxiong Buddhist Temple. But this too could add up to significant amounts. The client I interviewed, for example, only paid two or three hundred NT dollars (US$8–12) on each visit, but he went to the Noodle Vendor's home two or three times a month, and they had not set an end point to the appeasement process. ... To appease a fetus ghost the Noodle Vendor has his clients burn incense for them. After that he has the appeasers kneel on a pillow and bow three times for each ghost. That is it: quick, easy, and inexpensive. (2001: 96–7)

AN EXORCISM THAT INVOLVES BEHEADING A COCK

Now imagine you are in a village in northern Shaanxi Province (Shaanbei), northcentral China. This is a region famous for its arid and badly eroded loess plateau and having served as the base of the Central Red Army in the 1930s and 1940s. The houses here are the uniquely shaped vault homes (*yaodong*) either dug into the sides of slopes or built with cut-stone blocks or bricks. Every peasant home in this region has a sizable courtyard where the family can dry their crops, park their tractor, socialize with neighbors, and most importantly, host major household events such as weddings and funerals. We are inside the home of Mr. Zhu, an ordinary peasant in most regards but one: he is a spirit medium.

Mr. Zhu is in his forties and he is a "divine official" (*shenguan*, a type of spirit medium) in a small village in rural Shenmu County, Yulin Prefecture, in the northern part of Shaanbei.[13] He is married and has two unmarried children. Like the rest of his co-villagers, he is officially a peasant and has rural household registration. But because so many people come to consult him, he engages in spirit mediumism full time and does very little farm work nowadays, leaving it to his wife and neighbors. Three deities are his spirit familiars: the Azure Cloud Immortal (Qingyundaxian), the Red Cloud Immortal (Hongyundaxian), and the Fire Immortal (Huoyanzhenjun). During each spirit consultation session, one of the three deities would come down and possess the spirit medium.

Mr. Zhu's father, who is in his early seventies, was the first one in the family to be picked by an immortal to become a spirit medium. When he was a young man, one of his aunts died without bearing any children, and a few years after her death she cultivated herself into becoming an immortal (the Red Cloud Immortal) and asked her nephew to act as a spirit medium for her. After much resistance he eventually agreed. Sometime later, the Fire Immortal also became his spirit familiar as it is said that he is the boyfriend of the Red Cloud Immortal. The Azure Cloud Immortal used to live in a large temple in Shenmu City, the county capital. During the Cultural Revolution his temple was destroyed, so he fled the city and came to the village as a refugee. Old Zhu (the father) took him on as an additional spirit familiar. The temple in Shenmu City had been rebuilt in the early 1990s, but it had no medium for the deity. Some members of the temple in Shenmu City had visited Old Zhu to ask if the Azure Cloud Immortal would like to go back to Shenmu City, but apparently the immortal said no and decided to stay in Old Zhu's village out of gratitude for having been taken in during the hard times. Old Zhu used to also practice as a herbal doctor.

As Old Zhu became old and increasingly frail, he passed the ritual duty to his son and now lets the son handle most of the consultation sessions. Mr. Zhu usually works in his own home, an adobe-brick house with three vaulted-ceiling rooms (*yaodong*) and a sizable front courtyard enclosed by a brick wall. Two of the rooms are living quarters for the family of three generations (two elderly parents, Mr. Zhu and his wife, and their two children, a school-going teenage son and an older daughter who has just graduated from junior high school and is staying at home helping with farming and household chores).

Most of the medium's séance is conducted on the raised earthen bed (*kang*), the center of daily domestic life in all rural northern Chinese

Figure 13: A spirit medium (center) conducting a séance in a cave home in Shaanbei. Photo: Adam Yuet Chau

homes. Each time when the medium invokes the spirits with a long chant while beating rhythmically a drum made of goat skin and wrought iron in front of the painted deity scroll hanging on the wall, one of the three deities will come down to possess him. A series of big yawns and horse snorting sounds indicates that the deity is soon to arrive. The moment he is possessed, his head and whole body shake uncontrollably, and he makes more horse snorting sounds.

But he quickly calms down and sits down on his small chair on the *kang*, and in a sing-song tune the deity announces to the audience his or her identity (i.e. which of his three patron deities) and begins the consultation sessions with the visiting clients (in this particular session the possessing deity is the Azure Cloud Immortal). During the entire séance, which might last between half an hour and four to five hours depending on how many clients there are and how complicated the problems are, the deity speaks through the medium in the same sing-song tune, known as the "tune of the divine official" (*shenguandiao*), while occasionally making horse snorting noises and drinking small cups of hard liquor (the medium never drinks when not possessed). During the entire session there are always a few onlookers who are clients waiting for their turn and co-villagers and children "watching the fun" (*kanhonghuo*).

After dealing with a few cases concerning a spirit medium succession problem, a persisting leg pain that regular doctors failed to cure, and a missing person, two small children are brought to the side of the *kang* by their respective parents. While the children look on quietly, the parents tell the deity about the children's problems (crying incessantly at night, not having an appetite for a prolonged period of time, etc.). The deity diagnoses the problem as resulting from soul loss, i.e. the children's souls having been captured by some evil spirits. The solution is some exorcistic procedures. With a brush the medium writes two talismans in red ink on yellow paper and instructs the parents to make the children wear them on their bodies for a certain number of days. Then two flat, simple dough figurines about the length of ten inches are brought to him. The medium draws some talisman-looking strokes on different parts of the dough figurines while mumbling some chants. He sits up, comes down from the *kang* with his drum and stick, comes out to the courtyard with the clients, begins another session of drumming and chanting while instructing the children to go in and out in an intricate pattern through a five-foot tall, pavilion-looking wooden structure, which was erected earlier during the day for precisely such exorcism purposes.[14] A large hay chopper (*zhadao*) is placed nearby, and the dough figurines, together with a small bundle of hay and a white cock, are placed on the wooden seat/trough of the chopper. With one swift and firm downward movement on the handle, the heads of the figurines and the cock (and presumably those of the evil spirits) are chopped off together with the hay bundle. The medium throws the headless cock to the center of the courtyard and it flies and runs around for a minute or two, splashing blood all around, before lying dead in one corner.[15] Meanwhile, the medium smears one middle finger with the cock's blood and dots the foreheads of the two children (presumably to endow them with new lives, this procedure being very similar to that of "opening the light" of statues and spirit tablets). The smaller of the two children begins crying, to the amusement of all the onlookers. The medium returns to the altar on the *kang*, sits down, drops low his head, and a moment later he collapses into the sacks of grain next to the altar, looking dazed and exhausted, the Azure Cloud Immortal apparently having left his body. Like most mediums in Shaanbei, he can't recall what has happened during his possession.

While the spirit medium is engaged with one set of clients, the others might be crowding over to watch or chatting with one another. The crowd can be anywhere between ten and twenty people (many more during festival times), with people constantly coming and going. The atmosphere is not one of sacred solemnity but quite jovial and casual. There is absolutely no privacy as everybody can listen in onto anybody's else's consultation session. Some particularly eager onlookers might help other clients talk to the immortal, beseeching the immortal for divine assistance. It is not unusual for people to hang around the home of the spirit medium for an hour or two as they meet other clients and chat about all kinds of things that concern them. Because most of the clients are from surrounding areas, even if they have not met one another before, they would usually have some mutual acquaintances. In a way the spirit medium's home is the rural equivalent of a hair salon where people gather, information and gossip is spread, and there is plenty of red-hot sociality (*honghuo*).

"BEATING THE MEAN PERSON" (DAXIAOREN): RITUAL OF CURSING AND SPELLBINDING ONE'S ENEMY

We have seen that some spirits can cause troubles, but sometimes the trouble-makers are other people, and one can deal with unwanted human relations (e.g. a troublesome colleague or neighbor) with divine intervention, which in the anthropological literature would be classified as sorcery.

"Beating the mean person" (daxiaoren) is a form of sorcery common among the Cantonese and Tewchownese (but similar forms are found in other regions as well) (see Chiao 1986).[16] In its simplest form, a person who thinks that someone is bothering or hurting him or her can make a small cut-out paper figure with the alleged enemy's name written on it (the enemy is the "mean person"), go onto the sidewalk of the street after dark, invoke the power of a deity (usually the "tiger deity") with incense and offerings, and then beat savagely on the paper figure laid on the ground using a worn shoe or sandal while loudly cursing the enemy with extremely violent language (not unlike practices involving voodoo dolls). The hope is that the enemy will be subdued and will no longer harm the person in question. A typical curse would go like this (loosely translated from the original Cantonese with an attempt to rhyme as in the original):

Beat your bloody head, so that you will never get ahead;
Beat your bloody mouth, so that your breath can't come out;
Beat your bloody hand, so that you will always have a lousy hand
 [at gambling];
Beat your bloody feet, so that your shoes will never fit;
Beat your bloody lungs, so that you will be stung and hung; ...

The paper figurine will end up being beaten to shreds (note the similarity to the use of the dough figurine in the Shaanbei exorcism conducted by the spirit medium). This ritual will take just a few minutes. Though apparently quite common in the past and done by anyone with a grudge (because it is such a simple practice), nowadays in urban Hong Kong people who want to beat the mean person would hire a "specialist" (usually an old lady) to do it. The most famous place for beating the mean person is at the "Goose Neck Bridge" (Ejingqiao), a dark pad underneath the highway overpass between Causeway Bay and Wanchai (Canal Street, near Times Square). One can request and pay for the beating of a mean person any time in the year, even though in the spring, on the day of the "awakening of the insects" (*jingzhe*) (March 6 or 7 each year; the date apparently symbolizing evil people rearing their ugly heads), the need for a generalized anti-mean-people prophylactic treatment is the greatest and so is the effectiveness of such a treatment (similar to getting an immunization shot). On this day the Ejingqiao underpass would be overflowing with people requesting such sessions, and more "specialists" show up to meet the high demand. The cost of a "quick and dirty" *daxiaoren* session is around 50 Hong Kong dollars on an ordinary day but more on the Insect Awakening Day.[17]

RAMPANT COMMODIFICATION?

In the past two decades or so, thousands of Tibetan lamas have been active all over China in Han-majority areas, and hundreds of thousands of non-Tibetan Chinese (mostly Han urbanites) regularly host these lamas (many of whom are titled "Living Buddhas" [*huofo*]) or participate in gatherings during which the lamas would give *dharma* lectures, often through a Mandarin interpreter, and give blessings. Many of these gatherings take place in the devotees' homes, but some also take place in small temples. The Han devotees often shower the lamas with expensive gifts (e.g. cars) and donation money in exchange for privileged access to their charismatic power. Many celebrities (famous businessmen and actors) are known to have become disciples of this or that

"Living Buddha." Decrying such a trend of commodification, one senior Tibetan lama told the anthropologist Dan Smyer Yü (2012: 112–13):

> This is a perverted time. Everyone believes that one's merit comes from money and power. In Tibet, there is no such thing called "Living Buddha." This was an invention of the Han people. In recent years, there are many fake *tulkus* [reincarnate lamas]. Money or political power can buy this title. I dare say, those "Living Buddhas" and "Dharma Kings" roaming in Han areas have rarely sat down for practice in their lifetime, and have no sense of enlightenment – though they skillfully reap offerings from countless Han Buddhists who blindly worship their titles. Those who are truly masters of the Buddha's teaching have few chances to offer their teachings to worthy students of the Buddha Dharma. ... Now, many new *tulkus* have surfaced from the earth. ... In the 1980s when Tibetan tantric Buddhism just began to be known by Han Buddhists, the title of "lama" would be enough to win reverence from them. Now, nobody pays attention to lamas. The title of "Khenpo" worked for a while, but it soon lost its charm.[18] Now, "Living Buddha" is the catchy title.

Rampant commodification of religion seems to be found everywhere in today's China (but see Palmer 2011b for counterexamples). The story of a young man's visit to a temple run by the local state illustrates vividly the crass grab-what-you-can, fleece-whom-you-can spirit of religious commodification or profiteering that seems to be taking hold in many parts of mainland China today. Below is a translation of excerpts of his online discussion group entries recounting in detail his experience, interspersed by my comments. The entries are dated July 7, 2011.[19]

> I am from Shijiazhuang [provincial capital of Hebei Province]. My girlfriend and I have just booked a guided tour to visit Shandong [province] for the past two days. This morning the guide brought us to the

Tianhou temple in Qingdao. The deity enshrined in the Tianhou temple is Mazu. This place is actually not very large, just a small temple. One can make a round of it in ten minutes. When we went into the temple a staff member took over [from our tour guide] and gave us an introduction to the temple. After [hearing a] recounting of some legends and codes of conduct, we arrived at the main temple hall. We both made a few gestures of worship [to the deity]. As we were exiting the main hall, another staff member gave us a numbered card saying it was free and told us to go to another room. Since everyone took a card and went over there, we followed in.

Upon stepping into the room, I discovered 20 or so staff members spread out in a line, with a number behind each person. I found the "master" (*shifu*) corresponding to the numbered card I was given earlier. After the "master" bullshitted for a while (something like how we so match each other and that we should treasure our relationship, etc.), he wrote the number three on the card and told us to go outside for some staff member to receive us. As we came out of the room, there was indeed an auntie-aged staff member who, after having taken a look at my card, said: "The master asked you to burn three pairs of candles. Follow me." I walked over following her, and she gave me three pairs of small candles and said something like three pairs of candles symbolize good fortune, high rank, and longevity (*fulushou*) and they are for beseeching freedom from misfortune for family members, etc., after which she ended by saying that would cost 30 yuan. I was like "bloody hell!" but I was not in a position to object, so I handed over the dough – 5 yuan per stick! It's only 0.5 yuan per stick in the shops! At that moment I thought to myself, since my girlfriend is watching, I'd better pay up. Then we lit the candles and made our wishes.

The Tianhou temple in Qingdao is run by the Qingdao municipal tourism bureau. It is presented as a temple and museum-cum-tourist destination. Unlike most other temple sites all over China run by local tourism bureaus, there is no entrance fee to the temple complex; however, all visitors are subject to the kind of predatory harassment (or pecuniary predation) recounted by this young man (but it gets more horrendous below). The numbered-cards system is a clever institution. Like many temples in urban China operated by the local tourism bureau, individual halls and stalls of the Qingdao Tianhou Temple are subcontracted (*chengbao*) to private entrepreneurs. The individual contractors inside the temple have worked out a simple but clever mechanism to more equitably distribute the masses of visitors (hence income) among the stall-tenders (through the numbered cards and their corresponding "spiritual merchandise"). The "masters" manning the stalls would "prescribe" more expensive products for more wealthy-looking visitors. Some card-holders might end up buying more, or more expensive, temple "blessing" products than others, but in the long run the income should more or less be equitably distributed among the different stall-tenders. This arrangement certainly prevents unnecessary strife and jealousy among the contractors. The young man's story continues:

> After finishing that, this staff member slickly led us into another small room next door (why are there so many small rooms?). After we entered that room, there was another staff member who said to us: "Come on, buy a good-fortune-beseeching plaque (*qifupai*) so that you can pray for good fortune for your family members as well as each other. When you write both of your names on the plaque your relationship will be guaranteed to last as long as heaven and earth, etc." It "hurt my balls" but still I bought it. It cost 60 yuan and was just a red wooden plaque the size of half of a cigarette packet. Following the rules, we wrote our names on the plaque and hung it onto the tree outside. So many plaques were on the tree there was hardly any room left to hang ours. After hanging the plaque I thought to myself: "Let's get the hell out of here as quickly as possible. It hasn't even been ten minutes and a hundred

yuan is already gone! We can't afford to be bamboozled like this!" Then the two of us made our way for the exit.

In order to get to the exit, we had to pass through a small room. While passing through the room the staff member inside in her turn gave us a bouquet of fake flowers, saying it was free. After we passed through this room another staff member came up to us, saying "Come present a bouquet of flowers to your ancestors," and led us into another room. After we entered the room with our flowers, a staff member let us pay reverence (*baibai*) to our ancestors, following which she presented to us two sachets, saying "one for each so that your relationship will last for as long as heaven and earth, etc." Taking along the sachets, she brought us to where they collect money: "30 yuan for each so the total was 60." When I heard that, I turned to stone. At this point my girlfriend got upset as well and dragged me along to head out. I hardened my resolve and followed her out, not caring if I would be losing face or not. ... When I got out of that room I collapsed completely! I am just a poor student and I just spent money like running water! Let's get out of here quickly! As we were exiting we passed by a place where a young woman said she would like to give us a stick of incense, saying it's free! My girlfriend and I didn't even dare to look and ran out.

This visit [to the temple] was such a risky business. I almost coughed up 200 yuan. Even though I am someone who believes in science, I can't avoid wishing to beseech good fortune for my family members and friends. Because of this mentality and the fact that I was with my girlfriend, I was bamboozled by that bunch of people! 5 yuan for a candle! 60 for a wooden plaque! And an incense sachet! What kind of rationale is this! Ah, I only have my youthful inexperience to blame.

It seems that this young man and his girlfriend were particularly inexperienced temple-visitors; more experienced visitors would know about these money-grabbing tricks and how to refuse these persistent entreaties. Other than the numbered cards, several other features of revenue generation are worth noting here. First, the traditional modular layout of multiple halls in Chinese temples facilitates the kind of contracting-out arrangement seen at the Tianhou temple. Even a relatively modest temple typically has a few side halls that enshrine secondary deities or house temple staff or miscellaneous materials. This kind of contracting-out (*chengbao*) has become one of the most prominent socioeconomic arrangements in reform-era China, as large collectively- or state-owned work units or enterprises were privatized in flexible ways. Similarly, many communities have contracted out the running of their communal temples to entrepreneurs. Second, as the different halls have been contracted out to various private entrepreneurs, the tourism bureau can simply collect the contract fees without worrying about the day-to-day operations in order to generate income. The contract fee is most likely also partially tied to the actual amount earned by the contractors; therefore the more the contractors make, the more income the tourism bureau will receive (which is called "taking a percentage" [*ticheng*]). This way the tourism bureau can take in more income if business is good; hence it also has a vested interest in promoting the temple and bringing in more visitors. And yet it still can fall back on a fixed contract-fee income when business is slow, thus shielding itself to some extent from the vicissitudes of the market. Of course this is also the logic communities operate with when they contract out temples to entrepreneurs. Third, in addition to the main revenue-generating scheme with the numbered cards and the hall with all the stalls, each subsequent temple hall offers additional "blessing" products. This mimics the worshipers' traditional practice of paying respect to every deity enshrined in every temple hall, except that often these additional "blessings" products are recent innovations in the temple (e.g. the hanging of plaques on trees, the bouquet of flowers for one's ancestors). Fourth, there is a tendency for the temple staff to provide both targeted religious products (e.g. long-lasting relationships for couples) and generalized "blessing"-oriented (*qiufu*, literally "beseeching good fortune") religious products so as to appeal to the widest possible range of perceived desires. These products can all be seen as invented "religious financial instruments." Fifth, there is also the common practice of claiming one's religious products to be more efficacious, and so more expensive, than others as they have been further empowered through a ritual conducted by a famous monk or priest or at a famous temple.

Many readers might be disturbed by the degree of commodification shown in this account and the one on appeasing fetus ghosts in Taiwan. But we need to guard against any prejudice toward religious commodification as a phenomenon due to our own sensibilities toward the connection between money and religion. It might seem that religion in China was somehow not as commoditized in the past as it is today. A brief look at religious practices in dynastic China will quickly disabuse anyone of such a mistaken view. Some of the forms of commodification may be new or the scale of commodification might be greater and wider, but the commodification of religion itself is not a new phenomenon. Chinese religious culture has been commoditized for a very long time (at least since the Song Dynasty) and the effervescence of commoditized forms in contemporary Taiwan and reform-era mainland China should be understood in this longer historical context.[20]

Many people (including many Chinese) might think that the commodification of religion is somehow not right and therefore is a deplorable trend. However, this value judgment is out of place for observers who wish to understand the cultural logic behind native practices rather than passing judgments on these practices. The view that religion should somehow be a pure, spiritual pursuit freed from such worldly "ugliness" as monetary transactions and "vile" desires is a fundamentalist, elitist, and/or modernist-reformist position that itself needs critical deconstruction. For example, the current Chinese government approves and even encourages "pure" forms of religious practices such as monkish meditation, but considers ritual service for fee as deplorably superstitious and charlatan. Do we scholars and observers want to collude with the Chinese state in approving certain religious practices while suppressing (however indirectly) some other religious practices? Do we not inadvertently share with the traditional Confucian literati and high-minded religious elites an unwarranted disdain for these "vulgar" practices involving monetary transactions and sometimes seemingly unwholesome pursuits? For most Chinese people, paying cash for a ritual service is the right thing to do, and it allows them to establish a kind of meaningful relationship with the ritualist and the spirits (e.g. deities). The monetary amount is never perceived to be the equivalent of the benefits rendered and received. The performative utility of the monetary payment goes beyond the conclusion of the transaction. After all, how does one put a price tag on divine intervention?

Instead of condemning religious commodification, we should aim at better understanding its patterns. For example, all fieldworkers researching on Chinese religion should be encouraged to ask, record, and publish (even if just in footnotes) prices relating to Chinese religious life, such as for rebuilding or renovating temples (e.g. how much does it cost to have the donor's name inscribed on a piece of brick or roof tile or on a very visible feature of the temple building such as the columns by the front entrance); sponsoring opera performances at temple festivals; hiring Daoist or Buddhist priests for ritual work (including large ritual occasions such as "water and land *dharma* assemblies" and communal rituals such as *jiao* but also the so-called "small rites" conducted for individual households during a major ritual); incense money donations to temples; fees for spirit mediums, *fengshui* masters and ritual masters; fees for beseeching "trouble-freeness" (*ping'an*); fees for installing "bright lamps" (*guangmingdeng*) and "bushels" (*dou*); the cost of bundles of paper money and incense sticks (not how much they cost per item in the abstract but how much worshipers pay per visit of a particular temple and their patterns of use); costs of funeral and wedding banquets; amounts of "propriety money" guests bring to weddings and funerals and the return gifts from the hosts; the cost of sponsoring the printing of copies of morality books (*shanshu*) for free distribution; amounts donated to lamas and gurus; entrance fees for temples at tourist sites (not just for the main entrance but for individual halls and courtyards); fees for registering temples (and even bribes for officials of the religious affairs bureaus); subscription and membership fees for sectarians (e.g. the Yiguandao).[21]

THE RELATIONSHIP BETWEEN PROVIDERS AND CONSUMERS OF RITUAL SERVICES

The reader will notice that most of the ritual service providers presented above are household-based and live in the countryside, meaning their lives are otherwise similar to those of ordinary peasants except for their "trade." The householder religious service provider acts as an owner-operator of his family business, using the home as base and following petty capitalist principles in all matters of importance. He uses his family members and close kin as helpers and treats his son (or sons) as a target of expertise transmission and eventual succession (agnatic nephews are often suitable too). He benefits from the considerable trust obtained within this familial atmosphere and the power of a patriarch. He also enjoys the freedom, autonomy, and flexibility of an owner-operator.

This household idiom for religious service providers fits well with the household idiom of hosting spirits that we discussed in chapters 2 and 3. Despite the fact that the personal as well as the communal are important dimensions of Chinese religiosity, the household remains the most salient site in which most Chinese "do" religion because it is the most basic unit of ritual engagement. Dispersed into the ocean of Chinese households and adopting the household idiom themselves, these grassroots religious service providers fit snuggly in the midst of their clients. The clients feel most comfortable approaching them as they have built up neighborly relationships over time (sometimes over generations) (this is especially true in the case of spirit mediums, *yinyang* masters, and householder Daoist priests). Even though most Chinese are not averse to visiting large temples and praying to very powerful deities (e.g. the Buddha, Guanyin, the Jade Emperor), engaging with and hiring clerics stationed in these large temples is another matter. Because these temples and monasteries had extensive land endowment and substantial rent and donation income (or in today's China the clerics are salaried), the clerics felt little inclined to provide regular ritual service to the "small people." Hence their attitude to the common people tended to be condescending, aloof, if not callous and rude. The salaried clerics of major temples and monasteries in the PRC today tend to have similar attitudes. The householder ritualists, on the other hand, are usually models of good personal and business relations, for their livelihood depends on good *guanxi* (social relations).

A crucial advantage of the household idiom is that it allows the householder religious specialists to assume a very low profile to operate under the radar of the authorities. Larger religious institutions often draw too much attention to themselves, and often their spectacular success will eventually lead to their perhaps equally spectacular downfall (as a Chinese phrase would have it: "a tree, if too big, will surely draw storms and destruction to itself"). Householder religious service providers are, thanks to the household idiom, pre-adapted to suppression (be it from the state authorities, Confucian elites, or rival religious specialists such as the big temple clerics and sectarians). Dispersed among the people, a householder ritualist takes advantage of his familiarity with his home turf and makes friends with local state agents such as the local police (who are most likely his neighbors and clients) to avoid harsh treatment during oppressive times. Though recognized by the state as an average householder just like his neighbors, he avoids getting taxed for the money he makes in the ritual market (which sometimes can be substantial), partly because the state refuses to recognize his trade as legitimate (as taxation connotes recognition and approval) and partly because the tax officials probably have no idea that he exists or their families are themselves his loyal clients. And when times are really bad (e.g. at the height of Maoist anti-superstition campaigns), he can simply put aside his special trade and pick up farming again, quietly waiting for the next period of revival.

5 | Communities and Networks

THE FORMATION OF RELIGIOUS COMMUNITIES

In many locales in contemporary China there is a definite trend toward the atomization of society, where few people are organizing any collective or communal activities and people spend a large amount of time watching television in the comfort of increasingly nuclearized homes. People seem to be happy that they are no longer being forced to participate in collective labor, collective political study, or mass campaign rallies, all prevalent features of Maoist collectivist life. Yet there is also ample evidence to suggest that people in many parts of China have revived pre-Maoist forms of communal social life, sometimes even borrowing techniques of Maoist mobilization and social organization to good effect. Religion has provided one of the most important idioms through which Chinese people today engage in communal social life – in chapter 3 we have already seen examples of temple festivals and pilgrimages – and indeed to form communities of religious practitioners, be they monastic communities or communities based on common religious practices such as *qigong* or lay Buddhism.

In the previous chapter I mentioned that most Chinese people do not have confessional religious identities. When the need arises, they visit a temple, consult a spirit medium, or hire ritual specialists (e.g. for a funeral or a communal exorcism). They would not identify themselves as Buddhists or Daoists. On the other hand, both historically and in today's China, there are a significant number of people who do have a strong and definite religious identity (e.g. being a Buddhist, Daoist, or Christian; belonging to a sect). Even though small in numerical terms (but still in the millions), they are very important in the Chinese religious landscape. They are people who hope to reach certain spiritual goals (e.g. better reincarnation in the next life or Daoist immortality) through engaging in religious self-cultivation. Even though the religious "work" involved and the resultant benefits are individualistic, these individuals nevertheless form strong bonds through either becoming members in lineages of transmission of schools of cultivation or through forming communities of co-cultivators. In this chapter I will present a few case studies of these kinds of community-forming religious practices:

1. Monastic communities and networks;
2. Catholic and Protestant congregational communities;
3. communities of *qigong* practitioners that blossomed in the 1980s and 1990s (including Falungong) before the state cracked down on these widely influential spiritual-bodily pursuits;
4. "taking refuge in the three jewels" and the rise of lay confessional identity;
5. the ways in which Ciji, an immensely successful Taiwan-based lay Buddhist organization, molds its followers.

Before we look at the case studies, I would like to introduce a theoretical concept that will help us understand the religiosity of people who have developed a strong sense of religious identity and belonging. When looking at a particular religious tradition we can heuristically distinguish two crucial aspects (there are of course other aspects, but we will not be concerned with those for the purpose of this chapter). One aspect is the system of ideas, symbols, and ritual practices that make up this particular religious tradition. The other aspect is the mechanisms through which people actively mobilize this system of ideas, symbols, and ritual practices and are in turn mobilized (i.e. "interpellated," "called upon") by it. This second aspect we can call *religious subjectification*, i.e. how a certain kind of person (i.e. religious subject) is made through the dynamic interaction between "the system" and "the individual."[1] Under certain circumstances some religious traditions can become very powerful subjectificatory forces, subsuming all aspects of the followers' lifeworld within its fold. Religious subjectification brings about and facilitates the personal-cultivational modality of doing religion (see chapter 1).

MONASTIC COMMUNITIES AND NETWORKS

Compared to ascriptive membership that one is usually born into (e.g. a Catholic or sectarian identity that has been passed down from one generation to the next), membership in a monastic community is voluntary. The overwhelming majority of Buddhist and Daoist monastic communities were dispersed and forcibly laicized during the Maoist era (concluding a general trend of de-clericalization and de-monasticization that began at the end of the Qing Dynasty and during the Republican era). The re-establishment of monastic communities in the reform era meant the return to monastic life of some of the surviving older ex-monks and ex-nuns and the training and initiation of new clerics. Today there are hundreds of thousands of Buddhist and Quanzhen Daoist monks and nuns in China living as monastic communities in tens of thousands of temples (including Tibetan Buddhists in Tibetan areas and Theravada Buddhists in southwestern China). (Note that we are not including the even more numerous householder Daoist and Buddhist priests who are professional ritualists and who do not normally live in temples.) The largest temples can have several hundred monks (e.g. the Shaolin Temple in Henan Province). The Labrang monastery in the Amdo region of Gansu Province has over a thousand monks. The smallest temples just have a few monks or nuns. All monastics are supposed to lead a celibate lifestyle, though a few might have family members in the secular world from before they became monks. In pursuit of personal spiritual goals and a particular way of life, these monks and nuns form religious communities of spiritual kinship and lines of transmission (see Goldstein and Kapstein 1998; Davis 2005; Hillman 2005; Makley 2007; Herrou 2013).

But how does one become a monk or nun? In traditional times there were many more temples and monasteries in China, and monastic recruitment could be quite relaxed (see Goossaert 2000). Becoming a monk or nun was one of the options for poor people to seek a better life. Sometimes a poor family would leave a small child to the temple and the child would grow up in the temple and eventually become a monk. In Tibetan regions it was considered an honor to have one of the sons join the monastery. But the PRC government today has very strict rules on joining the monastery. First of all, one needs to be 18 or older. All temples have personnel quotas so they cannot admit a monk freely. All ordinations are regulated by the Buddhist Association and the Religious Affairs Bureau. In fact, in theory all monasteries (except those small, privately built ones) belong to the state even when they are managed by the resident clerics. The Buddhist Association has the power to appoint the abbots for major monasteries, and there are often conflicts among various stakeholders over these appointments (see Ashiwa and Wank 2006).

Because state restrictions on monastic recruitment (see Cabezón 2008 for the situation for Tibetan Buddhist monasteries), becoming a monk or nun is a path open to a very small number of people. More people who are devoted to Buddhism or Daoism as a personal religious pursuit become lay devotees instead, connected to particular temples, monks or nuns, or schools of teaching. In fact, lay devotees often form the backbone of local religious revival, temple rebuilding projects, and the organization of temple festivals. And in recent years some Buddhist monasteries have invented new ways of reaching out to the larger population, e.g. through summer camps for young people (Ji 2011) and temporary monastic retreats for both youth and adults, which would increase the base of lay devotion and widen the influence of Buddhism.

The anthropologist Adeline Herrou has conducted extensive field research on the revival of Daoist monastics' "wandering about" (*yunyou*) as a practice in the context of a wide network of Daoist temples (Herrou 2013). Her fieldwork, carried out in southern Shaanxi Province, shows that Daoist monks and nuns of the Hanzhong area, and more widely, of the region and of the whole country, are all connected and often meet one another on various occasions. She reveals four kinds of networks that are used by monks and lay followers: temples linked by the deity cults on which they are founded, both locally and regionally, and for which temple festivals and communal rituals are organized; the links between "small hereditary monasteries" and "large monastic centers" with a division of labor of levels of clerical training and ordination; monks and nuns connected to one another through master–disciple relationships and lineages of transmission; and the hierarchical networks of the official Daoist Association on the regional, provincial, and national levels, providing opportunities for monks to travel to the association's meetings and to network. But more essential to the Daoist monastics' spiritual training, the temporary residence (*guadan*) rule of hospitality allows these "brothers and fathers of apprenticeship" – nuns address one another in male kin terms as well – to stay in any monastery in the country, and thus to "wander like clouds." As Daoism becomes increasingly incorporated into the Western New Age movement, there are more and more non-Chinese Daoist practitioners in the West, many of whom are making trips to Daoist sacred sites in China on pilgrimage in search of masters, the sublime, and ordination certificates to authenticate their transmission lineages (see Palmer and Siegler 2017).

CONGREGATIONAL COMMUNITIES: CATHOLIC AND PROTESTANT

Unlike the history of conversion in European history, where the conversion of an emperor or king to Christianity would result in the wholesale conversion of the whole empire or kingdom, in China the early missionaries of the Jesuit, Franciscan, and Dominican orders during the Ming and Qing dynasties never managed to convince the Chinese emperor of the merits of Christianity. But they did convert a few members of the high literati-official class as well as founded a number of convert communities in various parts of China. Even when most of the missionaries were driven out of China during the Qing, most of these convert communities somehow managed to survive as Catholic communities, bound together by whatever sacraments they managed to conduct among themselves. After Western missionaries were allowed into China again as a result of the Nanking Treaty after the conclusion of the First Opium War in 1842, the Vatican sent Catholic priests to China, only to be horrified at the extent to which local ritual practices had deviated from church norms (some of the so-called deviations were merely the result of the Chinese convert communities having preserved practices that were standard in Europe during the time of the earlier missionaries). The newly-arrived priests were much preoccupied with rectifying these "deviant" ways and consolidating existing Catholic communities. Meanwhile, the opening up of China to Western imperialist powers in the treaty-port era coincided with the great Christian revival movement in the Western Protestant countries (Great Britain and the US in particular). Thousands of Protestant missionaries were sent to China from Great Britain, the US, Canada, Germany, Switzerland, the Scandinavian countries, etc., representing dozens of different denominations. The Taiping Rebellion (whose Chinese name was the Heavenly Kingdom of Great Peace [Taiping tianguo]), which almost succeeded in toppling the Manchu Qing Dynasty, was directly inspired by Protestantism, its leader Hong Xiuquan claiming to be Jesus's younger brother. Many of the missions founded schools and universities, hospitals, charitable organizations (e.g. orphanages, soup kitchens), and publishing houses. A few cohorts of Chinese elite were schooled in Western-style educational establishments in the treaty-port cities such as Shanghai, Guangzhou, Xiamen, and Tianjin as well as abroad (in the US and Japan), many of whom converted to Protestantism. Compared to the earlier Catholic missionaries, the Protestant missionaries were far more successful in this new era in converting the Chinese to Christianity. Thousands of churches and congregations were founded all over China. In the early twentieth century many indigenous Chinese churches emerged as well, some being explicitly against

Figure 14: A Sunday service at an officially-approved Protestant church in Wuhan, with around 300 persons in attendance. Photo: reproduced by permission of Carsten Vala

Western missionary domination and divisive denominationalism. Soon after the founding of the PRC, foreign missionaries were driven out and there followed systematic suppression of all religious life, though Christianity suffered much more because of the connection to Western powers that were deemed imperialists. The Chinese government forced all Catholic and Protestant communities to join the official patriotic church organizations (the "Three-Self" Church for Protestants[2] and the Catholic Patriotic Association for Catholics). Church leaders who did not cooperate were imprisoned and persecuted. Things got worse during the high Maoism period of the 1960s and 1970s when all visible religious activities ceased, though many Christians managed to hold gatherings underground, forming the basis of many of the underground and house churches of the reform era.

Because of its congregational nature, in addition to being based on intimate ties of kinship and locality, rural churches in China form strong communities. Because of a long, checkered history of conflicts between converts and non-converts in China (most violent of which was during the Boxer Rebellion of the late nineteenth century), many of the rural Catholic and Protestant communities have long been single-faith villages; some of these villages were founded by fellow converts who were expelled from their original villages. As a result of this histori-cal process, many Catholic and Protestant villages are tightly woven communities of kinsmen, not unlike single-surname lineage villages common in southern China. Because their faith was persecuted during the Maoist era, its revival during the reform era took on an unusual significance, just as the revival of lineage worship did for many lineages. With the revival of Catholic parishes and Protestant churches during the reform era, once again their regular, congregational worship can serve as a key idiom for building community solidarity (see Harrison 2013).

Catholics and Protestants each have their own distinctive linguistic usages that mark them out as different from non-Christians, which further enhances their collective identity (see Wang 2011). As soon as one joins a church community one becomes a "brother" (*dixiong*) or "sister" (*jiemei*) of all other church members. Church-goers' daily language is also peppered with words relating to God, the Bible, the church, the fellowship, the gospel, and one's spiritual growth, even though with non-Christians they tend to switch back to regular language. Hymn singing is central to Chinese Christians' ritual and spiritual life, so is miraculous healing through prayers and exorcisms (see Kao 2009; Harrison 2013; Inouye 2015).

In the past 40 years the Protestant population in both rural and urban China has grown spectacularly, primarily due to fervent evangelical activities. The services at official Three-Self churches are always packed, but the real scenes of fervent worship are found in the tens of thousands of unregistered "underground" churches (see Vala 2017) – they are not so underground since the local officials are keenly aware of their activities, but most choose to tolerate them. Many of these churches have grown so large that their numbers amount to several hundred or several thousand. Many of these "underground" congregations in the countryside have managed to build their own church buildings. In contrast, it is almost impossible for big urban "underground" churches to build their own churches due to much stricter official control, but they have developed ingenious ways to meet and evade official surveillance. For example, they would rent a large space in an office building which is empty on Sundays but only tell the congregants the location shortly before the Sunday service so that the police would not have sufficient time to plan and intervene. Many fellowships use public spaces such as fast-food restaurants (e.g. McDonald's) to conduct training sessions (see F. Yang 2005). For very popular churches the pastors have to conduct several services in order to accommodate the large number of congregants or those excess numbers have to sit in different spillover rooms and participate in the service via live-streaming on TV screens.

The anthropologist Cao Nanlai conducted extensive research on the Wenzhou Protestants (Cao 2010, 2013). Wenzhou is a region in southern Zhejiang Province in southeastern coastal China which is famous for having produced tens of thousands of rich entrepreneurs in the past few decades. There are many "boss Christians" (*laoban jidutu*) who donate large sums of money to build churches for their congregations. They are said to have the "blessing of building churches" (*jiantang de enci*). Ever competitive with one another, the local congregations have been building ever more magnificent churches, until the local government began a series of campaigns targeting such religious and architectural exuberance. In the past few years many large red crosses were taken down from the tops of these churches and quite a few churches were demolished completely, allegedly because of the violation of zoning and building codes (see Cao 2017).

Figure 15: A Christmas party performance at a migrant workers' church in Beijing. Photo: reproduced by permission of Huang Jianbo

Another Chinese anthropologist, Huang Jianbo, has researched on Christian migrant workers in big cities (Huang 2014). He found that even though these migrant workers are physically in the cities, their social setting has remained similar to their rural places of origin. As they seek out Christian fellowship, they tend to find established city churches too elitist and off-putting. Instead, they find comfort and support in "house churches" set up by fellow migrant workers. One migrant worker told Huang:

> I felt much at ease here [the migrant-worker church]. When I came to Beijing, I first went to Chongwenmen church [an officially-approved Three-Self church]. Just too many people there, I had no friends there. I went there once a week only for a Sunday service. Then I went to a house church in Guomao [central business district of Beijing]. The brothers and sisters were very nice to me, but I cannot understand the teaching there. Too theological. And I don't have much to say to brothers and sisters there. Only last year I finally found our church in this compound, I found many *laoxiang* [fellow countrymen] here. It is like a home to me.

The Catholics and Protestants in today's China are increasingly linked up to global Christian networks. Foreign-printed copies of the Bible and other Christian literature flow into China via a diverse array of channels, even though Bible-printing and distribution in China are no longer illegal (in fact China now prints the greatest number of Bibles in the world). Though proselytizing by foreigners is still illegal, it has not stopped tens of thousands of South Koreans and young Christians from other countries from coming into China to spread the gospel while enrolled as Chinese language students. Many members of unregistered churches in China go abroad to receive theological training (mostly short-term). Many of the Chinese students and scholars who have converted to Christianity when studying abroad (see Yang 1999) would go back to China and join or found local churches. There are even particularly ambitious Chinese churches that send missionaries to Central and South Asia and the Middle East and attempt to convert Muslims, Hindus, and Buddhists to Christianity (e.g. the Back-to-Jerusalem Movement). Because of Christianity's complicated links to foreign countries and the perceived troublesomeness of many of the Christian sectarian groups (e.g. the Shouters, Eastern Lightning), the Chinese government has continued to be very vigilant about the growth of Christianity.

THE RISE AND FALL OF QIGONG COMMUNITIES

The *qigong* movement was the largest expression of urban religiosity in the People's Republic of China in the 1980s and 1990s before the state cracked down on it in 1999, labeling a few of the most popular *qigong* groups "evil cults" (*xiejiao*) (Palmer 2007). Variously inspired by and clothed in concepts and practices gleaned from Confucianism, Buddhism, Daoism, popular religion, science, engineering, multilevel marketing, and even the latest corporate management theories (Palmer 2011a), these *qigong* "denominations" or schools emerged in the post-Cultural Revolution era of cognitive and bodily openness, economic optimism, improved physical mobility, rising consumerism, the retreat of the state healthcare system, and the coming to an end of party-state political orthodoxy and mass-mobilization politics (see Chen 2003; Palmer 2007). Most practices in *qigong* can be categorized as belonging to the self-cultivational modality of doing religion (see chapter 1). Even though *qigong* practices were extremely individualistic (e.g. enhancing personal health and vitality), they were at the same time resolutely collective (e.g. collective practice sessions; transmission networks). Followers were taught by thousands of self-proclaimed *qigong* masters whose networks of followers formed denomination-like organizations that became the largest popular organizations outside the Chinese Communist Party. The largest groups among them, such as Zhonggong and Falungong, claimed to have tens of millions of members. The *qigong* movement introduced many innovations to traditional Chinese body techniques and their forms of transmission, mostly because it was formed and flourished outside of any formal religious institution and thus was unconstrained by religious orthodoxy or strict state surveillance. Many of these innovative techniques and ideas were formed during the high Maoist period when established religious personnel were persecuted and most religious practices banned, leaving room for freer, underground adaptations of traditional practices. The state also played a key role in facilitating the flourishing of *qigong* because some of the early *qigong* practitioners served on the sanitaria staff for state leaders, and the potential for not just medical but also military and intelligence applications of extraordinary powers enabled by *qigong* was recognized by the military and state-run scientific research institutions. Many top party-state leaders and scientists endorsed the development of "qigong science" despite protests from some other scientists who accused the *qigong* masters of practicing superstition.

In reform-era urban China, the persistence of some aspects of the work-unit (*danwei*) culture and social organization continue to inform the contours of religious practice. For example, a lot of the *qigong* practice groups in the 1980s and 1990s were based on *danwei* spatial and social setups (Palmer 2011a) – though significantly, many of the *qigong* masters came from the margins of the *danwei* structure. One can hardly imagine how *qigong* could have thrived without the variety of public spaces that were the very product of Maoist revolutionary practice (e.g. squares, auditoriums, assembly halls, parks, *danwei* courtyards, athletic fields). And the state-organized larger *danwei* structure – in discrete domains like medicine, sports, education, religion, etc. – determined to a significant extent the ways in which *qigong* groups sought legitimacy and expanded their influence (Palmer 2009). This reliance on the larger state-determined organizational structure continues to be true for many religious groups in today's China.

For over two decades a so-called "*qigong* sphere" (*qigongjie*) emerged and flourished independently from the "religion sphere" (*zongjiaojie*) as it fashioned itself as closer to the sports and healthcare spheres. *Qigong* practitioners formed all kinds of communities and networks. Practicing in groups in parks, sports grounds, work unit courtyards, and other public spaces, many on a daily basis, they shared a kind of sometimes quiet sometimes exuberant sociality. They shared insights and methods, swapped stories of miraculous cures, went in droves to large auditoriums and stadiums to have their *qi* (invisible vital substance that supposedly circulates in the body and the universe) directed and boosted by famous *qigong* masters, participated in or ran *qigong* seminars (see Palmer 2011a), and went on pilgrimages to headquarters of *qigong* schools or other *qi*-conducive spots.

Alarmed by the exuberant sociality and wide network of the *qigong* activities and the potential disruption of social order, and catalyzed by the large Falungong protest around Zhongnanhai (the residence of top leaders in central Beijing) on April 25, 1999, the party-state cracked down on most of the *qigong* groups beginning in the summer of 1999. Many of them were labeled "evil cults" (*xiejiao*) (Palmer 2008), and membership in them became illegal. This caused most *qigong* practitioners to eventually quit their practices, partly in fear of official harassment but partly perhaps also because of the inevitable dissipation of a "fever," with or without official suppression. But as Palmer argues (2011a), the social energy behind the *qigong* movement did not disappear but instead resurfaced in other forms, such as the new "fever" around the revival of Confucian classics, which spawned new communities through group classics recitation and meditation sessions (see Billioud and Thoraval 2015).

"TAKING REFUGE": THE RISE OF LAY CONFESSIONAL IDENTITIES

The heightened importance of the personal-cultivational modality of doing religion in China as well as in Taiwan in the past two or three decades is manifested in the trend of "taking refuge" (*guiyi*) and becoming a more serious lay practitioner of Buddhism (a trend far less prevalent for Daoism). Many people are openly declaring their newly acquired identity as a "Buddhist disciple" (*jushi*, meaning "at-home practitioner," or *fomen dizi*, literally "disciple under the Buddha's gate") to their friends, colleagues, neighbors, and complete strangers. Similar to Christian evangelization, this kind of open advertisement of one's religious identity is a means of giving testimony and spreading the *dharma* (Buddhist teachings). Sometimes *guiyi* is translated as "conversion" in Western literature, but that would be misleading since *guiyi* is hardly the kind of conversions scholars in Religious Studies speak of (e.g. converting from one religion to another) but is rather an official confirmation of one's existing devotional tradition (or "faith"). It would be more accurate to translate *guiyi* as "affiliation" or "affirmation," though in our discussion here I have chosen to follow the emic (i.e. insiders') interpretation and translate it as "refuge-taking."

The phrase "taking refuge" (*guiyi*) is an abbreviation of "taking refuge in the three jewels" (*guiyi sanbao*), with the three jewels referring to the Buddha, the *dharma* (Buddha's teachings), and the *sangha* (the community of Buddhist clerics). Compared to Buddhist monks and nuns, the ordinary Buddhist practitioner who takes the refuge will only need to abide by a few precepts that are not overly demanding and can be easily followed even when one lives in the hustle and bustle of secular life (which, for example, might prevent one from refraining from eating meat, hence indirectly contributing to killing sentient beings). The word *gui* has the following explicit meanings and connotations: to come back to, to submit, submission, to convert, conversion.

The word *yi* has the following meanings and connotations: to lean on, to depend on, dependence. To *guiyi* is to become a confirmed Buddhist practitioner, a much more serious student of the Buddha/dharma; to distinguish oneself from the masses of occasional and non-serious worshipers; to enter into the "gate of dharma" (*fomen*); to begin a life-long pursuit of the *dharma*; to be protected and guided and ultimately to even "achieve Buddhahood." In terms of relationships, once one becomes a serious Buddhist practitioner, one enters into a thick web of relationships: master–disciple relationship (*shitu*); temple-devotee relationship; disciple–disciple or co-cultivator relationship (*tongxiu*, literally "practice together"); and religion-follower relationship. But how seriously one treats one's *dharma* pursuit very much depends on the individual practitioner. Below is a report of Mrs. Chen (pseudonym) who took refuge a few years ago. She is a secondary-school teacher who lives and works in a large city in the lower Yangtze Delta region not too far from Shanghai.[3]

> I am in my early 40s. Having been born and raised in the Jiangnan region [i.e. lower Yangtze Delta region] where there is a very strong presence of Buddhism, I have been exposed to many Buddhist practices since I was very young (for example, I had seen Buddhist funeral rituals). Up until a few years ago my own religious practices relating to Buddhism were very casual, consisting mostly just visiting Buddhist temples and burning incense on occasions. But a few years ago I had a miscarriage, losing my first child (now I have a daughter). I got quite depressed and began going to temples and praying more often. One day I met up with a former university teacher of mine visiting from Beijing (she is now nearly 80 years old). She had already taken refuge. She was planning to visit her *dharma* master at his temple (which is in the same city where I live) and seeing that I was depressed she offered to bring me along. If I had gone by myself I wouldn't have been able to see the *dharma* master. When we went to the temple it happened to be the

day when the temple was conducting its refuge-taking ceremony, so I just decided on the spot to take refuge. It happened quite naturally. At that moment I thought to myself: this is something I am supposed to do; it's a matter of course; after taking refuge I will feel at peace. This particular temple has refuge-taking ceremonies on set dates, three or four times each year. People who wish to take refuge need to read some instructions beforehand, something like taking a simple course, but because I was taking refuge on the spur of the moment I didn't take the course. Because I was being received by the head monk of the temple, they allowed me to be added on the spot. The ceremony was conducted for the whole group altogether. There were rites of taking refuge in the three jewels presided by the head monk. We acted according to the ritual instructions, including kowtowing to the Buddha statues a number of times and listening to the head monk read out some precepts and sutra passages. The refuge-taking ceremony was free of charge. I received a refuge-taking certificate (*guiyizheng*), which in addition to my name and date of birth also has my new dharma name and the date of refuge-taking. I have kept the certificate in a drawer in a red velvet pouch. I have not used it.

After having taken refuge I have not subjected myself to the constraints of the precepts. Take the example of not eating meat. Sometimes I don't feel like eating meat, so I would eat vegetarian for a while. When I feel like eating meat, I would just start eating meat again. Take the example of venerating the Buddha. I don't really follow the proper protocols. There are a lot of protocols and rules in Buddhism, but I am more of an easy-going person. I prefer doing what comes naturally. Just as it was natural for me to get closer to the Buddha (*yu fo de qinjin*), I also let things flow naturally whenever I meet other people related to the Buddha (e.g. *dharma* masters, other lay Buddhist practitioners), never forcing myself to seek them out. I see day-to-day living as a kind of cultivation, accepting things as they happen, be they smooth or difficult. I normally carry the sutra with me. It is entitled the *Diamond*

Sutra (*Jingang bore boluomi jing*). It is the first and only sutra that I
have read. It is a small book which I got from a temple. Inside this
book there is another, much shorter sutra entitled the *Heart Sutra*
(*Bore boluomiduo xinjing*), which is regarded as a condensed version of
the *Diamond Sutra* as there are only 260 Chinese characters, so it is
easy to recite. I have memorized the *Heart Sutra* and can recite it from
memory. But I won't require myself to chant or copy the sutra every
day but rather follow my inclinations. I have been very busy, so I don't
have a lot of time to visit temples. Nor do I make deliberate efforts to
meet *dharma* teachers. But I do want to develop kindness, for example
not to be wasteful, be appreciative of blessings, trying my best to help
others, having the heart to forgive others, etc.

I have established some relationships with people because of our
shared orientation to Buddhism. Recently I have paid a few visits to a
60-year old "auntie" [older woman friend] who just had an operation
to remove cancer. I got to know her about ten years ago. At first I only
knew her daughter and son-in-law. One day I ran into the whole family
in a restaurant and she and I got talking. We got in touch from time
to time. She has been a devout Buddhist since she was in her thirties.
Her family background is Hui [Chinese Muslim] but one day she was
touched by Buddhist teaching and decided to become a Buddhist. She
is a strict lay practitioner, following a vegetarian diet and chanting
sutras daily. Every day she would get up at four in the morning to
chant sutras and meditate in the evenings. She would also visit the
temple near her home frequently to chat with the monks and to volunteer at different temples. She had a major operation to remove the
cancer and also underwent chemotherapy. Her body has been completely
wrecked. She has become bedridden and can no longer take care of
herself. I went to see her after her operation. In her room a recording
of sutra-chanting was playing; I presumed that she no longer had the
strength to chant sutras herself. She was told by the doctor to drink
some non-vegetarian soup so that she could recover faster, but it was

very difficult for her as she would throw up frequently. When she was eating vegetarian, she wouldn't even eat eggs or drink milk; her digestive system can't cope with the changed diet.

A few years ago I met a famous Rinpoche [accomplished Tibetan lama] in a temple in Suzhou before a long trip abroad and he helped me by giving me blessings (*jiachi*) right there and then in the temple courtyard. I felt very thankful. I found his Weibo [popular Chinese microblog platform] site and tried to get in touch with him. He often publishes on his Weibo site Buddhist content that I felt I could read and get enlightened. After I returned to China from the trip abroad I tried to know where and how to learn from the Rinpoche so I sent a personal message to him through his Weibo site. I got a response but it was not from him; the response came from his disciple who told me that the Weibo was actually managed by the disciple, not by the Rinpoche himself. After that I stopped accessing the Weibo site. Now I can't even remember the password of that Weibo site and haven't logged onto it for at least a year and a half.

I have given this rather detailed narrative from Mrs. Chen to show not only an example of refuge-taking but how as a lay Buddhist practitioner the nature of one's social world changes in certain ways (i.e. more meaningful contacts with *dharma* masters and other lay Buddhists) even if one is a self-proclaimed casual practitioner. Mrs. Chen's encounter with the Tibetan lama is typical of many such enchanted encounters between Han Buddhist practitioners and Tibetan lamas (see section on "rampant commodification" in chapter 4).

All over China, Buddhist temples are conducting refuge-taking ceremonies to encourage more people to become more serious lay practitioners. Some of these lay practitioners are wealthy businesspeople who donate large amounts of money to temples (which goes into building and charity projects). Less wealthy lay practitioners often contribute their time and energy as volunteers, helping out at temples when there are major *dharma* events, but their monetary contribution to temples collectively is also significant. Some lay practitioners are officials, but most try to maintain a low profile because Communist Party members are not supposed to practice any religion. All these donation and volunteering activities are understood to be generating karmic merits for the believers.

Having taken refuge in one temple does not necessarily bind the follower to that temple since most Chinese Buddhist temples are not divided along sectarian lines.[4] The high monk at one's refuge-taking ceremony, typically the abbot of the temple, is merely one's initiating *dharma* master. One is free to seek Buddhist teachings from many sources. In theory one can participate in more than one *guiyi* ceremony at different temples thus making official *dharma* links with different *dharma* masters (though some temples and practitioners frown upon such behavior). Many lay Buddhists and Daoists, armed with their *guiyi* certificates, travel widely throughout China to visit temples and monasteries. At some temples they might be provided food and lodging due to their lay practitioner status. Some people get the refuge-taking certificate so as to get into officially-run temples without having to pay the often exorbitant entrance fees, though many major sites do not recognize the refuge-taking certificates issued by other temples.

One of the most visible manifestations of the revival of Buddhism is the ready availab ility of Buddhist-themed literature in the form of sutras as well as commentaries, especially those by famous contemporary monks and Buddhist scholars. These books can be found in bookstores under "Buddhism," but many are available for free, distributed by lay Buddhists or piled up at entrances to temples and vegetarian restaurants. This free literature is collectively known as "morality books" (*shanshu*) since their purpose is to exhort people to act kindly to all humans and other sentient beings. Many lay Buddhists sponsor the printing and distribution of these morality books as a means to accumulate karmic merit, and this practice has been around for more than a thousand years. The anthropologist Gareth Fisher has conducted a study on these groups of lay Buddhists who gather together and distribute morality books to visitors in the outside courtyard of Guangji Temple (Temple of Universal Rescue, Guangjisi) in Beijing (Fisher 2014). Some of these lay Buddhists come to the temple to preach their own understandings of the sutras and distribute pamphlets they have written themselves. Other visitors gather around them to seek wisdom or just to see what they have to say. The monastic clerics at Guangji Temple tolerate these lay preachers and try to keep them far away from the main halls where worshipers attend the *dharma* assemblies, but some of these lay preachers are quite charismatic and develop followings of their own. Many admirers of these lay preachers gather around them on a regular basis in the monastery courtyard, but they also go to the homes of the lay preachers to discuss sutra teachings and share their insights with one another, forming a loosely connected but nevertheless real community brought together by a common religious pursuit. Many of these lay preachers and their followers were state-sector employees in the past who had been laid off and forced to live on a meager pension or people who are experiencing serious personal and familial problems and wish to seek spiritual advice. Some of the lay preachers highlight the moral decline of the present age and the necessity to reform society according to Buddhist principles. It is interesting to note that with this example we witness the coming together of three modalities of doing religion that I introduced in chapter 1: the discursive-scriptural modality (i.e. the writing and reading of morality books; discussing sutras), the self-cultivational modality (i.e. accumulating merit through printing and distributing morality books and developing one's "Buddhahood"), as well as the relational modality (i.e. new communities developed around lay Buddhist preachers).

For some lay Buddhists, "taking refuge in the three jewels" means taking on a much stronger and more exclusivist religious identity similar to the kind of confessional religious identities founded in Christianity and Islam. Some of the newly found Buddhist sects certainly wish to promote this kind of exclusivist identity, binding the believer to their sects rather than loosely to Buddhism more generally. For example, the refuge-taking certificate (*guiyizheng*) granted by Foguangshan (Buddha's Light), one of the three most successful Buddhist sects headquartered in Taiwan, contains the following three injunctions:

> 1) From this day forth until the end of this and future lives, I will take refuge in the Buddha and will neither place my faith in nor practice the heretical teachings of other religious teachers; 2) From this day forth until the end of this and future lives, I will take refuge in the Dharma and will neither place my faith in nor practice the heretical teachings of other religious doctrines; 3) From this day forth until the end of this and future lives, I will take refuge in the Sangha and will never follow disciples of other religious teachings.

By taking refuge with Foguangshan one is pledging one's allegiance to Foguangshan. Sometimes entire families take refuge. Under the charismatic leadership of its founder, Master Xingyun (Hsing Yun), Foguangshan (founded in 1967 in southern Taiwan) has expanded into a well-endowed and powerful global organization, with branch temples in dozens of countries, over one thousand monks and nuns, and over one million followers. Once joining the Foguangshan as a lay Buddhist, one becomes a "Foguang person" (*Foguangren*), and is enveloped in the myriad of activities organized by Foguangshan including environmental protection, tree planting, disaster relief, summer camps, meditation retreats, etc. In other words, one becomes a particular kind of "religious subject" in Foguangshan's fold.

BEING A CIJI PERSON/BEING A RELIGIOUS SUBJECT

The frail, soft-spoken yet charismatic Taiwanese nun Master Zhengyan's (Cheng Yen) Ciji gongdehui (Tzu Chi) has inspired millions of followers in the past few decades – the worldwide number of followers is estimated to be around ten million – to practice a kind of engaged lay Buddhism. The central aim is to see and confront all the sufferings in the world and to transform oneself into a kind of bodhisattva so as to spread love and caring to others through concrete actions. For example, housewives and mothers are asked to build upon but ultimately to transcend their selfish love for their children and family members to cultivate a universal love for humanity, especially those who are less fortunate and those who are suffering (see Huang and Weller 1998; Ting 1999; Huang 2009; Lu 2011). Ciji followers are enjoined to be ever mindful of notions of compassion and merit, and how they can contribute to alleviating others' sufferings. Moved by the frail but incredibly inspiring nun and founder-leader Master Zhengyan, people are literally converted to Ciji and a new life. The emotional charge of such episodes of conversion is a powerful driving force motivating Ciji members (*Cijiren*) to maintain their commitment over a long period (Huang 2009). We may say that Ciji is a powerful religious-subjectificatory force and Ciji members are the ideal-typical interpellated religious subjects.

Ciji has developed a vast subjectificatory apparatus to envelop its members into the Ciji world and to help them consolidate their resolve in "being a Ciji person." The most common Ciji activities are compassionate volunteering, especially in the concrete acts of helping and consoling the sick and injured in hospitals and at sites of disasters. Ciji members are enjoined to nurture a compassionate worldview and to act compassionately almost upon impulse and not to think too much before acting. The famous motto Ciji members wear on their lips is "Just do it" (*zuo jiu duile*) (see Ting 1999: 482–6).[5] Ciji members even address one another as bodhisattvas (*pusa*), which helps construct a particular Ciji personhood and subjectivity. And the immenseness of the task of turning this world into an ideal Buddhist pure land necessitates all members' tireless commitment.

A 2011 "Great Love" (da'ai, the Ciji TV channel in Taiwan) episode has the following message for the viewers:

"In order to achieve a beautiful realm people need to engage in this pursuit collectively. The compassionate ritual arena for repentance must be inspired by our coming to realization of the sufferings in life" [a Zhengyan quote]. Looking back at the earthquake in Japan, the natural and human disasters in Afghanistan, the Venerable Zhengyan rallies us to carry the burden of responsibility truthfully, using Great Love (da'ai) to pave a grand boulevard of Bodhi starting in Taiwan, and to open up a sentient-compassionate great road all around the globe. The Venerable Zhengyan said: "Everyone needs to hurry up and unceasingly engage in deep repentance and deep fast, and to let *dharma* enter their mind-heart, and to enter deeply into the sutras so as to grasp the wondrous lessons of the *dharma* and to apply them in our daily lives.[6]

In a recent large-scale Ciji gathering in Taipei (in December 2011) Master Zhengyan had the following exchange with her disciples and followers:[7]

Master Zhengyan: Therefore we must use our left shoulder to carry Amitabha's mission, spreading the spirit of the Buddha; and our right shoulder to carry the Ciji spirit. The key to being in the Ciji lineage is to enter the masses, and to wear our special quality on our chests. Therefore from today onward, we all have one common name: the Ciji person (*Cijiren*). A Ciji person is one who makes a vow to be a model for the entire world. Can you do it?

The followers: Yes we can!

Even though Ciji is clearly engaged in providing public goods in the forms of education (the Ciji university), medicine (medical training and hospitals), social welfare (volunteer carers), and the environment (recycling centers), more broadly and more ambitiously Ciji is aiming at transforming society at large with its message of compassion in action. In other words, it is not only providing public goods but more importantly trying to bring into being a *good public* (defined in its own terms) composed of Ciji-interpellated religious subjects. These religious subjects might ultimately be motivated by their self-centered desire for their own "ontological improvements" in the form of accruing more karmic merits (*jigongde*) (see Ting 1999: 398–473), but the ensemble of subjectificatory practices developed within Ciji – including a variety of volunteering activities but also group testimonialism and pilgrimages – ensures that its members are firmly interpellated.

The ideal situation in Ciji is that all members would embody the teachings of their master Zhengyan. In the world of Ciji, Master Zhengyan does not act like a schoolmaster laying down rules of conduct (the more obvious form of disciplining); rather, she inspires sustainable acts of sacrifice and commitment (a much more subtle and "deeper" form of disciplining). When confronted with an otherwise unfamiliar situation, a Ciji follower would ask "What would Master Zhengyan do in this situation?" (Huang 2009). In other words, rules for conduct are exhaustible and easily transgressed or undermined whereas true inspired exemplarity is a lot more versatile and effective.

It might be instructive to compare "being a Ciji person" with some people's devoted practice of recycling as a form of "environmentalist subjectification." People who have been fully interpellated into the discourse and practice of assuming personal responsibility for protecting the environment usually become so meticulous and obsessive with recycling that it seems that their very personhood is constituted by their everyday practices of recycling at home, in the workplace, and in public. Any small negligence or infraction becomes a source of psychic agony, and any small act of successful recycling becomes evidence of triumph (over the global evil of ever-expanding carbon footprint due to human activities) and is cause for quiet celebration. The kind of environmentalist subjectivity fostered by the daily practices of mindful recycling certainly bears striking resemblance to the kind of religious subjectivity fostered by the equally mindful and detail-focused practices of "being a Ciji person."

Ciji had a very humble beginning more than five decades ago in a small city in eastern Taiwan, one of the island's most neglected regions. At that time it was merely a small group of nuns headed by Zhengyan and a small following of devout lay Buddhist housewives. It then spread steadily and later explosively, eventually becoming the richest and most powerful Buddhist organization in Taiwan. In the past two or three decades, Ciji also became thoroughly globalized, not just in its charitable activities but also in organization expansion. There are hundreds of Ciji branches all over the world. At first the members of these branches were primarily Taiwanese émigrés, but nowadays many more locals join in to become Ciji volunteers even if they do not always share the same Buddhist thinking behind the charitable acts. When examined from a sociology-of-religion perspective, Ciji could be characterized as a sectarian movement or a new religion. Even though the PRC government has in recent years permitted Ciji to carry out charitable activities in mainland China, it is unlikely that it will allow Ciji to develop formally as a religious organization on the mainland precisely because of the potential for spectacular growth.

NEW TECHNOLOGIES AND RELIGIOUS TRANSMISSION

The media and technological revolution in contemporary China in the past three to four decades also has broad implications for religious transmission and innovation and the formation of translocal religious communities. The *qigong* movement of the 1980s and 1990s would not have been possible without the aid of the pager and messaging centers (when most Chinese households did not have landlines). Though the sponsoring of the printing of morality books and their distribution might appear traditional, the technologies of desktop printing and photocopying enable a much more decentralized production (see Fisher 2014). The use of computers is now pervasive in most temples, to print stelae inscriptions as well as menus for vegetarian meals, manage temple personnel and volunteers, and operate temple websites and social media outreach. Unhappy with the new Dai (also Tai) script that was a product of reform and "rationalization" by Chinese linguists during the Maoist period, the Theravada Dai monks of Xishuangbanna in southern Yunnan have used computers to reintroduce the old Dai script in monastic education – the computer and old Dai font software having been "smuggled in" from Thailand by Thai visiting monks – and to print old sutras in the classical script (see Davis 2005). The Longquan Monastery near Beijing has recently created the first talking monk robot, triggering immense interest all over China and abroad.[8] Whereas a decade ago there were sutra chanting or Daoist liturgical music on CDs and DVDs and Buddhist chanting karaoke DVDs on sale in the larger temples and monasteries for personal devotional practice, today anyone can download any number of Buddhist chanting sound files and *dharma* lectures onto his or her smartphone. The mass availability of classical religious texts from the Buddhist and Daoist canons to the Bible and the Qur'an in print form as well as in digital forms on the internet has the potential of radically changing the knowledge and power dynamics between the clerical elite and the average devotee (even if allowing charismatic "masters" to reach out to a heretofore unimaginably wide base of prospective disciples) (see Huang 2017; Laliberté 2016; Tarocco 2017). The long-term implications for religious life of microblogging (*weibo*) and WeChat (*weixin*) are yet to be researched, but we already know that various forms of social media and instantaneous communication have allowed closer connections between masters and disciples and among religious group members (many using disguised group names to evade the authorities). These technological applications demonstrate how modern technologies and other non-traditional elements can often be effortlessly incorporated into the framework of traditional idioms and practices, which in turn reveals the dynamic innovativeness of the religious traditions themselves. And more importantly, these technological advancements allow the creation of ever wider circles of religious co-practitioners and the formation of ever more dynamic religious communities.

6 | State–Religion Relations ───────

In chapter 4 I have briefly mentioned the potentially tense relationship between religion and the state in Chinese history. The dynastic state (pre-1911) was primarily run by an elite that was steeped in Confucian ideologies of governance (benevolent and virtuous rulers vis-à-vis loyal subjects, caring parents vis-à-vis filial children, etc.). These ruling ideologies were accompanied by an elaborate system of state-sponsored rites regularly enacted according to the ritual calendar from the court in the capital to the magistracies in the provinces, prefectures, and counties. These rites involved making offerings to Heaven and Earth, the imperial ancestors, a variety of important deities on the state's "worship registry" (e.g. the Emperor of the Eastern Peak, Guandi, the Empress of Heaven, the city gods, etc.), and even hungry ghosts. In other words, the emperor and the Confucian elite were the chief officiants at these rites. However, this did not make Confucianism a state religion in the same way Christianity was a state religion in the Roman Empire in the wake of the conversion of Emperor Constantine because there was no imposition of the same set of rites and associated beliefs and practices on the general populace (even if Confucian values certainly were pervasive in the entire Chinese society). Some of the emperors and imperial houses had strong private religious orientations (Daoist or Buddhist and often both), but these rarely impinged upon state attitudes toward religious life except during certain short periods with a few particularly fervently devout emperors.

But how did the dynastic state control and manage the wide variety of religious practices that were outside the imperially endorsed rites? Indeed, deity cults that were "in excess" of the state-sanctioned ones were labeled "licentious cults" (*yinsi*) (licence meaning excess liberty rather than sexual wantonness). Do current religious policies reflect any long-standing Chinese state penchants irrespective of its modern Marxist dominant worldview? And how has the dynamics of the state regulatory framework on religious life enabled certain kinds of relationships between the state and religious groups, among the different religious groups and ritualists, among different modalities of doing religion, etc.? One crucial thing we should be constantly reminded of is that even when state policies are repressive, they can be *productive* of certain relationships rather than merely inhibiting practices and relationships. In this chapter we will look at the range of relationships in spite of, and often *because of,* state regulations and control. First, I will explain the overall state regulatory framework for religion. Second, I will explain a potent Chinese notion, the "religion sphere" (*zongjiaojie*), that has been instrumental in structuring state–religion relations in modern and contemporary China. I will then illustrate state–religion relations in China with a few pertinent cases, including the impact on religion of the state's preference for certain kinds of religiosity; the increasing legitimization of popular religion in China; the discursive construction of the label "superstitious specialist household"; and the tightening of state control over funerals and burial practices.

SOCIALIST PERSECUTION OF RELIGIOUS INSTITUTIONS

The Maoist party-state has been understood as a so-called Leninist state, i.e. it is governed by ideological discipline (via disciplinary practices internal to the CCP itself [see Apter and Saich 1995]) as well as outreach disciplinary practices that were endemic within the entire society) and centralized political organization (via a bureaucratic state fused with the party that acts as the former's command center at every level). What is less discussed is the Leninist state's inability to tolerate any social organization even when it is not political.

Traditionally, Chinese religious institutions included many with strong institutional forms. For example, the Quanzhen school of Daoism was organized as branches of lineages of transmission, as were most of the Buddhist sects. And there were the numerous sectarian groups. However, there was a tendency toward decentralization (not only because of the dynastic state's attempt to curtail overly strong religious institutions), so none of the religious groups reached the kind of centralized authority and control wielded by the Catholic Church in pre-modern Europe, the Church of England in Britain, or the Russian Orthodox Church in pre-Revolutionary Russia. But the attitude and accompanying suppressive practices adopted by the Maoist state against the religious institutions resembled the kind of radical anti-clerical stance of the French Revolution and the Russian Revolution, which did face the religious establishment as formidable enemies (the Catholic Church in the case of eighteenth-century France and the Russian Orthodox Church in the case of early twentieth-century Russia). So the Maoist state constructed a strawman enemy called 'clerical authority' (or 'power of the gods') (*shenquan*) to justify their suppressive, and often violent, measures against religious institutions and personnel, when these measures seemed out of proportion to the power that these religious institutions and personnel actually wielded, not to mention that the overwhelming majority of religious personnel were household-based religious service providers without any institutional base. The real reason behind the severe suppression of religious institutions during the Maoist period is a general intolerance of *any* social institution outside the orbit of the party-state. In other words, it was not the *religiousness* of Chinese religious institutions that invited suppression but their *institutionality*.

Not unlike religious institutions in the more familiar case of Western Christianity (with the Catholic Church being the most exemplary), traditionally Chinese religious institutions were also avid accumulators of real estate (see Gates 2000; Fisher 2008). In addition to monastic grounds proper with their grand buildings (including temple halls and dormitories for monks and nuns) and large courtyards, large Buddhist and Daoist monastic centers owned large expanses of land, collecting rent on farm lands and urban rental properties (in addition to being exempt from taxation). Some of these properties were granted by imperial favor; some were expropriated from other, rival religious institutions (for example when one sect gained imperial favor at the expense of another that lost favor or was persecuted); some were donated by devotees; and some were straightforwardly purchased in the property market by astute estate managers. The smaller temples had at least some land dedicated to raising funds (usually through rent collection) for the annual temple festivals and other festivities (as well as temple maintenance and repairs and the hiring of any resident cleric). The native place associations almost always had deities from their native places enshrined in dedicated halls within the native place association compounds and staged annual festivals celebrating their deities' "birthdays."

Religious real estate suffered a big blow during the late Qing movement to turn temple properties into schools and/or fund local education with temple income (*miaochan xingxue*) (see Goossaert 2006) (though most schools were owned and run by local lineages and communities, so it wasn't an issue of state expropriation of property). The Republican government continued with a similar program, this time more aggressively in expropriating religious real estate, though because of war disruptions and the short-lived nature of their regime on the mainland the impact was not sustained (see Nedostup 2010). It was really the early Maoist period that spelled the end of religious real estate. During the Land Reform of the early 1950s, land and property of all "evil landlords" were forcibly redistributed to poor peasants. Land and property owned by temples, native place associations, guilds, and communities were either taken away by various government agencies hungry for offices and turf or redistributed. Anyone resisting or protesting was met with the harsh "dictatorship of the proletariat." As a result, there was no longer a physical site on which to celebrate the deities' birthdays, now that the temple grounds and halls had turned into schools, government offices, factories, etc. Even today in urban China, many long-standing primary and secondary schools sit on the former grounds of temples. Again we see that it was not the *religiousness* of the temples that invited Maoist "wrath" but rather their *status as property owners*.

The persecution of religious institutions and the appropriation of religious real estate obviously dealt a great blow to all forms of institutionalized religious life. However, it had unintended consequences for the household idiom of religious engagement. One would imagine that the elimination of larger and more powerful religious institutions might open the space up for household-based ritual specialists. Of course, while institutional religion was being persecuted, household-based ritual specialists were also being persecuted. There was the famous "campaign against spirit mediums" (*fanwushen yundong*) launched by the Communist government as early as during the Yan'an days (1930s), and once in power the Communist government continued with their efforts to stamp out these "superstitious cheats" and tried to reform them into productive citizens of the new society. However, because of the decentralized and relatively private nature of household-based ritualists (more on this below), the attacks on them were far less thorough when compared to those on temples, lineages, and major cult centers.

Interestingly, the household-based ritualists' homes sometimes even became the refuge of deities that were driven out of their temples. During my fieldwork in Shaanbei, I came across a spirit medium in a village. He was an elderly man and had, by that time, already passed most of the work to his son. He proudly told me how, during the height of the Cultural Revolution, the Azure Cloud Immortal had to flee his abode (temple) situated in the town of Shenmu because the red guards were destroying his temple. So he took in the Azure Cloud Immortal as an additional tutelary deity (on top of the Red Cloud Immortal, which was a female deity, and the Fire Immortal). When he or his son went into trance any one of the three tutelary deities would come down to possess the spirit medium. He said that because he was a poor peasant and had good relations with local cadres (because he had cured the illnesses of their family members, among other kinds of help), he was never persecuted. In fact, he even practiced during the Cultural Revolution, though more discreetly. In the 1990s the urban devotees of the Azure Cloud Immortal wanted to rebuild the temple (though in a different site since the old temple ground was still occupied by government offices) and invite the deity back to Shenmu City. But since the deity had become quite used to life in the countryside, he apparently didn't want to go back, at least not yet at the time of my fieldwork. Even though this is an isolated case, one can imagine that similar cases of refugee deities must have been quite widespread during the Maoist period; in other words, the deities didn't get destroyed or disappear; they simply changed residence and continued with their lives, though admittedly with far less glamour than before. And the key to their survival was the household idiom of religious service provision.

STATE–RELIGION INTERACTIONS: THE OFFICIAL REGULATORY FRAMEWORK

The Chinese state has always been very bureaucratically oriented, from dynastic times to today's Communist regime. One important expression of this orientation is the desire of the state to regulate religious life. In dynastic times this state regulation took the form of:

1. instituting a system of state-sponsored ritual programs dedicated to officially recognized deities and cosmic forces (mentioned above);
2. bestowing recognition to certain popular local cults while trying to prohibit, albeit never successfully, certain others; and
3. instituting a hierarchical clerical management system that granted certificates of practice to monastics and priests, though the majority of religious service providers practiced without such certificates (as we saw in chapter 4 on grassroots ritual service providers).

In today's China and Taiwan, the state is deploying not only many regulatory strategies from the past regarding religious life but also new ones befitting modern secularist ideologies and requirements of different regime environments. In reform-era China, the state recognizes citizens' right of religious beliefs – freedom of religion is enshrined in the PRC constitution – and supports the officially established religious organizations for the five recognized religions (Buddhism, Daoism, Islam, Catholicism, and Protestantism). These religious organizations act as bureaucratic management structures that assess and grant official recognition to temples (or churches or mosques), run clerical training schools, assign jobs to clerics, organize a hierarchical nationwide system of branch associations (from the capital and provincial levels down to the prefectural and county levels), publicize useful information in newsletters and websites (e.g. policy and news), manage and facilitate interactions with foreign co-religious institutions, and advise on laws and policies regarding religious affairs. The five national religious organizations are the Buddhist Association of China (Zhongguo fojiao xiehui), the Daoist Association of China (Zhongguo daojiao xiehui), the Islamic Association of China (Zhongguo yisilanjiao xiehui), the Three-Self Patriotic Movement (Sanzi yundong), and the Patriotic

Catholic Association of China (Zhongguo tianzhujiao xiehui). Together they are supervised by the State Administration of Religious Affairs (SARA), which is in turn supervised by the United Front Department of the Chinese Communist Party (in the PRC all state agencies have a corresponding CCP supervisory organ). Just like the associations for the five officially recognized religions, SARA itself has branches at the provincial, prefectural, county, and city levels, allowing it to carry out "religion work" (zongjiao gongzuo) effectively. These branches are normally referred to as religious affairs bureaus (zongjiaojü). One of the main tasks of the local religious affairs bureau in recent years is to accredit and register local popular religious temples (more on this below).

These multifaceted and complex regulatory structures have spawned interesting sociopolitical relationships. People who had no previous connections are administratively categorized as co-religionists (e.g. Buddhists, Daoists). Some of them are then appointed as their leaders and brought together to run the religious associations and to meet regularly at the various administrative levels. This has facilitated the traffic in personnel, ideas, and practices across the vast expanse of China's territories. Interesting sociopolitical relationships also arise between leaders and members of different religious traditions. Under the watchful eye and the auspices of the religious affairs bureau, the leaders of all five recognized religions come together regularly to study official documents and to discuss shared issues, which has resulted in their learning from one another's experiences and poaching one another's strategies and techniques of survival and expansion in ever shifting political environments. The system of registering temples has also resulted in considerable local temple activism that attempts to seek official recognition for popular religious temples that would otherwise face harassment and persecution.

The new fad since the beginning of the new millennium in getting registered as "intangible cultural heritage" (feiwuzhi wenhua yichan) at the national, provincial, and local levels has spurred yet another wave of interactions between local stage agents and religious activists championing their temples or religious festivals. A surprisingly large number of religious traditions which previously would either be considered within the domain of "religion" or "superstition" have now been given the intangible cultural heritage seal of approval at various prestige levels (national, provincial, prefectural, county) and thus come under the protection of a whole new set of laws, this time administered by the Ministry of Culture, in addition to existing regulations on religion. But some of these registered religious traditions are faced with pressures of standardization and "upgrading" (e.g. with state-approved "cultural workers" coming up with "improvements" to make local traditions more palatable to outsider elite tastes).

THE WORKINGS OF THE RELIGION SPHERE

Beside the five officially recognized religions and their concomitant associations and state regulatory framework, the PRC state deploys another concept and political apparatus to control, manage, and especially to mobilize people who have religious orientations: the "religion sphere" (*zongjiaojie*).[1] The religion sphere as a concept is not formally defined in government documents, but in its wide usage it refers to the overall sociopolitical domain to which people with (proper) religious orientations belong and within which they conduct themselves. It is a state-sanctioned domain that carries a certain degree of legitimacy (though always contested and never stable). In the broadest sense it refers to "all religious people" (however vaguely you define them) as a "constituency," to be dealt with politically but also to be mobilized for state-initiated agendas. The most common usages of this term are in expressions such as: "The religion sphere has responded enthusiastically to the call of the state to donate blood for the urgent need of disaster victims of the Wenchuan earthquake"; "President Xi warmly received the leaders of the religion sphere and gave a speech on how they can play a crucial role in the One Belt One Road initiative." But this domain is not so much a top-down imposition of the state as a product resulting from the negotiation between state actors, the "religious people," and other social actors who have an interest in this domain (e.g. social critics, journalists, bloggers). Many "religious people" are activists in the religion sphere and contribute to the shaping of this domain, not to mention deriving legitimacy and power in the process. But where has this notion of religion sphere come from? Why has it become such a potent sociopolitical domain in modern and contemporary China?

In the political constitution of the modern Chinese state (from the Republican times through the Maoist times to the current era), a process emerged that was very much driven by a desire to conform to hegemonic Western standards and practices. This process involved the recognition and production of different functional *spheres* in society that are similar to (or rather imitative of) the functional constituencies or interest groups in Western liberal states. These spheres included the education sphere, health and medicine sphere, the manufacture and commerce sphere, the labor sphere, the intellectual sphere, the scholarly sphere, the women's sphere, the minority nationalities sphere, the overseas Chinese sphere, the arts sphere, the science sphere, the sports sphere, the political sphere, etc.[2] And of course along with these spheres one finds the "religion sphere."

A sphere is a relatively fuzzy, semi-formal sociopolitical domain comprising certain publicly acknowledged social actors accompanied by related institutions and activities. Each sphere is made up of social actors who, consciously or unconsciously, construct and help maintain the sphere so that they can gain from their membership in, or association with, the sphere. Some of these social actors have been assigned or appointed to occupy their positions within this sphere by the authorities (not always the government), while some others self-appoint or have fought their way into it. Many other social actors not operating within a sphere can also exert considerable influence over the development and shape of that sphere. For example, journalists, scholars, and bloggers can have discussions on the activities within a sphere and thus contribute to the overall construction of this sphere (for example, they can criticize the behavior of some practitioners within a particular sphere).

In theory, the totality of the nation-state is to be composed of the seamless collaboration among these various spheres as structural-functionalist components, together forming the nation-state's socio-taxonomical order (though admittedly this taxonomy is not as explicitly articulated as, for example, the taxonomy on minority nationalities in the PRC). Each sphere is a structural-functional equivalent of all the other spheres, while within each sphere there are sub-spheres which are in turn structural-functional equivalents of one another. For example, within the religion sphere in China today one finds, corresponding to the five officially-recognized religions, the Buddhism sphere (*foji-aojie*), the Daoism sphere (*daojiaojie*), the Protestantism sphere (*jidu-jiaojie*), the Catholicism sphere (*tianzhujiaojie*), and the Islam sphere (*yisilanjiaojie*). Unlike the institutional setup of the official religious associations such as the Buddhist Association and the Three-Self Patriotic Movement, the religion sphere is a fuzzy sociopolitical domain in which, and *with* which, the public/political presence and significance of China's religious "constituencies" are constructed and negotiated. I have put constituencies in quotation marks because they are more of a product of discursive construction and political will than a real social entity (not so dissimilar to race, ethnicity, and class).

The construction of the various spheres and the resulting constituencies during the early years of the PRC contributed crucially to the perceived legitimacy of the new regime since the party-state wanted to form alliances with all useful elements of society (as part of the United Front strategy). The historian Thomas Mullaney (2011) has detailed how the urgent need for representatives of minority nationalities to participate in the first People's Congress in the early 1950s formed the impetus for the Nationalities Identification (*minzu shibie*) project, which was the foundation of the "minority nationalities sphere." We can understand the official recognition of the five religions (Buddhism, Daoism, Islam, Protestantism, and Catholicism) as a kind of "Religions Identification" project, with the concomitant construction of the five religion sub-spheres and the overall religion sphere.

Religion and nation have had a complicated relationship in history, especially in the modern era of ethnonationalism. Religious adherence (especially the exclusivist, confessional kind) was often the foundation of ethnic group identity, which could serve as the foundation of nationhood (especially in early modern Europe). The nation, once formed, often served as the territorial and institutional basis for fostering and elaborating a nation-centric religiosity and religious identity (from Henry VIII's Church of England to Emperor Meiji's state Shinto, Gandhi's Hinduism, and even Taiwan's island-wide Mazu cult). Though not historically inevitable, such nation-centric religiosity and religious identity often led to more explicit forms of religious nationalism in which religious actors and institutions engaged in explicitly pro-home-nation, patriotic practices (see Kuo 2017).

One of the most revealing aspects about the religion sphere (as well as all the other spheres) is how it fills up the sociopolitical space of the nation. Precisely because the religion sphere has to be coextensive with the nation (in its institutional and imaginary reach), it is as much an *imagined community* (Anderson 1983) as the nation: a lay Buddhist practitioner or a Protestant church-goer is led to imagine himself or herself as a member of the Buddhism sphere or Protestantism sphere of China. In theory, a nation can have only one religion sphere (even if underneath this there can be a multitude of local spheres or a number of sub-spheres, e.g. the Shanghai religion sphere is a local religion sphere subordinate to the national religion sphere), and each sphere can only occupy one nation. The very act of constructing all the spheres constituting a society is to accentuate and solidify the boundaries of the nation. We may even go as far as saying that the formation of the spheres is necessary to the construction and maintenance of the sovereignty of the nation. Each nation has its own spheres. One nation's sphere of a certain kind (e.g. religion) can interact with its analogous bodies in other nations, but they do so based on the principle of nation-based, "sphere-ized" autonomy. The religion sphere in China should never be invaded by foreign bodies. This is one of the conceptual-structural reasons why the Chinese state is so wary and intolerant of any foreign interference with affairs within its own religion sphere; the nation's "religious sovereignty" (i.e. the inviolability of the [imagined] borders of the nation's religion sphere) is coextensive with the nation's political sovereignty and neither is to be violated.[3]

The reader will notice that I have translated *zongjiaojie* into *"religion sphere"* rather than *"religious sphere"*; this is because I want to avoid any inadvertent misunderstanding of the nature of the sphere itself as religious, which it is not (just as the education sphere is not educational).[4] In fact, not only is the religion sphere not religious in nature, its existence is constitutive of the overall construction of secularity (the very existence of the religion sphere as a discrete social category attests to the efficacy of state secularism), i.e. the existence of the religion sphere *qua* sphere presumes secularity. In fact, China's state secularism stands out as an exception among many Asian nations. In contrast, most other Asian countries have placed far more emphasis on the nation's (presumably indigenous) religious identity: modern Japan from the Meiji era to the end of World War II, with Shinto enshrined as the state's spiritual foundation; post-colonial/Independence India, with the nation considered fundamentally Hindu; post-colonial/Independence Indonesia, with the requirement that all citizens must believe in God and belong to one of five officially recognized religions, Islam, Protestantism, Catholicism, Hinduism, and Buddhism; post-colonial/Independence Malaysia, with Islam as the "religion of the Federation"; modern Thailand, with Theravada Buddhism as quasi-state religion; not to mention Pakistan and Bangladesh, with Islam as state religion, or Nepal up to 2006, with Hinduism as official religion.[5]

The political utility of the religion sphere concept in contemporary China is manifest in its frequent appearance in the speeches of the PRC top leaders as well as official press. For example, in recent years there have been debates within the CCP about whether or not the Party can welcome prominent figures in the religion sphere into its membership despite the fact that in the Party constitution it states explicitly that a Communist Party member must be an atheist. And in a recent United Front speech, President Xi Jinping spoke of the importance of mobilizing the religion-sphere leaders for building socialism.[6]

COMPETITION WITHIN THE MODERN RELIGION SPHERE AND THE RISE OF THE DISCURSIVE-SCRIPTURAL MODALITY OF DOING RELIGION

The religious elite and modern state regulatory apparatus in China have a vested interest in constructing certain Chinese religious traditions in the image of monotheistic religions (especially in the process of constructing the "religion sphere" as a secularist and nationalist approach to religious life). However, such a construction is carried out at the expense of the vast majority of the providers and consumers of religious services in China, as it favors the discursive modality of doing religion and suppresses most of the practices encompassed by the other four modalities (especially those in the liturgical and immediate-practical modalities), many of which are labeled as superstition or counter-revolutionary sectarianism.

The Dean of the Shanghai Daoist Academy has the following to say about the importance of Daoist discursive knowledge in the contemporary field of competition between Daoism and Buddhism:

In the Political Consultative Conference (*Zhengxie*) and the People's Congress (*Rendaihui*, abbreviated as *Renda*) of the Shanghai Municipality, the seats allotted to Daoism are normally the fewest, compared with those for the other religious groups. The reason is simple: because their followers are richer, more influential, *have more "culture"* (*wenhua*, meaning formal education), and are more organized than our followers. Besides, many prominent clergymen of other religions have received BA or even higher degrees, while hardly any Daoist priest has ever been to university. Recently, I heard from the Bureau of Religious Affairs that the municipality has decided to implement a tacit rule to enforce the policy of "improving leadership quality" (*tisheng lingdao suzhi*). Principally, among those under 45 years old, only holders of a BA or higher degrees can be nominated as candidates for membership of the Political Consultative Conference and representatives of the People's Congress. This is the reason why the representatives of Daoism are mostly old masters or lay Daoist practitioners (*jushi*) over 70 years of age – there are no qualified younger priests to replace them! So, strictly speaking, the two or three young priests now serving as the representatives of Daoism are not actually qualified for their posts. The Political Consultative Conference and People's Congress cannot but bend the rule and recruit some young priests to substitute for their aged predecessors because they cannot do without some representatives from Daoism.

An even more pitiful situation is that, even though they have been given the nominally equal status as representatives of the "religion sphere," our young priests are still ignored or looked down on by the representatives of other religious or social groups, *because the quality of their knowledge and speech is too poor to impress the other representatives.* As a result, our young priests can do no more than "sitting on a cold stool" (*zuo lengbandeng*) in those meetings like idiots without saying anything that can represent the Daoist perspective. How sad! Therefore, if we don't try our best to improve our education, encourage young priests to get BA or higher degrees to make up for the qualification requirements, it's highly possible that some day, if the superiors decide to tighten up the rules, the Daoist community may end up with no political representatives. That's not just a humiliation but also a declaration that there will be nobody able to talk to the government on behalf of Daoism in the future. If this is the case, then we cannot develop or breathe freely. It's like being suffocated. ...

Daoism will definitely be replaced by other religions if there is no talented youth coming to join us. The Chinese Buddhist Association is keenly aware of this trend, so they have made great efforts during these years. Despite the creation of quite a few Buddhist colleges, as far as I know, they have quietly implemented a large-scale human-resource development program which basically aims to cultivate intensively talented young graduates of Buddhist colleges, so as to produce a targeted pool of elite monks and nuns within the next ten years who have PhD, MA, and BA degrees. Ten years from now, it is hoped that these elite monks and nuns can gradually replace senior leaders of the Buddhist circle. The implications of this case cannot be clearer: modern schooling and the generalized, modern hierarchy of degrees are an inevitable challenge. If you don't face it and try to "keep up with the Joneses" now, you will be put out sooner or later. Meanwhile, our current students need to be trained with the capability to *talk about Daoist knowledge.* Actually, I have suggested that the leadership of the City God Temple should institute "Sunday lectures" in the temple and ask our graduates to give lectures by turn. Yes, *Daoism does not have a tradition of talking about our religion,* but we need to prepare ourselves for the challenge of missionary acts if we want to keep our presence in the religious sector [i.e. religion sphere] in such an age of mass communication. Without propagating our stuff through preaching, how can we attract young talents? (Yang 2011: 98–100; emphasis added)

The curriculum of the Daoist academies in today's China is over-whelmingly oriented toward enhancing the students' discursive knowledge about Daoism, so much so that when the students graduate and are posted to local temples, they hardly know how to provide ritual services to the local people. But because their discursive knowledge is not what is useful to the local people, these young graduates have to learn ritual skills that were not taught at the Daoist academies (see D. Yang 2005, 2011).

But a better command of Daoist knowledge does increase the self-confidence of the Daoist academy students, and when the occasion arises to defend their religion and their own dignity, this knowledge proves indispensable. D. Yang (2011: 100–1) recounts an anecdote where one of the Shanghai Daoist Academy students was once manning the Daoism booth at a multi-religion exhibition organized by the local religious affairs bureau and, because of his young age and probably the low prestige of Daoism in today's China, he was harassed by a number of passers-by. But this young man successfully fended off these challenges and defended the dignity of Daoism by drawing upon the extensive knowledge on Daoist thought he had learned from his courses and readings.

THE EMERGENCE OF A "POPULAR RELIGION SPHERE"?

In previous chapters we have already encountered the Black Dragon King Temple in northern Shaanxi Province (known locally as Long-wanggou, the Dragon King Valley). It is a popular religious temple dedicated to a local deity, the Black Dragon King (Heilongdawang).[7]

Through the arduous efforts of the temple officers, led by their charismatic leader Temple Boss Lao Wang ("Old Wang"), the temple managed to gain various official statuses and recognitions and thus consolidated its legitimacy. These efforts culminated in its being granted the status of a Daoist temple and thus official incorporation into the religion sphere. In fact, as the temple's activities expanded into different officially recognized domains, it in effect accrued legitimacy through entering these officially sanctioned "spheres" one by one (cultural relic protection, forestry and environmental protection, education, charity, religion). To turn messy reality (i.e. popular religious practices on the ground) into a few simpler categories (i.e. Daoism or Buddhism) is a process James Scott has called "seeing like a state" (Scott 1998). The "Dao-ification" of the Heilongdawang Temple and other similar popular religious temples in a way made these temples "legible" to the state even if it involved a willful misreading.

Even though the Black Dragon King Temple had been successfully registered as an officially recognized Daoist venue of religious activities, it was to remain marginal to the official Daoist establishment in the local Daoism sphere and the broader religion sphere for as long as it resisted any attempt by the local and regional Daoist associations to incorporate it further into the Daoism sphere (e.g. by taking over the management of the temple). And because of a lack of proper religious training in the temple personnel – the two or three Daoist priests that the temple did eventually decide to host are merely there to man a newly built "Daoist" side temple hall that is peripheral to the main temple complex, and they are paraded out in the procession during temple festivals but otherwise play no part in the management of temple affairs – it would be difficult to imagine that the temple can participate in any significant way in the broader religion sphere in the region (except perhaps during times of disaster relief and other state-prompted charity activities). In other words, the case of the Dao-ification of the Black Dragon King Temple shows us that the great majority of grassroots temples (despite their local eminence), even after they have joined the officially recognized religions, will never count much in the constitution of the religion sphere. But perhaps they don't care to either?

The successful entry of many popular religious temples into the Daoism or Buddhism (sub-)sphere during the past 20 years or so – though not without expending strenuous efforts – suggests the attractiveness for popular religious temples to enter an officially approved sphere. However, in recent years the Chinese government is giving more and more space to popular religion, so much so that in some provinces (mostly in the southeastern coastal regions such as Fujian), there is a new bureau within the local religious affairs bureau that is in charge of registering and supervising popular religious temples, *as* popular religious temples rather than as Daoist or Buddhist temples. This is a new development that might be introduced to other parts of China in the future.

Even more astonishing is the very recent emergence of the term "popular religion sphere" (*minjianxinyangjie*) in official media, which suggests that popular religion might be in a position to openly develop its own sociopolitical persona with relative autonomy from the different sub-spheres of the religion sphere (primarily the Daoism and Buddhism spheres). The news excerpt below (China News Agency Xiamen dated June 17, 2012) reports on a recent "make friends and learn from one another" conference in the city of Xiamen in Fujian Province attended by representatives of popular religious temples from mainland China and Taiwan.[8] Over 100 Taiwanese temples and over 50 mainland Chinese temples were represented. These representatives are referred to as being from the "popular religion sphere." Here is an English translation of the news excerpt:

> The "Come together and celebrate dharma connections conference for folk temples and shrines of both sides of the Taiwan Strait" took place in Xiamen in the afternoon of the 17th [of June]. One hundred and

fifty-eight temples and shrines from mainland China and Taiwan got together to "trace and celebrate their dharmic connections, discuss harmonious society and to promote development." Ever since mainland China and Taiwan began interactions relating to folk beliefs (popular religion), this was the first time representatives of temples and shrines of different folk beliefs from the "two shores" got together in one place for discussions.

Those participating included more than one hundred temples and shrines from Taiwan and more than fifty temples and shrines from mainland China, including folk religious beliefs involving Mazu [the Goddess of the Sea], Guandi [the Emperor Guan], Baoshengdadi, Qingshuizushi, Kaizhangshengwang, Guangdewang, Chen Jing'gu, the city god temple, etc.

As soon as they entered the conference venue, old and new friends of the two shores' "popular religion sphere" [*minjianxinyangjie*] greeted one another and sent one another regards. All over the conference venue, there were slogans such as "one hundred temples gather together thanks to karmic/dharmic connections; the two shores are connected thanks to the deities," "the Eight Immortals crossing the sea; they bless the two shores with good fortune"; etc., all testifying to the beautiful wishes of the representatives of the two shores' temples and shrines. ...

While Mr. Ye Kedong, representing the Chinese Taiwan Bureau [Guotaiban of the PRC], thanked the "religion-sphere friends" [*zongjiaojie pengyou*] from Taiwan for having contributed to the development of peace between the two shores, he hoped that the representatives of the two shores' folk religious temples and shrines can discuss and share among themselves, interact closely, with long-term view in mind, benefit from one another's wisdom, open and expand channels, widen the scope of exchange, strengthen their cooperation, explore deeper the precious resources in the two shores' folk religious beliefs and cultures, promote together the inheritance and transmission of the brilliant culture of the Chinese nation, and maintain actively the peaceful development of the relationships between the two shores.

It is not surprising that this neologism ("popular-religion sphere") should be invented in the context of PRC–Taiwan exchanges since the Chinese government has been actively using popular religious ties between the mainland and Taiwan as part of their effort to bolster the Taiwanese people's ties to the mainland (where all of the popular religious deities originated) and to enhance their sense of Chinese national and cultural identity (i.e. part of the United Front strategies aiming at the eventual reunification of mainland China with Taiwan).

The invention of this term opens the door to millions of local activists like temple boss Lao Wang at the Black Dragon King Temple to construct, fill up, and expand this new field of sociopolitical action without needing to resort to be affiliated with the Daoism sphere or Buddhism sphere. It will be extremely interesting and instructive to watch how this new sphere gains further legitimacy and in time becomes more robust.[9] The truth is that the vast majority of temples in China are so-called popular religious temples, and they have been growing at a much faster rate than the officially recognized religion since, though illegal in status, they have not been subjected to the same degree of state control and regulation as the registered temples. So the irony is that what is in theory illegal has been the most vibrant and expansive, while many of the officially supported temples, especially those in urban areas, remain stagnant or at best expand at a far more modest rate (see also Yang 2012, chapter 5).

THE DISCURSIVE CONSTRUCTION OF THE "SUPERSTITION SPECIALIST HOUSEHOLDS"

In the past three decades or so the Chinese official media often report on the social ills posed by the many so-called "superstition specialist households" (*mixin zhuanyehu*) active in rural China. According to these media portrayals, these superstitious specialist households contribute to the re-surfacing of "feudal superstitious grime" (*fengjian mixin chenzha fanqi*), and that grassroots-level cadres and the Public Security Bureau should be vigilant and try to crack down on these undesirable elements. By superstition specialist households the authorities seem to be referring to all kinds of people who make a living doing what are considered superstitious activities in the popular religious realm. These include fortune tellers, *fengshui* masters, spirit mediums, ritual healers, uncertified Daoist priests, folk musicians who play at weddings and funerals, storytellers, opera singers and orchestra members of private folk opera troupes performing at temple festivals, makers of votive paper offerings, printers of hell bank notes, full-time temple caretakers, etc.[10] Many of these are precisely what I have labeled "household-based ritual service providers," some of whom we have met in chapter 4.

Continuing to use the label "superstition" to refer to the activities *yinyang* masters and spirit mediums are engaged in, the authorities may sound like they are reviving the virulent Maoist anti-superstition campaigns. However, except in a few locales where such anti-superstition attitudes are occasionally turned into concrete action (e.g. demolition of temples, banning of lavish funerals, leveling of conspicuously large graves on supposedly valuable farmland), most of the talks of cracking down on superstition remain at a rhetorical level. Most local cadres not only tolerate apparently superstitious activities but even encourage and actively participate in them (see Chau 2006a). The central government has so far avoided using Maoist-era campaign-style strategies to deal with the "superstition boom."

Even though the term *mixin* (superstition), imported as a modern neologism from Japan, has been in use in China for a century by now, the term *zhuanyehu* (specialist household) seems to be a new, reform-era invention. After the long Maoist suppression of private businesses of all sorts (from the 1950s to the 1970s), privately owned and operated businesses finally came back in the 1970s and flourished thereafter, contributing significantly to China's dynamic economic growth in the past four decades. Most of these businesses are very small, family operations, continuing a long tradition in Chinese political economic history of what Hill Gates calls petty capitalist enterprises (Gates 1996). Along with the slogan "To get rich is glorious," new terms such as *getihu* (private business households), *zhuanyehu, xiangzhen qiye* (village and township level enterprises), and *chengbao* (contract enterprises) came into vogue. The term *getihu* became especially ubiquitous. *Geti* (private, independent) is of course in contradistinction with *jiti* (collective), the latter referring to the Maoist collectivization of farming, industrial and other kinds of production, goods distribution, and even consumption (e.g. in the extreme form of collective canteens during the Great Leap Forward). In the Maoist era, *geti* was considered petty bourgeois (*xiaozichanjieji*) or of peasant consciousness (*xiaonong xixiang*) and thus politically suspect; it smacked of selfishness and immorality, while *jiti* connoted morality and revolutionary civic-mindedness. During the reform era, the overall socioeconomic atmosphere is a sea change from that of the Maoist era; now the most important and celebrated qualities in a person are self-initiative, a spirit of adventure and risk taking, flexibility (*linghuo*), a keen sense of market opportunities, sociability (including skills in banqueting and drinking; key to building and maintaining *guanxi* with business partners and political patrons), imagination, management and negotiation skills, personal flair and charisma, skills in talking and persuading, etc. These are necessary qualities for successful entrepreneurs. In addition to these qualities, one would be even more "of the reform spirit" if one specializes in a particular trade or profession, that is if one becomes a "specialized household" (*zhuanyehu*). The term *zhuanye* connotes professional, expert, dedicated trade. The money-making, commercial aspect of these professionals is highlighted, so much so that, ironically, an even more professional (in the sense of full-time pursuit and professional accreditation), certified Daoist priest or Buddhist monk who draws a salary from the Daoist or Buddhist Association but does not sell his service for money would not even be included in this *zhuanyehu* category (the same goes for the Muslim *ahongs* [imams], Protestant ministers, and Catholic priests).

Though sardonic and condemning in tone, "superstition specialist household" as an appellation in fact inadvertently puts the different kinds of religious service providers in the larger categories of *getihu* and *zhuanyehu* that are not only legitimate but even celebrated in reform-era China. Indeed, most of these religious service providers have the same qualities mentioned above that are crucial for successful entrepreneurs. However, curiously, the authorities continue to consider householder religious service providers as "people who gain without laboring" (*bulao-erhuozhe*). In the current political economic climate, to make money and get rich is glorious, but not if it is through mongering superstition or engaging in otherwise morally dubious activities (such as regularly selling one's blood for money), so the party-state argues.

An important fact to keep in mind about the category *zhuanyehu* is that even though the term *hu* refers to households, in reality it sometimes refers to an individual entrepreneur alone, not necessarily including his or her household members. The reason why the authorities still prefer to use the term household as a shorthand (i.e. a metaphor) reveals the extent to which the household idiom has become a hegemonic idiom in statist mentality, i.e. the household is the state's most basic unit of engagement with society because of the long history of the household registration system in Chinese statecraft.

REFORMING FUNERARY AND BURIAL PRACTICES

In earlier chapters we have encountered ancestor worship (chapter 2) and funeral rituals (chapter 4). In recent times, how to treat the body of the deceased has become an increasingly pressing problem for the state as well as for the family members (urbanites certainly do not have ready access to a piece of land to bury the dead). In "traditional China" (see Conclusion), the body of the deceased was always embedded in a dense social universe of symbols and meanings, what some scholars have called the "local moral world" (see Zhang, Kleinman, and Tu 2011). As a result, the corporeal-physical nature of the dead body did not feature prominently in people's consciousness. In other words, (appropriately-embedded) dead bodies were rarely conceived of as corpses. Of course bodies did matter. For example, it is a traditional practice in Shaanbei for an old person to save money and prepare his or her own coffin. This coffin will be kept in one of the family *yaodong* (cave-dwelling) in the same courtyard and he or she would frequently go and check on the coffin. It is not unheard of that the person would climb into the coffin from time to time to "test it out" (or "try it on"), so to speak. The body of the deceased would be washed and elaborately clothed before being put into the coffin. But overall the corporeal aspects of the deceased body is not highlighted in traditional conceptions of dead family members.

During the Maoist period the work units (*danwei*) in urban areas began the practice of holding memorial services (*zhuidaohui*) for their deceased *danwei* employees. To the extent that a deceased person was always somebody embedded in the *danwei* (with a name, a position [*gangwei*], a career, a network of relationships) the *danwei* thus was also a "local moral world." In fact, the structure of these memorial services was such that the *danwei* can be said to have trumped the family in being the main host of the funeral (the family having been relegated to a secondary position after the *danwei* representatives). In other words, the *danwei* usurped the "household sovereignty" of the grieving family (see chapter 2; also Chau 2014). The same happened in the collective farms in the countryside, with the party secretary of the production team presiding over the memorial service. And no religious service would be allowed (all funerary ritualists were prohibited).

In the cities cremation also replaced burial as the preferred method of treating the bodies of the deceased, even though the funerary urns containing the ashes of the cremated bodies would be buried in public cemeteries. The rich and colorful traditional ritual culture surrounding death disappeared completely.

During the reform period we have witnessed the decline of the work unit as the main organizational medium of urban society, which led to the disembedding of the employees from this world of meaningful socialist work, so the *danwei* literally gave the bodies back to the households to which the bodies supposedly really belonged. In the countryside the de-collectivization of the rural political economy happened even earlier (in the early 1980s). In other words, the household has returned as the most basic unit of ritual engagement and the most meaningful local moral world.

The current Chinese state has had an almost four-decade long experience of implementing nationwide family planning and birth control policies, and it has finally reached a point where it wants to meddle with dead bodies in a more systematic manner (see Fang and Goossaert 2008). For almost a decade, an institute within the Chinese Academy of Social Sciences has published annually a high-profile, officially sponsored study on the state of affairs around death and funerary matters in China: *The Green-Cover Book [Green Paper] on Funerals and Burials* (*binzang lüpishu*) – the choice of the color green is, according to the compilers, evocative of an environmentally friendly approach to dealing with death and dead bodies. The book contains empirical studies on funerary reforms in particular locales, the improvement in cremation technologies, funeral customs in foreign countries, etc. The seriousness of these studies more than hints at the intention of the state to advocate nationwide funeral-burial reforms, and possibly even draconian policies in the near future.

With about ten million deaths each year (thus producing about ten million dead bodies each year to be dealt with) and limited land supply,

China is apparently facing a crisis relating to the oft-mentioned "battle for land between the living and the dead" (*huoren yu siren zhengdi*). Employing a *national-statistical approach* to dead bodies as has been the case with fertile bodies and bodies conceived and prohibited to be conceived, the Chinese state is attempting to dislodge dead bodies from their "local moral worlds" and "elevate" them, collectively and anonymously, into the "strategic heights" (*zhanlüe gaodu*) of national planning for scientific and sustainable development. In such a conception, dead bodies are mere corpses. The Civil Affairs Bureau (*minzhengjü*) and other related agencies in local governments are charged with the task of providing more numerous, more convenient, and cheaper ways to "process" (*chuli*) dead bodies (through providing state-operated cremation and accompanying services), in the same spirit as illegal pregnancies are to be "processed" with the family planning policies. Meanwhile, all kinds of "green" and "ecological" "burials" have been invented (e.g. scattering ashes in the woods). When bodies are made to disappear completely, they can no longer resonate with other bodies (live or equally dead). As the notorious recent cases of the Zhoukou (Henan Province) tomb-flattening incident and the Jiangxi coffin-confiscating incident show, the struggle over dead bodies between local moral worlds and the state has greatly intensified, revealing the contested and shifting nature of symbolic investments in (and divestments from), and physical treatments of, dead bodies. For the time being, however, the ritual services of funerary specialists (i.e. the so-called "superstition specialist households") are still *de rigueur* in China's vast agrarian hinterland.

Conclusions

THE REVIVAL OF RELIGIOUS TRADITIONS IN CONTEMPORARY CHINA

Traditional China had one of the richest religious cultures in the world because of the mixing of diverse peoples, the exchange and trafficking of ideas, the invention and continuous innovation of practices and institutions, the expansion of territories, and the integrating power of the Chinese written language that ensured effective borrowing (e.g. the translation of Buddhist, Islamic, and Christian texts) as well as substantial continuity in transmission of a large body of religious knowledge over a very long period of time. The radical anti-traditionalist policies of both the Republican and Communist regimes as well as other broader sociohistorical forces (e.g. the Cold War, urbanization, migration, globalization) have posed formidable challenges to China's religious traditions, but these conditions have also presented new opportunities for regeneration, reinvention, and innovation. In the past four decades or so we have witnessed the incredible revitalization of Chinese religious life; while so much of it is new, the vast majority of contemporary religious practices would not look too unfamiliar to a historian of Chinese religion of the late imperial period. If anything, the continuity is astonishing. How is this substantial continuity possible?

It would be easier to understand this continuity if we understood religious traditions as complex, dynamic, ever-changing clusters of institutions, practitioners and consumers, knowledge and practices, sociopolitical relations and hierarchies, fully amenable to innovations, inventions, and reinventions all the time. Religious traditions are not static.

It is instead necessary to adopt a dynamic and processual understanding of "tradition," to see "tradition" as *generative* and *grounded*. Any particular religious tradition (be it rural Catholicism, lay Buddhism, the transmission of Daoist ritual knowledge, pilgrimage networks, etc.), is *always* in the process of being made and re-made by social actors in response to changing concrete, local circumstances. This understanding of religious traditions is premised on a more

Figure 16: Pilgrims chanting scriptures in front of a Buddhist temple. Photo: reproduced by permission of Wu Nengchang

on-the-ground perspective, looking at the unfolding of elements of religious traditions as they relate concretely to one another in actual historical and sociopolitical contexts rather than reifying *supposedly* related elements into a putative, abstract "tradition." In other words, instead of speaking of grandiose, overarching "traditions" such as Buddhism or Daoism (which necessarily exist only as abstractions or, one may even say, fetishes), it is far more sensible and meaningful to speak of, for example, particular deity cults, particular pilgrimage networks, particular kinds of household-based ritual specialists and their local ritual ecology/economy; particular monastic traditions of sutra chanting and ritual music making; etc. This is why an anthropological disciplinary approach can be so fruitful in uncovering the lived experience of people's religious lives.

Though both religious reproduction and innovation take place within the larger generative structure of tradition, "religious traditions" themselves do not do things; *it is people who do things with religious traditions,* though within the possibilities offered and limitations imposed by these traditions. A particular religious tradition (in the sense specified above, i.e. as generative and grounded) continues to be viable or can be revitalized when three conditions are met: *First,* the substantive elements of the tradition have to be available to be mobilized. These can include symbols, rituals, knowledge, texts, ritual paraphernalia and other material culture, ritual specialists, methods of transmission, networks, particular kinds of spaces, etc. They might be readily accessible or are at least retrievable (e.g. ritual protocols recorded in manuscripts or ritual music "hibernating" in scores). *Second,* there are people who have the interest and desire to mobilize elements of this religious tradition, be they religious specialists who want to make a living using their religious expertise, local elites who derive authority and prestige from sponsoring or organizing local cult activities, or ordinary people who seek divine assistance from deities or ritual specialists, etc. *Third,* the political and socioeconomic environment is conducive to such mobilization. In other words, we need to explain adequately all these conditions before we can understand the revitalization and innovation of any religious tradition (see Chau 2011c).

On the other hand, "tradition" can be mobilized as a legitimizing device, as a claim to meaningful connection to the past. The "invention of traditions" literature has amply demonstrated such instrumental uses of "tradition" (Hobsbawm and Ranger 1983). In other words, the struggle between "the modern" and "the traditional" has more often than not spawned *traditionalism* as a conscious conservationist or revivalist strategy (including most so-called fundamentalisms). The modern application of Islamic Law (the *sharia*) in many Islamic countries is more a product of such a revivalist traditionalism than an uninterrupted legacy from the past.[1] Forms of religious fundamentalism are no less products of modernity and desires for renewal than forms of religious modernism. The same is true for seemingly traditional forms of relational and communal life enabled by religion as a social technology.

THE RELATIONAL APPROACH TO STUDYING RELIGION AND SOCIETY

My aim for this book has been to highlight the centrality of relationality in Chinese religious life. This new, relational approach reveals how Chinese people, through *doing religion*, establish and maintain all kinds of relationships: between different categories of people; between people and all kinds of supernatural entities, be they deities, ancestors, or ghosts; as well as between people, things, and spaces.

This "relational approach to studying religious life" as presented in this book is for understanding religious life not just in the contemporary Chinese world but in other societies and other historical periods as well. Relationality is not incidental to religion, which is often conceived mostly as something residing in, and practiced by, the individual, and which is premised on the existence of a soul no less (the soul being an ego-centric religious notion). Rather, relationality in all its diverse aspects is the very enabling engine and the very "stuff" of religious life. People interact with spirits (deities, God, the Holy Spirit, saints, ancestors, ghosts, evil spirits) as well as with one another *through* their interactions with spirits. These interactions have been created by, and in turn help reproduce countless ritual séances, funeral processions and banquets, temple festivals, worship communities, spirit-cultivation gatherings, and pilgrimage networks. The scale of these interactions can be at the interpersonal, household, village, neighborhood, regional level and even up to the national, transnational, and global level. All these different kinds of relations and interactions interweave into a complex web of ongoing activities, each having an impact on all the others. This complex and colorful amalgamation (yet variedly diffused and locale-specific) of "doing religion" does include texts (e.g. the so-called "sacred texts"), the traditional source of "religious ideas" in Religious Studies, but it is *so much more* than texts. Such a complexity also defies any attempt to delineate any clear-cut "religions." One is even tempted to call it a mess, but it is precisely the job of the social scientist to disentangle this "mess" and elucidate its intricate patterns. "Relationality" and the "five modalities of doing religion" schema I have introduced in this book are productive approaches to understanding religious life in an increasingly complex and interconnected world.

I hope this book has brought the reader closer to Chinese people's religious lives as concrete, on-the-ground practices rather than "Chinese religions" as "systems of thought." Most Westerners and other non-Chinese people are normally introduced to Buddhism and Daoism as systems of philosophical ideas rather than religious conceptions and rituals. For example, the most central idea in Buddhism is understood to be "desires are the sources of suffering," whereas the most central wisdom from Daoism is commonly understood to be "go with the flow rather than against the flow" or "the Way (*dao*) that can be explained is not the true Way," etc. There are often courses on Buddhism and

Daoism in Philosophy departments at universities and, even when they are taught in Religious Studies departments, they are often presented as "Oriental thought," emphasizing ideas at the expense of practice. Presenting a non-Abrahamic religious tradition "systematically" might seem a respectful thing to do, as if granting equal dignity to these traditions that only a century ago were considered unworthy pagan superstitions. This kind of scholarly and pedagogical systematizing owes its inspirations to the Christian tradition of systematic theology, which attempts to formulate Christian doctrines as a coherent whole (but of course ordinary Christians in fact do not necessarily *practice* their Christianity "coherently"). We might not be able to readily throw off this intellectual baggage, but we must always be aware of such epistemological habits (or "habits of the mind") when we try to understand any religious tradition. With this book I argue that relationality is the key anchor of religious lifeworlds in China, and this insight calls for an entirely new way of approaching religion everywhere.

List of Chinese Terms

Even though this book is primarily about the PRC (mainland China), where simplified characters have been used since the character reforms in the 1950s, I have elected to use traditional (non-simplified) characters in the list below. The main reason for this is considerations of historical continuity: most of the place names, deity names, and native terms are not creations of the socialist era. In the past two decades or so, one observes increasingly more frequent use of traditional characters in the mainland alongside the revival of traditional cultural practices.

ahong 阿訇
badahui 八大會
bagua 八卦
bai 拜
baibai 拜拜
Baishatun 白沙屯
baishi 白事
baoda shen'en 報答神恩
baojuan 寶卷
Baoshengdadi 保生大帝
Beigang 北港
benling 本靈
binzang lüpishu 殯葬綠皮書

Bore boluomiduo xinjing
　　般若波羅蜜多心經
buhe shendao 不合神道
buke buxin, buke quanxin
　　不可不信, 不可全信
bulaoerhuozhe 不勞而獲者
chaojin 朝覲
chaojin gongzuo 朝覲工作
Chaotiangong 朝天宮
Chegongmiao 車公廟
chengbao 承包
Chen Jing'gu 陳靖姑
Chongyang 重陽

chuli 處理
Ciji 慈濟
Ciji gongdehui 慈濟功德會
Cijiren 慈濟人
da'ai 大愛
dabao shen'en 答報神恩
dahuizhang 大會長
Dai 傣
Dajia 大甲
danwei 單位
dao 道
Daodejing (Tao Te Ching) 道德經
daojiao 道教
daojiaojie 道教界
Datong 大同
daxiaoren 打小人
Dimu 地母
dixiong 弟兄
dizi 笛子
dou 斗
Ejingqiao 鵝頸橋
fahui 法會
falun 法輪
Falungong 法輪功
fanwushen yundong 反巫神運動
fashi 法事
fashi 法師
feiwuzhi wenhua yichan 非物質文化遺產
fengjian mixin 封建迷信

fengjian mixin chenzha fanqi 封建迷信沉渣泛起
fengshui 風水
fodao 佛道
Foguangren 佛光人
Foguangshan 佛光山
fojiao 佛教
fojiaojie 佛教界
fomen 佛門
fomen dizi 佛門弟子
fu 符
Fujian 福建
fulushou 福祿壽
fuyao nenghao 服藥能好
gangwei 崗位
Gansu 甘肅
Gaoxiong 高雄
geti 個體
getihu 個體戶
gong'an 公案
gongde 功德
gongzhu 宮主
gua 卦
guadan 掛單
Guangdewang 廣德王
Guangjisi 廣濟寺
guangmingdeng 光明燈
guanxi 關係
Guanyin 觀音
guanzi 管子
guhun 孤魂
guhun yegui 孤魂野鬼

gui 鬼
guiyi 皈依
guiyi sanbao 皈依三寶
guiyizheng 皈依證
guoguan 過關
haoxiongdi 好兄弟
Heilongdawang 黑龍大王
Heilongdawangmiao
　黑龍大王廟
Henan 河南
Hong Xiuquan 洪秀全
honghuo 紅火
Hongyundaxian 紅雲大仙
hu 戶
Hualian 花蓮
Huangdaxian 黃大仙
huansu 還俗
Hui 回
huiling 會靈
huilingshan 會靈山
huizhang 會長
huofo 活佛
huoju 火居
huoju daoshi 火居道士
huoren yu siren zhengdi
　活人與死人爭地
Huoyanzhenjun 火焰真君
jia 家
jiachi 加持
Jiangnan 江南
jiantang de enci 建堂的恩賜
jiao 醮

jidujiao 基督教
jidujiaojie 基督教界
jiebei 揭碑
jiemei 姊妹
jigongde 積功德
Jingang bore boluomi jing
　金剛般若波羅蜜經
jingshen shenzai, bujing buguai
　敬神神在, 不敬不怪
jingsi jingshe 靜思精舍
jingzhe 驚蟄
Jinmu 金母
jinxiang 進香
jiti 集體
jushi 居士
Kaizhangshengwang 開漳聖王
kanbu 堪布
kang 炕
kanhonghuo 看紅火
kanyinyang 看陰陽
Kejia 客家
keyi 科儀
kouyuan buming 口願不明
laiwang 來往
Lanzhou 蘭州
laoban jidutu 老闆基督徒
laoxiang 老鄉
Liang Congjie 梁從誡
lianhuan wanhui 聯歡晚會
Lin Moniang 林默娘
ling 靈
linghuo 靈活

lingji 靈乩
lingmai 靈脈
lingyan 靈驗
lingying 靈應
lisheng 禮生
Longquansi 龍泉寺
Longwanggou 龍王溝
Lugang 鹿港
luopan 羅盤
luzhu 爐主
Maijia 麥加
matong 馬童
Mazu 媽祖
Meizhou 湄洲
menkou tudi caishen
　門口土地財神
miaochan xingxue 廟產興學
Miaofengshan 妙峰山
minghun 冥婚
minjianxinyangjie 民間信仰界
minzhengjü 民政局
minzu 民族
minzu shibie 民族識別
mixin 迷信
mixin zhiye fenzi 迷信職業分子
mixin zhiyezhe 迷信職業者
mixin zhuanyehu 迷信專業戶
Mizhi 米脂
namo amituofo 南無阿彌陀佛
Nanyang 南洋
nengren 能人
Nezha 哪吒

Ningbo 寧波
Ningxia 寧夏
nongjiale 農家樂
paiwei 牌位
ping'an 平安
ping'an chaojin, youxu chaojin,
　wenming chaojin 平安朝覲,
　有序朝覲, 文明朝覲
pinyin 拼音
pudu 普渡
qi 氣
qian 簽
qianxin qidao 虔心祈禱
qifupai 祈福牌
qigong 氣功
qigong re 氣功熱
qigongjie 氣功界
Qingdao 青島
Qingming 清明
Qingshuizushi 清水祖師
Qingyundaxian 青雲大仙
qingzhu huigui qifu fahui
　慶祝回歸祈福法會
qiqi 七七
qiu 求
qiufu 求福
Quanzhen 全真
quyao daishui 取藥帶水
re'nao 熱鬧
Renda 人大
Rendaihui 人代會
renmin 人民

sangshi zhuanyehu 喪事專業戶
sanju 散居
sanzi jiaohui 三自教會
Sanzi yundong 三自運動
Shaanbei 陝北
Shaanxi 陝西
shang xitian 上西天
shangshang daji 上上大吉
shanshu 善書
Shaolin 少林
Shatin 沙田
Shaukeiwan 筲箕灣
shehuizhuyi hexin jiazhiguan 社會主義核心價值觀
shen 神
sheng 聖
sheng (musical instrument) 笙
shenguan 神官
shenguandiao 神官調
shenling xianying 神靈顯應
Shenmu 神木
shenquan 神權
shenzhupai 神主牌
shifu 師傅
shigong 師公
shitu 師徒
shuilu fahui 水陸法會
siren gongtan 私人公壇
suanming zhuanyehu 算命專業戶
Taidong 台東
Taiping tianguo 太平天國

Taixu 太虛
tan 壇
tanggua 趟卦
tian 天
tiandi 天地
Tianhou 天后
Tianjin 天津
tianren heyi 天人合一
tianzhujiao 天主教
tianzhujiaojie 天主教界
ticheng 提成
tisheng lingdao suzhi 提升領導素質
tongxiu 同修
waishengren 外省人
Wangmu 王母
Wanhua 萬華
weibo 微博
weixin 微信
Wenchuan 汶川
wenhua 文化
wenhuajie 文化節
Wenzhou 溫州
Wujilaomu 無極老母
Wujishengbaodian 無極聖寶殿
wushen 巫神
wuxing wenhua zichan 無形文化資產
wuyi laodongjie 五一勞動節
Xi Jinping 習近平
Xiamen 廈門

xian 仙

xiang 香

Xianggang daojiao lianhehui
香港道教聯合會

xiangzhen qiye 鄉鎮企業

xiantian 先天

xiaonong sixiang 小農思想

xiaozai jie'e qifu fahui
消災解厄祈福法會

xiaozichanjieji 小資產階級

xiaxia zhongping 下下中平

xiejiao 邪教

xingren zaohui 行人早回

Xingyun (Hsing Yun) 星雲

Xinjiang 新疆

Xinpu 新埔

Xinzhu 新竹

Xishuangbanna 西雙版納

xitong 系統

Xuejia 學甲

xuyuan 許願

yangge 秧歌

yangzhai 陽宅

yankou 燄口

yanmenzi 沿門子

yaodong 窯洞

Yiguandao 一貫道

Yilan 宜蘭

yimin 義民

Yinchuan 銀川

ying 應

yingling 嬰靈

yinhunfan 引魂幡

yinsi 淫祀

yinyang 陰陽

yinyang xiansheng 陰陽先生

yinzhai 陰宅

Yisilanjiao 伊斯蘭教

yisilanjiaojie 伊斯蘭教界

youqiu biying 有求必應

youshen 遊神

yu fo de qinjin 與佛的親近

yuan 元

yuanling 元靈

yulanpen 盂蘭盆

Yulin 榆林

yunluo 雲鑼

Yunnan 雲南

yunyou 雲遊

zaojun 灶君

zhadao 鍘刀

zhanlüe gaodu 戰略高度

Zhejiang 浙江

zhencai 真才

Zhenchuan 鎮川

Zhengxie 政協

Zhengyan (Cheng Yen)
證嚴

Zhengyi 正一

zhizha 紙紮

Zhonghua Jidu jiaohui
中華基督教會

Zhongguo daojiao xiehui
中國道教協會

Zhongguo fojiao xiehui 中國佛教協會

Zhongguo musilin chaojin shiyong shouce 中國穆斯林朝覲實用手冊

Zhongguo tianzhujiao xiehui 中國天主教協會

Zhongguo yisilanjiao xiehui 中國伊斯蘭教協會

Zhongtanyuanshuai 中壇元帥

zhongyuan 中元

Zhoukou 周口

zhu 主

Zhuangzi 莊子

zhuanye 專業

zhuanyehu 專業戶

zhuchi 住持

zhuidaohui 追悼會

zhujia 主家

Ziran zhi you 自然之友

zizhi, ziyang, zichuan 自治, 自養, 自傳

zongjiao 宗教

zhongjiao gongzuo 宗教工作

zongjiao huodong changsuo 宗教活動場所

zongjiaojie 宗教界

zongjiaojie pengyou 宗教界朋友

zongjiaoju 宗教局

zongling 總領

zuo gongde 做功德

zuo jiu duile 做就對了

zuo lengbandeng 坐冷板凳

Notes

Introduction: Relationality at the Heart of Religion in China

1 The Pew-Templeton Foundation "Global Religious Futures" project website: http://www.globalreligiousfutures.org/countries/china#/?affiliations_ religion_id=0&affiliations_year=2010&region_name=All%20 Countries&restrictions_year=2016

2 The English version of the full text can be found at http://english.gov.cn/ archive/white_paper/2018/04/04/content_281476100999028.htm

3 The original uses "Taoism" and "Taoists," but I have changed them into Daoism and Daoists for consistency's sake. Today, most academic writings on Chinese religion adopt "Daoism" and "Daoists" while popular works continue to use "Taoism" and "Taoists."

1 Understanding Religious Diversity: Five Modalities of Doing Religion

1 For a detailed treatment of these "modalities of doing religion" see Chau (2011a, 2011b, and 2013a).

2 Note that the Daoist conception of immortalhood is not the same as immortality, the latter implying the continuous use of the same worldly body. Daoist immortals are supposed to take other forms.

2 Interacting with Gods, Ghosts, and Ancestors

1 It requires analytical ingenuity and quite a bit of imagination to understand other people's experience, especially when they live in a completely different lifeworld. But this is precisely the task of anthropology.

2 For an experimental ethnography on the Hakka righteous martyrs festival involving the sacrifice and public display of dozens of specially-fed giant pigs, see Chau (2013c).

3 Nowadays weddings are almost entirely secular with only some rural areas retaining the practice of reporting to the ancestors about the joyful event.

4 In the Judeo-Christian religious tradition, the figure of the stranger has theological significance: one had better offer hospitality to the stranger who shows up at one's door since he might very well be an angel or God himself. On the other hand, in the Chinese religious tradition, there are hardly any such figures of stranger-spirits.

5 For a detailed exposition on the key role households have played in the revival of religious and ritual life in the reform era, see Chau (2015).

6 The bread used in the Eucharist is known as "host" as well, although the etymology is entirely different.

7 Both historical studies of Christianity and the gradually maturing field of "the anthropology of Christianity" have revealed very many different forms of practicing Christianity. I have no doubt collapsed a wide diversity of possible forms of Christian practices into a generic image, but I have constructed these images in such sharp relief for heuristic purposes.

3 Festivals and Pilgrimages

1 See Feuchtwang (2001: chapters 4 and 5) for a detailed description of how temple festivals are organized in Taiwanese communities, especially the ones involving the selection of main organizing households by divination and the institution of the "incense pot master/host" (*luzhu*).

2 There are always moments at funerals where the band plays joyous tunes because the death of a person in old age is considered a joyous occasion despite the sadness.

3 The French scholar Patrice Fava has recently made an ethnographic film on these associations.

4 In contrast, saints do not visit other saints in Catholicism.

5 For the ethnographic accounts and some analyses, I rely on the work of Marshall (2003) and Ting (2005). I obtained further information on the *lingji* and their activities from Alison Marshall via email. I am very grateful to her for her kind help.

6 Scholars generally make a distinction between spirit mediums and shamans. Spirit mediums are human agents who are possessed by their tutelary spirits during séances and normally do not remember what has happened during

the séance once they come out of it. On the other hand, shamans themselves are endowed with supernatural powers that allow them to roam in the spirit realm, and they are aware of what is happening during the "trip." China has both spirit mediums and shamans, though among the Han Chinese spirit mediumship is usually the norm. There are also very many "magical healers" in all parts of China who help their patients or worshipers without getting possessed.

7 For studies on Chinese Muslim communities, see Gladney (1996), Jaschok and Shui (2000), Gillette (2003), Ma (2006), Erie (2016), and Stewart (2017).

8 In 2017, three Chinese airlines (Air China, Southern Airlines, Eastern Airlines) were tasked to operate 39 hajj chartered flights, taking hajj pilgrims from Beijing, Kunming (Yunnan Province), Lanzhou (Gansu Province), Urumqi (Xinjiang Muslim Autonomous Region), and Yinchuan (Ningxia Muslim Autonomous Region).

9 https://www.nxmslcj.cn/tzgg/260551.shtml (accessed October 29, 2018).

10 The notes underneath the table indicate that the costs in Saudi Arabia include accommodation, meals and water, contribution to ritual slaughter, transportation, Saudi surcharges, etc. The cost of meals in Saudi Arabia is calculated at RMB45 per day (a total of 31 days).

11 In 2017, most hajj pilgrims departed from Beijing, but there were also hajj delegations that departed from Ningxia, Xinjiang, Yunnan, and Gansu.

12 http://www.chinaislam.net.cn/cms/zjsw/news/internal/201708/09-11237.html

13 Intending to stimulate consumption and leisure activities, the reform-era Chinese state expanded the May First International Labor Day into a long vacation that is enjoyed by schoolchildren and state and private enterprise employees alike. The other long vacation is during the Chinese New Year. Both can last for up to ten days. To go on a tree-planting expedition during vacation seems to be a legacy of the Maoist era, when different urban work units and schools organized collective volunteer labor activities such as planting trees and rice seedlings, harvesting, building dams and terraced fields, etc.

14 As if blessed by the Heilongdawang, most of the trees actually survived through at least the summer of 1998, thanks to the abundant spring rain, the availability of irrigation, and the care of the arboretum staff.

15 A female Beijing student was bitten by a peasant home guard dog (she was trying to take a picture with the dog thinking that it was a pet while in fact peasants use dogs primarily as guard dogs and they can be extremely fierce). She was rushed to the local hospital to be checked if she had contracted

rabies (fortunately she did not). One of the Friends of Nature members was known to be physically weak, but she worked very hard until she got sick and had to lie down in the dormitory.

16 Some of the Longwanggou Primary School children's parents complained that the temple and Lao Wang were exploiting their children in entertaining the Beijing guests. But the Beijingers did reciprocate appropriately by donating a large number of books to the schools of the nine villages affiliated with Longwanggou. The majority of the books went to the Longwanggou Primary School. See Chau (2006c and forthcoming) for an analysis on youth and youth cultural production in rural China.

4 Ritual Service Providers and Their Clients

1 By "sectarian" I am referring to the mostly Buddhist-inspired millenarian cults that developed around charismatic leaders that demanded exclusivistic membership adherence. Their occurrence was sporadic in Chinese history and they were often targets of state crackdowns.

2 The form of competition may include Buddhist temples against Daoist temples, Daoist temples against spirit mediums, Buddhist temples against other Buddhist temples, Daoist temples against other Daoist temples, householder Daoist priests against other householder Daoist priests, spirit mediums against magical healers, etc.

3 In Japan, the two major religious traditions Shinto and Buddhism have worked out an amiable division of labor (and, one may add, share of income), in which the Shinto priests are in charge of matters relating to life-stage rites of passage and marriage while the Buddhist monks take care of the funeral and after-death matters.

4 I have modified the expression which was first coined by the anthropologist of South Asia Michael Carrithers (2000).

5 Following a *dharma* (teaching) is like following a path; one can only be on one path at any one time. Being a Hindu, a Jain, or a Buddhist is like following a path, embodied in the teaching (*dharma*). Although following a *dharma* is not as strong as confessing one's faith in the sense of belonging to one of the Abrahamic religions, it is nonetheless a form of confessionality (often conflated with ethnic identities in South Asia). See Chau (2012a) for a more detailed argument.

6 See Mollier (2008) for a historical analysis of the extensive mutual borrowings between Buddhism and Daoism during medieval times.

7 The most important reason for most ritual specialists to adopt the household idiom is to keep a low profile in order to dodge the attention of the state, which has not always been friendly toward these ritual service providers (Chau 2006b).

8 In 1997 and 1998 when I conducted my year-long fieldwork near Zhen-chuan Town (Yulin County, Yulin Prefecture), the standard fee for a *yinyang* master's funeral service was between 150 and 300 yuan, not a bad income considering that the average daily wage of an unskilled laborer (e.g. a crew member of a labor gang working on building roads) at that time was between 20 and 30 yuan.

9 This *jiao* took place in 1969, but the essential structure is the same today.

10 See Schipper (2008) for details of this ritual.

11 All information in this paragraph is derived from Yau (2003).

12 Marc Moskowitz conducted field research in Taiwan in the 1990s. The fees for ritual services should be adjusted to the standard of living at that time.

13 This section is taken from Chau (2006b), based on field research in rural northern Shaanxi Province (Shaanbei), northcentral China. The ethnographic present is circa late 1990s.

14 This ritual is called "passing the obstacles" (*guoguan*).

15 See Katz (2009) for rituals of oath-taking involving beheading a chicken.

16 The information in this section is based on brief ethnographic fieldwork and various websites on the *daxiaoren* practice. One particularly graphic episode can be found at: https://www.youtube.com/watch?v=YJO39B7e1pk (accessed October 29, 2018).

17 In recent years some protestors have used this ritual to symbolically beat up and curse any unpopular Chief Executive of Hong Kong.

18 *Khenpo* (*kanbu* in Chinese) is a formal title for a lama who has undergone substantial learning.

19 The blog can be found at http://dzh.mop.com/whbm/20110707/0/gO3378I27022d2FO.shtml (last accessed on October 1, 2013). Unfortunately, this blog has since vanished from the web, but I have kept a copy of the contents of this blog entry as a Word document.

20 For a fuller analysis of commodification in contemporary Chinese religious practices, see Chau (2016).

21 We should at the same time ask for some contextual financial information since the cost of religious services will have no meaning unless juxtaposed against the cost of other items in daily life (e.g. the cost of a packet of cigarettes, a kilo of rice, lottery tickets, movie tickets, lunch at a fast-food restaurant) and certain major household expenses (such as building a house, buying a car, sending children to school).

5 Communities and Networks

1 This perspective owes its inspiration to Louis Althusser (1971) and Michel Foucault (1982). For more detailed treatments of the concept of "religious subjectification," see Chau (2013b and 2014).

2 "Three-Self" churches are churches under the jurisdiction of the Three-Self Patriotic Movement (TSPM). The three-self principles are self-governance, self-support (financial independence from foreign church bodies), and self-propagation (proselytization by native Chinese) (zizhi, ziyang, zichuan).

3 The report is a product of an informal interview conducted in the spring of 2018 for a new project on "taking refuge" and lay Buddhism in contemporary China.

4 Some lay Buddhist practitioners do not want to go through any official guiyi ceremony and get a certificate since they believe their devotion is about the heart, whereas the guiyi ceremony is merely a matter of formality (Remoiville 2013).

5 An accompanying expression is "willing to do and happily receive [e.g. inconveniences, suffering, etc.]" (see Ting 1999: 484).

6 http://www.youtube.com/watch?v=K_0nPIQGgHU (last accessed on February 2, 2013).

7 http://www.tzuchi.org.my (last accessed on February 2, 2013).

8 See a report in the Guardian: https://www.theguardian.com/world/2016/apr/26/robot-monk-to-spread-buddhist-wisdom-to-the-digital-generation

6 State–Religion Relations

1 For a more detailed treatment of the workings of the "religion sphere" concept in modern and contemporary China, see Chau (2017).

2 Some of these spheres are labeled differently depending on the historical period. In more recent years new spheres have emerged in the PRC, e.g. the law sphere, the qigong sphere, the stocks and securities sphere, the charity sphere, the classical learning sphere, the NGO sphere, and the internet sphere.

3 This "religious sovereignty" should not be confused with any sense of autonomy which is the goal of some religious practitioners; the latter is referring to autonomy from state interference. Religious sovereignty is about the religion sphere as a key constituting element of the nation being autonomous from foreign influence; it is therefore always entangled with the state.

4 All spheres, despite their stated functional references (e.g. religion, education, science), are ultimately political in nature.

5 Given the ideological dominance of the Chinese party-state, one might suspect that PRC secularism is based on the party-state's monopoly power or control over cosmological truth. Such a monopoly might have been in place during the high Maoist era but does not exist today, even during the Xi Jinping era when there has been much tightening of the party's ideological discipline and promotion of "core socialist values" (*shehuizhuyi hexin jiazhiguan*). The considerable liberalization in the religion sphere during the reform era has produced a plethora of cosmological truths, the monitoring of which by the state is nearly impossible.

6 According to Xi, leaders of the religion sphere: (1) must persist in the direction of indigenization; (2) must raise the level of the rule of law in "religion work"; (3) must view the social role of religion dialectically; and (4) must try hard to make good use of people in the religion sphere. A fuller report can be found at: http://news.china.com.cn/2015-05/21/content_35621328.htm

7 For detailed studies on various aspects of this temple's revival and operations, see Chau (2004, 2006a, 2009, 2018).

8 *Liang'an bai yu jia gongmiao 'Baxian guohai' gongxu fayuan"*. Source: http://www.chinataiwan.org/hxlt/zhuti/ztltfour/gongmiao/bobao/201206/t20120617_2746823.htm

9 Judging from the paucity of usage I can locate on the internet, it seems that this term has not taken off yet.

10 Other terms for these people include *mixin zhiyezhe* (superstition professionals) and *mixin zhiye fenzi* (superstition professional elements).

Conclusions

1 For a detailed ethnographic account of the negotiations between *sharia*, Chinese law, and the party-state, see Erie (2016).

Further Reading

The following works are useful guides to more focused investigations into various dimensions of Chinese religion life in contemporary Chinese societies. I have limited the selection to works in the English language and those that are more recent, in book form (mostly available in paperback), accessible, and based on extensive ethnographic fieldwork. Readers with more specialized interests are encouraged to explore the bibliography of this book and those of the following books for further relevant literature.

Ashiwa, Yoshiko and David. L. Wank, eds. 2009. *Making Religion, Making the State: The Politics of Religion in Modern China*. Stanford, CA: Stanford University Press.

Billioud, Sébastian and Joël Thoraval. 2015. *The Sage and the People: The Confucian Revival in China*. Oxford: Oxford University Press.

Blake, C. Fred. 2011. *Burning Money: The Material Spirit of the Chinese Lifeworld*. Honolulu, HI: University of Hawai'i Press.

Bruun, Ole. 2003. *Fengshui in China: Geomantic Divination Between State Orthodoxy and Popular Religion*. Honolulu, HI: University of Hawai'i Press.

Cao, Nanlai. 2010. *Constructing China's Jerusalem: Christians, Power, and Place in Contemporary Wenzhou*. Stanford, CA: Stanford University Press.

Chan, Selina. C. and Graeme Lang. 2014. *Building Temples in China: Memories, Tourism, and Identities*. London: Routledge.

Chau, Adam Yuet. 2006. *Miraculous Response: Doing Popular Religion in Contemporary China*. Stanford, CA: Stanford University Press.

Chau, Adam Yuet, ed. 2011. *Religion in Contemporary China: Revitalization and Innovation*. London: Routledge.

Chu, Cindy Yik-yi. 2012. *The Catholic Church in China: 1978 to the Present*. New York: Palgrave Macmillan.

DeBernardi, Jean. 2006. *The Way that Lives in the Heart: Chinese Popular Religion and Spirit Mediums in Penang, Malaysia.* Stanford, CA: Stanford University Press.

Fisher, Gareth. 2014. *From Comrades to Bodhisattvas: Moral Dimensions of Lay Buddhist Practice in Contemporary China.* Honolulu, HI: University of Hawai'i Press.

Gillette, Maris B. 2001. *Between Mecca and Beijing: Modernization and Consumption Among Urban Chinese Muslims.* Stanford, CA: Stanford University Press.

Gladney, Dru C. 1996. *Muslim Chinese: Ethnic Nationalism in the People's Republic,* 2nd edn. Cambridge, MA: Harvard East Asian Monographs.

Goldstein, M. C. and M. T. Kapstein, eds. 1998. *Buddhism in Contemporary Tibet: Religious Revival and Cultural Identity.* Berkeley, CA: University of California Press.

Goossaert, Vincent and David A. Palmer. 2011. *The Religious Question in Modern China.* Chicago, IL: University of Chicago Press.

Harrison, Henrietta. 2013. *The Missionary's Curse and Other Tales from a Chinese Catholic Village.* Berkeley, CA: University of California Press.

Herrou, Adeline. 2013. *A World of Their Own: Daoist Monks and Their Community in Contemporary China.* Dunedin, FL: Three Pines Press.

Huang, C. Julia. 2009. *Charisma and Compassion: Cheng Yen and the Buddhist Tzu Chi Movement.* Cambridge, MA: Harvard University Press.

Ji Zhe, Gareth Fisher, and André Laliberté, eds. Forthcoming. *Buddhism after Mao: Negotiations, Continuities, and Reinventions.* Honolulu, HI: University of Hawai'i Press.

Jing, Jun. 1996. *The Temple of Memories: History, Power, and Morality in a Chinese Village.* Stanford, CA: Stanford University Press.

Jones, Stephen. 2017. *Daoist Priests of the Li Family: Ritual Life in Village China.* Magdalena, NM: Three Pines Press.

Kang, Xiaofei and Donald S. Sutton. 2016. *Contesting the Yellow Dragon: Ethnicity, Religion, and the State in the Sino-Tibetan Borderland.* Leiden: Brill.

Katz, Paul R. 2009. *Divine Justice: Religion and the Development of Chinese Legal Culture.* New York: Routledge.

Katz, Paul R. 2014. *Religion in China and Its Modern Fate.* Waltham, MA: Brandeis University Press.

Kuah-Pearce, Khun Eng. 2011. *Rebuilding the Ancestral Village: Singaporeans in China.* Singapore: National University of Singapore Press.

Lagerwey, John. 2010. *China: A Religious State.* Hong Kong: Hong Kong University Press.

Lin Wei-Ping. 2015. *Materializing Magic Power: Chinese Popular Religion in Villages and Cities*. Cambridge, MA: Harvard Asia Center Publications.

Madsen, Richard. 2007. *Democracy's Dharma: Religious Renaissance and Political Development in Taiwan*. Berkeley, CA: University of California Press.

Moskowitz, Marc L. 2001. *The Haunting Fetus: Abortion, Sexuality, and the Spirit World in Taiwan*. Honolulu, HI: University of Hawai'i Press.

Naquin, Susan and Chün-fang Yü, eds. 1992. *Pilgrims and Sacred Sites in China*. Berkeley, CA: University of California Press.

Oakes, Tim and Donald S. Sutton, eds. 2010. *Faiths on Display: Religion, Tourism, and the Chinese State*. Lanham, MD: Rowman and Littlefield.

Palmer, David A. 2007. *Qigong Fever: Body, Science, and Utopia in China, 1949–1999*. New York: Columbia University Press.

Palmer, David A. and Elijar Siegler. 2017. *Dream Trippers: Global Daoism and the Predicament of Modern Spirituality*. Chicago, IL: University of Chicago Press.

Sun, Anna. 2013. *Confucianism as a World Religion: Contested Histories and Contemporary Realities*. Princeton, NJ: Princeton University Press.

Travagnin, Stefania, ed. 2018. *Religion and Media in China: Insights and Case Studies from the Mainland, Taiwan and Hong Kong*. London: Routledge.

Vala, Carsten. 2017. *The Politics of Protestant Churches and the Party-State in China: God Above Party?* New York: Routledge.

Vermander, Benoît, Liz Hingley, and Liang Zhang. 2018. *Shanghai Sacred: The Religious Landscape of a Global City*. Seattle, WA: University of Washington Press.

Wellens, Koen. 2011. *Religious Revival in the Tibetan Borderlands: The Premi of Southwest China*. Seattle, WA: University of Washington Press.

Weller, Robert P., C. Julia Huang, and Keping Wu, with Lizhu Fan. 2017. *Religion and Charity: The Social Life of Goodness in Chinese Societies*. Cambridge: Cambridge University Press.

Yang, Fenggang. 2012. *Religion in China: Survival and Revival under Communist Rule*. Oxford: Oxford University Press.

Yang, Mayfair Mei-hui, ed. 2008. *Chinese Religiosities: Afflictions of Modernity and State Formation*. Berkeley, CA: University of California Press.

Yü, Chün-fang. 2013. *Passing the Light: The Incense Light Community and Buddhist Nuns in Taiwan*. Honolulu, HI: University of Hawai'i Press.

Yü, Dan Smyer. 2012. *The Spread of Tibetan Buddhism in China: Charisma, Money, Enlightenment*. London: Routledge.

References

Ahern, Emily M. 1981. *Chinese Ritual and Politics*. Cambridge: Cambridge University Press.

Al-Sudairi, Mohammed. 2017. "Changing State-Religion Dynamics in Xi Jinping's China: And its Consequences for Sino-Saudi Relations." *Dirasat*, No. 19, January.

Althusser, Louis. 1971. "Ideology and Ideological State Apparatuses." In *Lenin and Philosophy and Other Essays*. Translated by Ben Brewster. London: Monthly Review Press, pp. 121–76.

Anderson, Benedict. 1983. *Imagined Communities: Reflections on the Origin and Spread of Nationalism*. New York: Verso.

Apter, David E. and Tony Saich. 1995. *Revolutionary Discourse in Mao's Republic*. Cambridge, MA: Harvard University Press.

Ashiwa, Yoshiko and David L. Wank. 2002. "The Globalization of Chinese Buddhism: Clergy and Devotee Networks in the Twentieth Century." *International Journal of Asian Studies* 63(3): 719–56.

Ashiwa, Yoshiko and David L. Wank. 2006. "The Politics of a Reviving Buddhist Temple: State, Association, and Religion in Southeast China." *The Journal of Asian Studies* 65(2): 337–59.

Billioud, Sébastian and Joël Thoraval. 2015. *The Sage and the People: The Confucian Revival in China*. Oxford: Oxford University Press.

Blake, C. Fred. 2011. *Burning Money: The Material Spirit of the Chinese Lifeworld*. Honolulu, HI: University of Hawai'i Press.

Brown, Michael F. 1999. *The Channeling Zone: American Spirituality in an Anxious Age*. Cambridge, MA: Harvard University Press.

Cabezón, José Ignacio. 2008. "State Control of Tibetan Buddhist Monasticism in the People's Republic of China." In Mayfair Mei-hui Yang, ed. *Chinese Religiosities: Afflictions of Modernity and State Formation*. Berkeley, CA: University of California Press, pp. 261–94.

Candea, Matei and Giovanni da Col. 2012. "The Return to Hospitality: Strangers, Guests, and Ambiguous Encounters." *Journal of the Royal Anthropological Institute* 18(s1): s1–s217.

Cannell, Fenella, ed. 2006. *The Anthropology of Christianity*. Durham, NC: Duke University Press.

Cao, Nanlai. 2010. *Constructing China's Jerusalem: Christians, Power, and Place in Contemporary Wenzhou*. Stanford, CA: Stanford University Press.

Cao, Nanlai. 2013. "Renegotiating Locality and Morality in a Chinese Religious Diaspora: Wenzhou Christian Merchants in Paris, France." *The Asia Pacific Journal of Anthropology* 14(1): 85–101.

Cao, Nanlai. 2017. "Spatial Modernity, Party Building, and Local Governance: Putting the Christian Cross-Removal Campaign in Context." *China Review* 17(1): 29–52.

Carrithers, Michael. 2000. "On Polytropy: Or the Natural Condition of Spiritual Cosmopolitanism in India: The Digambar Jain Case." *Modern Asian Studies* 34(4): 831–61.

Chang, Hsun. 2008. *Mazu: xinyang de zhuixun/Zhang Xun zixuanji* [*Mazu: The Pursuit of Beliefs/A Selection of Chang Hsun's Work*]. Taipei: Boyoung.

Chau, Adam Yuet. 2004. "Hosting Funerals and Temple Festivals: Folk Event Productions in Contemporary Rural China." *Asian Anthropology* 3: 39–70.

Chau, Adam Yuet. 2006a. *Miraculous Response: Doing Popular Religion in Contemporary China*. Stanford, CA: Stanford University Press.

Chau, Adam Yuet. 2006b. "Superstition Specialist Households?: The Household Idiom in Chinese Religious Practices." *Minsu quyi, the Journal of Chinese Ritual, Theatre, and Folklore* (special issue on religious specialists) 153: 157–202.

Chau, Adam Yuet. 2006c. "Drinking Games, Karaoke Songs, and Yangge Dances: Youth Cultural Production in Rural China." *Ethnology* 45(2): 161–72.

Chau, Adam Yuet. 2009. "Expanding the Space of Popular Religion: Local Temple Activism and the Politics of Legitimation in Contemporary Rural China." In Yoshiko Ashiwa and David Wank, eds., *Making Religion, Making the State: The Politics of Religion in Contemporary China*. Stanford, CA: Stanford University Press, pp. 211–40.

Chau, Adam Yuet. 2011a. "Modalities of Doing Religion and Ritual Polytropy: Evaluating the Religious Market Model from the Perspective of Chinese Religious History." *Religion* 41(4): 547–68.

Chau, Adam Yuet. 2011b. "Modalities of Doing Religion." In David A. Palmer, Glenn Shive, and Philip L. Wickeri, eds., *Chinese Religious Life: Culture, Society, and Politics*. Oxford: Oxford University Press, pp. 67–84.

Chau, Adam Yuet, ed. 2011c. *Religion in Contemporary China: Revitalization and Innovation.* London: Routledge.

Chau, Adam Yuet. 2012a. "Efficacy, Not Confessionality: Ritual Polytropy at Chinese Funerals." In Glenn Bowman, ed., *Sharing the Sacra: The Politics and Pragmatics of Inter-communal Relations around Holy Places.* Oxford: Berghahn Books, pp. 79–96.

Chau, Adam Yuet. 2012b. "Actants Amassing (AA)." In Nick Long and Henrietta Moore, eds., *Sociality: New Directions.* Oxford: Berghahn Books, pp. 133–55.

Chau, Adam Yuet. 2013a. "Religious Diversity from the Perspective of Religious Consumers." In Perry Schmidt-Leukel and Joachim Gentz, eds., *Religious Diversity in Chinese Thought.* New York: Palgrave Macmillan, pp. 141–54.

Chau, Adam Yuet. 2013b. "Religious Subjectification: Cherishing Written Traces and Being a Ciji (Tzu Chi) Person." In Chang Hsun, ed., *Studies on Chinese Popular Religion: Integrating Fieldwork and Theory.* Taipei: Boyang Publishers, pp. 75–113.

Chau, Adam Yuet. 2013c. "Actants Amassing (AA): Beyond Collective Effervescence and the Social." In Sondra L. Hausner, ed., *Durkheim in Dialogue: A Centenary Celebration of The Elementary Forms of Religious Life.* Oxford: Berghahn Books.

Chau, Adam Yuet. 2014. "Household Sovereignty and Religious Subjectification: China and the Christian West Compared." *Studies in Church History* 50: 492–504.

Chau, Adam Yuet. 2015. "Chinese Socialism and the Household Idiom of Religious Engagement." In Tam T. T. Ngo and Justine B. Quijada, eds., *Atheist Secularism and its Discontents: A Comparative Study of Religion and Communism in Eurasia.* New York: Palgrave Macmillan, pp. 225–43.

Chau, Adam Yuet. 2016. "The Commodification of Religion in Chinese Societies." In Vincent Goossaert, Jan Kiely, and John Lagerwey, eds., *Modern Chinese Religion II: 1850–2015.* Leiden: Brill, pp. 949–76.

Chau, Adam Yuet. 2017. "The Nation in Religion and Religion in the Nation: How the Modern Chinese Nation Made Religion and Was at the Same Time Made by Religion." In Cheng-tian Kuo, ed., *Religion and Nationalism in Chinese Societies.* Amsterdam: Amsterdam University Press.

Chau, Adam Yuet. 2018. "Of Temples and Trees: The Black Dragon King and the Arbortourists." In Michael Stausberg, ed., *Religion and Tourism in China and India.* Oxford: Berghahn.

Chau, Adam Yuet. Forthcoming. "Spaces of Youth Cultural Production in Rural China." In Vanessa Frangville and Gwennaël Gaffric, eds., *China's Youth Cultures and Collective Spaces.* London: Routledge.

Chau, Adam Yuet. Under review. "Ritual Terroir: The Generation of Site-Specific Vitality." In Vincent Goossaert, ed., Special Issue on "Religion in a Plural Society: Comparing the Chinese and Indian Worlds." *Archives des Sciences Sociales des Religions.*

Chen, Nancy. 2003. *Breathing Spaces: Qigong, Psychiatry, and Healing in China.* New York: Columbia University Press.

Chiao, Chien. 1986. "'Beating the Petty Person': A Ritual of the Hong Kong Chinese." *New Asia Academic Bulletin* 6 (Special Issue on Anthropological Studies of China): 211–18.

Chio, Jenny (Director). 2012. Peasant Family Happiness (Nong Jia Le). Ethnographic film, 71 minutes. Distributed by Berkeley Media.

Davis, Sara L. M. 2005. *Song and Silence: Ethnic Revival on China's Southwest Borders.* New York: Columbia University Press.

Dean, Kenneth. 1998. *Lord of the Three in One: The Spread of a Cult in Southeast China.* Princeton, NJ: Princeton University Press.

Dean, Kenneth and Zheng Zhenman. 2010. *Ritual Alliances of the Putian Plain. Volume One: Historical Introduction to the Return of the Gods.* Leiden: Brill.

Deleuze, Gilles and Félix Guattari. 1987 [1980]. *A Thousand Plateaus: Capitalism and Schizophrenia.* Translated by Brian Massumi. Minneapolis, MN: University of Minnesota Press.

Derrida, Jacques and Anne Dufourmantelle. 2000. *Of Hospitality.* Stanford, CA: Stanford University Press.

Eng, Irene and Y. Lin. 2002. "Religious Festivities, Communal Rivalry, and Restructuring of Authority Relations in Rural Chaozhou, Southeast China." *Journal of Asian Studies* 61(4): 1259–85.

Erie, Matthew S. 2016. *China and Islam: The Prophet, the Party, and Law.* Cambridge: Cambridge University Press.

Fang, Ling and Vincent Goossaert. 2008. "Les réformes funéraires et la politique religieuse de l'État chinois, 1900–2008", *Archives de sciences sociales des religions* 144: 51–73.

Feuchtwang, Stephan. 2001. *Popular Religion in China: The Imperial Metaphor.* London: RoutledgeCurzon.

Fisher, Gareth. 2008. "The Spiritual Land Rush: Merit and Morality in New Chinese Buddhist Temple Construction." *The Journal of Asian Studies* 67: 143–70.

Fisher, Gareth. 2014. *From Comrades to Bodhisattvas: Moral Dimensions of Lay Buddhist Practice in Contemporary China.* Honolulu, HI: University of Hawai'i Press.

Foucault, Michel. 1982. "The Subject and Power." *Critical Inquiry* 8(4): 777–95.

Gates, Hill. 1996. *China's Motor: A Thousand Years of Petty Capitalism*. Ithaca, NY: Cornell University Press.

Gates, Hill. 2000. "Religious Real Estate as Indigenous Civil Space." *Bulletin of the Institute of Ethnology (Academia Sinica)* 88 (Special issue in honor of Professor Li Yih-yuan's retirement I): 313–33.

Gillette, Maris B. 2003. "The 'Glorious Returns' of Chinese Pilgrims to Mecca." In C. Stafford, ed., *Living with Separation in China: Anthropological Accounts*. London: RoutledgeCurzon, pp. 130–56.

Gladney, Dru C. 1996. *Muslim Chinese: Ethnic Nationalism in the People's Republic*, 2nd edn. Cambridge, MA: Harvard East Asian Monographs.

Goldstein, M. C. and M. T. Kapstein, eds. 1998. *Buddhism in Contemporary Tibet: Religious Revival and Cultural Identity*. Berkeley, CA: University of California Press.

Goossaert, Vincent. 2000. "Counting the Monks: The 1736–1739 Census of the Chinese Clergy." *Late Imperial China* 21(2): 40–85.

Goossaert, Vincent. 2006. "1898: The Beginning of the End for Chinese Religion?" *Journal of Asian Studies* 65(2): 307–36.

Goossaert, Vincent. 2017. *Bureaucratie et salut: Devenir un dieu en Chine*. Geneva: Labor et Fides.

Harrison, Henrietta. 2013. *The Missionary's Curse and Other Tales from a Chinese Catholic Village*. Berkeley, CA: University of California Press.

Heal, Felicity. 1990. *Hospitality in Early Modern England*. Oxford: Oxford University Press.

Herrou, Adeline. 2013. *A World of Their Own: Daoist Monks and Their Community in Contemporary China*. Dunedin, FL: Three Pines Press.

Hillman, Ben. 2005. "Monastic Politics and the Local State in China: Authority and Autonomy in an Ethnically Tibetan Prefecture." *The China Journal* 54: 29–51.

Hobsbawm, Eric J. and Terence Ranger, eds. 1983. *The Invention of Tradition*. Cambridge: Cambridge University Press.

Huang, C-Y. Julia. 2009. *Charisma and Compassion: Cheng Yen and the Buddhist Tzu Chi Movement*. Cambridge, MA: Harvard University Press.

Huang, Julia C-Y. and Robert P. Weller. 1998. "Merit and Mothering: Women and Social Welfare in Taiwanese Buddhism." *Journal of Asian Studies* 57(2): 379–96.

Huang, Jianbo. 2014. "Being Christians in Urbanizing China: The Epistemological Tensions of the Rural Churches in the City." *Current Anthropology* 55(suppl. 10): 238–47.

Huang, Weishan. 2017. "WeChat Together about the Buddha: The Construction of Sacred Space and Religious Community in Shanghai through Social

Media." In Stefania Travagnin, ed., *Religion and Media in China: Insights and Case Studies from the Mainland, Taiwan and Hong Kong*. London: Routledge, pp. 110–28.

Inouye, Melissa W. 2015. "Miraculous Modernity: Charismatic Traditions and Trajectories within Chinese Protestant Christianity." In J. Lagerwey, V. Goossaert, and J. Kiely, eds., *Modern Chinese Religion II: 1850–2015*. Leiden: Brill, pp. 884–919.

Islamic Association of China. 2005. *Zhongguo musilin chaojin shiyong shouce [Practical Pilgrim Handbook for Chinese Muslims]*. Yinchuan, Ningxia: Ningxia People's Press.

Jaschok, Maria and Shui Jingjun. 2000. *The History of Women's Mosques in Chinese Islam: A Mosque of Their Own*. Richmond, Surrey: Curzon Press.

Ji, Zhe. 2011. "Religion, jeunes et modernité: Le camp d'été, nouvelle practique rituelle du bouddisme chinois." *Social Compass* 58(4): 525–39.

Jones, Stephen. 2017. *Daoist Priests of the Li Family: Ritual Life in Village China*. Magdalena, NM: Three Pines Press.

Kao, Chen-yang. 2009. "The Cultural Revolution and the Emergence of Pentecostal-style Protestantism in China." *Journal of Contemporary Religion* 24(2): 171–88.

Katz, Paul. 2009. *Divine Justice: Religion and the Development of Chinese Legal Culture*. New York: Routledge.

Kipnis, Andrew B. 1997. *Producing Guanxi: Sentiment, Self, and Subculture in a North China Village*. Durham, NC: Duke University Press.

Kuo Cheng-tian, ed. 2017. *Religion and Nationalism in Chinese Societies*. Amsterdam: Amsterdam University Press.

Lagerwey, John. 1987. *Taoist Ritual in Chinese Society and History*. London: Macmillan.

Laliberté, André. 2016. "Engaging with a Post-totalitarian State: Buddhism Online in China." In Stefania Travagnin, ed., *Religion and Media in China: Insights and Case Studies from the Mainland, Taiwan and Hong Kong*. London: Routledge, pp. 129–50.

Lin, Wei-ping. 2015. *Materializing Magic Power: Chinese Popular Religion in Villages and Cities*. Cambridge, MA: Harvard Asia Center Publications.

Liu, Xin. 2009. *The Mirage of China: Anti-Humanism, Narcissism, and Corporeality of the Contemporary World*. Oxford: Berghahn.

Lu Hwei-syin (Lu Huixin). 2011. *Renqing hua da'ai: duo mianxiang de Ciji gongtongti [The Transformation of Human Sentiments into Greater Love in the Buddhist Tzu Chi Community]*. Taipei: SMC Publishing.

Ma Qiang. 2006. *Liudong de jingshen shequ: renleixue shiye xia de Guangzhou Muslim zhemati yanjiu [Fluctuant Spiritual Community: A Study of the Jamma'at of Guangzhou Muslims from an Anthropological Perspective*]. Beijing: Zhongguo shehuikexue chubanshe.

Makley, Charlene E. 2007. *The Violence of Liberation: Gender and Tibetan Buddhist Revival in Post-Mao China*. Berkeley, CA: University of California Press.

Marshall, Alison. 2003. "Moving the Spirit on Taiwan: New Age *Lingji* Performance." *Journal of Chinese Religions* 31: 81–99.

Mollier, Christine. 2008. *Buddhism and Taoism Face to Face: Scripture, Ritual, and Iconographic Exchange in Medieval China*. Honolulu, HI: University of Hawai'i Press.

Moskowitz, Marc L. 2001. *The Haunting Fetus: Abortion, Sexuality, and the Spirit World in Taiwan*. Honolulu, HI: University of Hawai'i Press.

Mullaney, Thomas S. 2011. *Coming to Terms with the Nation: Ethnic Classification in Modern China*. Berkeley, CA: University of California Press.

Nedostup, Rebecca. 2010. *Superstitious Regimes: Religion and the Politics of Chinese Modernity*. Cambridge, MA: Harvard University Asia Center.

Orsi, Robert A. 2010 [1985]. *The Madonna of 115th Street: Faith and Community in Italian Harlem, 1880–1950*, 3rd edn. New Haven, CT: Yale University Press.

Palmer, David A. 2007. *Qigong Fever: Body, Science, and Utopia in China, 1949–1999*. New York: Columbia University Press.

Palmer, David A. 2008. "Heretical Doctrines, Reactionary Secret Societies, Evil Cults: Labelling Heterodoxy in 20th Century China." In Mayfair M.-H. Yang, ed., *Chinese Religiosities: Afflictions of Modernity and State Formation*. Berkeley, CA: University of California Press, pp. 113–34.

Palmer, David A. 2009. "China's Religious *Danwei*: Institutionalising Religion in the People's Republic." *China Perspectives* 2009(4): 17–30.

Palmer, David A. 2011a. "Chinese Religious Innovation in the Qigong Movement: The Case of Zhonggong." In Adam Yuet Chau, ed., *Religion in Contemporary China: Revitalization and Innovation*. London: Routledge, pp. 182–203.

Palmer, David A. 2011b. "Gift and Market in the Chinese Religious Economy." *Religion* 41(4): 569–94.

Palmer, David A. and Elijar Siegler. 2017. *Dream Trippers: Global Daoism and the Predicament of Modern Spirituality*. Chicago, IL: University of Chicago Press.

Park, Choong-hwan. 2008. "Delights in Farm Guesthouses: Nongjiale Tourism, Rural Development and the Regime of Leisure-Pleasure in Post-Mao China." PhD dissertation, University of California, Santa Barbara.

Remoiville, Julie. 2013. "Le renouveau religieux en Chine urbaine contemporaine: Le rôle social de la religion dans la vie quotidienne à Hangzhou." Doctoral thesis, l'École pratique des hautes études, Paris.

Robbins, Joel and Naomi Haynes, eds. 2014. "The Anthropology of Christianity: Unity, Diversity, New Directions." *Current Anthropology* 55(S10).

Roberts, John M., Chien Chiao, and Triloki N. Pandey. 1975. "Meaningful God Sets from a Chinese Personal Pantheon and a Hindu Personal Pantheon." *Ethnology* 14(2): 121–48.

Sangren, P. Steven. 1987. *History and Magical Power in a Chinese Community.* Stanford, CA: Stanford University Press.

Sangren, P. Steven. 2000. *Chinese Sociologics: An Anthropological Account of the Role of Alienation in Social Reproduction.* London: Continuum.

Schipper, Kristofer. 2008. "Comment on crée un lieu saint local." In Kristofer Schipper, ed., *La religion de la Chine: la tradition vivante.* Paris: Fayard, pp. 305–27.

Schmidt-Leukel, Perry and Joachim Gentz, eds. 2013. *Religious Diversity in Chinese Thought.* New York: Palgrave Macmillan.

Scott, James L. 1998. *Seeing Like a State: How Certain Schemes to Improve the Human Condition Have Failed.* New Haven, CT: Yale University Press.

Scott, Janet Lee. 2007. *For Gods, Ghosts and Ancestors: The Chinese Tradition of Paper Offerings.* Seattle, WA: University of Washington Press.

Stark, Rodney and Roger Finke. 2000. *Acts of Faith: Explaining the Human Side of Religion.* Berkeley, CA: University of California Press.

Stewart, Alexander B. 2017. *Chinese Muslims and the Global Ummah: Islamic Revival and Ethnic Identity among the Hui of Qinghai Province.* London: Routledge.

Sutton, Donald S. 2003. *Steps of Perfection: Exorcistic Performers and Chinese Religion in Twentieth-century Taiwan.* Cambridge, MA.: Harvard East Asian Monographs.

Tarocco, Francesca. 2017. "Technologies of Salvation: (Re)locating Chinese Buddhism in the Digital Age." *Journal of Global Buddhism* 18: 155–75.

Ting, Jen-Chieh (Ding Renjie). 1999. *Shehui mailuo zhong de zhuren xingwei: Taiwan fojiao Ciji gongdehui ge'an yanjiu* [Helping Behavior in Social Contexts: The Case of the Buddhist Ciji gongdehui in Taiwan]. Taipei: Linking Publishing Company.

Ting, Jen-Chieh (Ding Renjie). 2005. "Huilingshan xianxiang de shehuixue kaocha: qudiyuhua qingjing zhong minjian xinyang de zhuanhua yu zailianjie [A Sociological Analysis of the Collective Trance Movement "Converging with the Spirit-Mountain": The Transformation and Re-Embedding of Folk

Religion under the Situation of De-Territorialization]." *Taiwan zongjiao yanjiu* [*Research on Religion in Taiwan*]. 4(2): 57–111.

Vala, Carsten. 2017. *The Politics of Protestant Churches and the Party-State in China: God Above Party?* New York: Routledge.

Wang Ying. 2011. *Shenfen jiangou yu wenhua ronghe: zhongyuan diqu jidujiaohui gean yanjiu* [*The Construction of Identity and Cultural Incorporation: The Case Study of a Protestant Church in the North China Plain*]. Shanghai: Renmin chubanshe.

Watson, James L. 1985. "Standardizing the Gods: The Promotion of T'ien Hou ('Empress of Heaven') along the South China Coast, 960–1960." In David Johnson, ed., *Popular Culture in Late Imperial China*. Berkeley, CA: University of California Press, pp. 292–324.

Watson, James L. 1996. "Fighting with Operas: Processionals, Politics, and the Spectre of Violence in Rural Hong Kong." In David Parkin, Lionel Caplan, and Humphrey Fisher, eds., *The Politics of Cultural Performance: Essays in Honor of Abner Cohen*. London: Berghahn Books.

Weller, Robert P. 1994. *Resistance, Chaos and Control in China: Taiping Rebels, Taiwanese Ghosts and Tiananmen*. London: Macmillan.

Yan, Yunxiang. 1996. *The Flow of Gifts: Reciprocity and Social Networks in a Chinese Village*. Stanford, CA: Stanford University Press.

Yang, Der-Ruey. 2005. "The Changing Economy of Temple Daoism in Shanghai." In Fenggang Yang and Joseph B. Tamney, eds., *State, Market, and Religions in Chinese Societies*. Leiden: Brill, pp. 113–48.

Yang, Der-Ruey. 2011. "From Ritual Skills to Discursive Knowledge: Changing Styles of Daoist Transmission in Shanghai." In Adam Yuet Chau, ed., *Religion in Contemporary China: Revitalization and Innovation*. London: Routledge, pp. 81–107.

Yang, Fenggang. 1999. *Chinese Christians in America: Conversion, Assimilation, and Adhesive Identities*. State College, PA: Penn State University Press.

Yang, Fenggang. 2005. "Lost in the Market, Saved at McDonald's: Conversion to Christianity in Urban China." *Journal for the Scientific Study of Religion* 44(4): 423–41.

Yang, Fenggang. 2012. *Religion in China: Survival and Revival under Communist Rule*. Oxford: Oxford University Press.

Yang, Mayfair Mei-hui. 1994. *Gifts, Favors, and Banquets: The Art of Social Relationships in China*. Ithaca, NY: Cornell University Press.

Yang, Mayfair Mei-hui. 2000. "Putting Global Capitalism in Its Place: Economic Hybridity, Bataille, and Ritual Expenditure." *Current Anthropology* 41(4): 477–509.

Yau Chi On. 2003. "Xianggang daojiao songwen qifu fahui ji qi biwen jingwen" [The Hong Kong Daoist ritual of prayer to expel epidemics and its exorcistic scriptures]. *Huanan yanjiu ziliao zhongxin tongxun* [Bulletin of the South China Research Centre] 32: 21–7.

Yü, Dan Smyer. 2012. *The Spread of Tibetan Buddhism in China: Charisma, Money, Enlightenment*. London: Routledge.

Yue Yongyi. 2010. "Jiazhong guohui" ["Making Temple Festivals at Home"]. In Yue Yongyi, *Lingyan, Ketou, Chuanshuo* [Efficacy, Kowtow, Legends]. Shanghai: Sanlian Publishers, pp. 169–240.

Zhang, Everett, Arthur Kleinman, and Weiming Tu, eds. 2011. *Governance of Life in Chinese Moral Experience: The Quest for an Adequate Life*. London: Routledge.

Index